PRODUCERS

VERSUS

CAPITALISTS

*Constitutional*

*Conflict in*

*Antebellum America*

# PRODUCERS VERSUS

# CAPITALISTS

*Constitutional*

*Conflict in*

*Antebellum America*

*TONY A. FREYER*

UNIVERSITY PRESS OF VIRGINIA

*Charlottesville and London*

*More than any of the books*
*I have written*
*this one represents*
*the intellectual debt I owe*
*Willard Hurst, Harry Scheiber, and*
*Forrest and Ellen McDonald.*

# CONTENTS

# ACKNOWLEDGMENTS

Over the years this study was in preparation, I benefited from the aid of many individuals and institutions. Glenn Porter, Director of the Hagley Museum and Library, helped to provide support for me and my family during the summer of 1977 and the year 1979–80 so that I was able to accomplish much of the basic research on the four states of Delaware, Maryland, New Jersey, and Pennsylvania. For assisting me in that work I am grateful to the staffs of the Hagley Museum and Library, the Federal Record Centers located in Philadelphia and (at the time) Suitland, Maryland, the Historical Society of Pennsylvania, and the Maryland Hall of Records, Annapolis, Maryland. During the same period others who gave generously of their insights and time were Lee Benson, Joyce Appleby, Diane Lindstrom, Joan Jenson, and Thomas C. Cochran. Chris Baer kindly shared with me his impressive knowledge of many obscure sources. For later stages of research I was fortunate to have support from the Charles Warren Center, Harvard University, during 1981–82, and from the Earhart Foundation for the summer of 1982 and the fall of 1985. The staffs of Harvard's Baker, Langdell, and Widner libraries were most helpful.

I wish to thank, too, Harry N. Scheiber, Thomas K. McCraw, Steven Hahn, Lawrence M. Friedman, Eugene D. Genovese, Joyce Appleby, James Willard Hurst, Leslie Hannah, Lawrence F. Kohl, Stanley Katz, and Glenn Porter, who read all or portions of earlier drafts of the manuscript. In this same connection I am particularly indebted to Forrest and Ellen McDonald. I am grateful too to Chris Baer for sharing with me an early draft of a manuscript.

Helpful, too, were the participants in seminars given under the auspices of the following forums where I presented the initial drafts of several different chapters: the Regional Economic History Research Center of the Hagley Museum and Library, the Charles Warren Center of Harvard University, the Legal History Workshop of Princeton University, the Social History Seminar of the University of California, San Diego, and the Jurisprudence and Social Policy Center of the University of California, Berkeley School of Law (Boalt Hall). In addition, the

*Wisconsin Law Review* and the *Kentucky Law Journal* published in other forms portions of chapters 2 and 4.

It is a pleasure to have had the opportunity of working with the University Press of Virginia. As series editors Kermit Hall and David M. O'Brien have been just what a harried writer might hope for. Richard Holway and Boyd Zenner have rendered invaluable editorial assistance.

I am pleased to thank yet again members of the Word Processing Center of the University of Alabama School of Law, especially Patricia Lovelady Nelson, Alesia White Darling, and Anderson Wynn. I also continue to be indebted to the Law Library's Paul M. Pruitt.

Unless otherwise noted, the pamphlets cited throughout the book are located in the Hagley Museum and Library, including those by or about the railroads and banks.

Finally, I wish to thank my wife, Marjorie, and son, Allan, for their continuing support during the long years it took me to complete this book. Of course, neither they nor others are responsible for what is written. For that I alone am accountable.

PRODUCERS

VERSUS

CAPITALISTS

*Constitutional*

*Conflict in*

*Antebellum America*

# Prologue

Throughout much of American history the relationship between the Constitution and the nation's economic system has been contentious. To a certain extent the proponents and opponents of the drafting and ratification of the Constitution itself framed their arguments in terms of a struggle between mercantile and agricultural enterprise. Following the triumph of political party politics in 1800, various party organizations supported different interpretations of the Constitution in order to legitimate their conflicting visions of society and economic policy. Meanwhile, under chief justices John Marshall and Roger B. Taney the Supreme Court's steadily growing role in setting the bounds of economic opportunity was the object of repeated attack. Contrary appeals to constitutional legitimacy were also fundamental to the clash between slave and free labor that culminated in the Civil War. After the war generations of historians and commentators followed a path popularized by Charles A. Beard. They debated the meaning of the Constitution with reference to an enduring confrontation between groups advocating and resisting capitalist values.[1]

More recently, however, consensus replaced conflict as the framework for understanding capitalism's relationship to constitutional de-

velopment. Scholars, jurists, and popular commentators accepted the pervasive regard for private property and comparatively free markets that dominated the nation's culture as the starting point for explaining how constitutional institutions influenced the triumph of American capitalism. As the primary expounder of the values that the Constitution embodied, the Supreme Court, particularly, received credit or blame for having virtually always legitimated a capitalist economy. This characterization of the Court's market function and impact, like that of the constitutional order as a whole, emphasized continuity. Thus the repeated struggle that once made controversies involving constitutional legitimacy seem so important became simply politically manageable tensions within a liberal-capitalist consensus. The entire constitutional system was the agent of capitalism now.[2]

Studies of constitutional development and policy making during the decades preceding the Civil War supported the consensus view. After 1800 liberal individualism increasingly eroded the anticapitalist republican values identified with the protagonists in the initial struggles over the Constitution. Summing up decades of impressive research that examined this complex transition, one prominent historian observed that "by 1860 the nascent outline of the modern American economy of mass consumption, mass production, and capital-intensive agriculture was visible." Drawing upon many of the same rich sources, another incisive scholar emphasized the central role that the constitutional order played. "Notwithstanding small budgets, tiny bureaucracies, and great hostility among some policy makers to capitalism, the constitutional system that divided power between a national government and strong states provided potent encouragement for capitalism," he concluded.[3]

As the constitutional system enforced capitalist values, it transformed social class and market relations. "State and federal governments together regulated markets, allowing capital to grow: they financed internal improvements, encouraged banking and interregional trade, . . . and rewrote the common law to protect developmental uses of property." The changes that the constitutional order furthered and formally sanctioned in turn "transformed productive relations, impelling the decline of traditional systems of unfree and craft labor and the growth of classes of wage laborers and capitalists."[4]

Whether the constitutional system was so impervious to deeper social conflicts, however, is problematic. Alexis de Tocqueville was

one of many antebellum contemporaries commenting upon the "new-ness" of American federalism. Exploring the cultural implications of this observation, Michael Kammen has argued that conflict more than consensus molded the popular perception of the Constitution, at least throughout the period before the Civil War. In a pathbreaking assess-ment of the Marshall Court's relation to culture, G. Edward White found that the Court reconciled republican and liberal ideologies, thereby facilitating society's accommodation to wrenching change. Both studies suggested that the struggles within American society were too profound for constitutional institutions to have been immune to values and interests outside the emerging liberal capitalist con-sensus.[5]

This present study further explores constitutionalism's role in the conflicted antebellum culture. I define constitutionalism in terms of the constituent institutions and values that comprise a working sys-tem. Thus I am concerned with what may be called the constituent constitution. Approached in this light, the understanding of constitu-tional development must consider the degree to which the system as a whole shaped and was shaped by the wide range of ideological and social struggles pervading antebellum society. The interaction be-tween these conflicts and constitutional institutions suggests, more-over, a policy-making role which was dynamic, reflecting a multi-plicity of values and supporting diverse interests, many of which resisted corporate and mercantile capitalism.

The public discourse of political leaders was often critical of capitalist values. Both Jeffersonian and Jacksonian Democratic party rhetoric attacked aristocracy and monopoly, harkening back to a republican ideology which condemned the corrosive financial and market be-havior and institutions identified with corporate and large mercantile capitalism. To a certain extent Whigs and Republicans endorsed ele-ments of this same ideology in their advocacy of a "harmony of inter-ests." A case in point was Whig and later Republican Henry C. Carey. A chief proponent of the "harmony of interests" philosophy and the foremost American political economist of his time, Carey argued that large-scale corporate and mercantile capitalism threatened the modest-sized farmers, artisans, and traders whom he favored as the foundation of the nation's economic order.[6]

Most political leaders and publicists contended that the producing classes were most important to American prosperity. The proponents

of a labor theory of value, producers were those who made and deserved the fruits of all true wealth. The manipulative creators of false paper wealth-bankers, lawyers, corporations generally, and big merchants-were agents of capitalist enterprise that threatened the producing classes. To modern perceptions this distinction between producers and capitalists may not seem meaningful. After all, to moderns, "producers" as small-to-middling-scale proprietors of business, contrasted with wage laborers, were capitalists, standing as they did for their own relative autonomy in private markets as against government control of the economy. According to these perceptions attacks upon privilege, monopoly, corporations, and whatnot did not indicate that the critics identified these evils with specific men or groups. What people feared were the consequences of the tendencies of capitalism, a system in which they all participated.[7]

This study does not follow the modern conception, favoring instead that of antebellum political economists. I use the distinction that these commentators made between producers and corporate or large mercantile capitalists for several reasons. First, the people and institutions I write about in this study operated in a world in which the great majority of white adult males were self-employed in some form of small or modest-size, independent, unincorporated enterprise. Also, most of these people and their families lived in rural areas and small towns. In 1830 only 9 percent of Americans resided in cities; by 1860 the percentage of city dwellers had risen to just 20 percent. While most forms of enterprise involved farming, there was considerable occupational versatility. As one historian has summarized, "Most American artisans, even those in larger cities, grew gardens and kept cows, hogs, or chickens. Likewise, most workers in rural areas, even those on the more specialized farms, engaged in nonagricultural tasks, in various types of processing, in local commercial exchange, and in the providing of services."[8]

Even so, *independent* generally did not mean *self-sufficient*. Throughout the period occupational versatility and primary exchange took place largely within local markets supplemented by foreign trade. Yet within local neighborhoods existed "complex, overlapping networks of control" in which reciprocity prevailed. Accordingly, the "economic man" whom political economists such as Carey knew "still depended upon a high degree of cooperative interchange, or a complex swapping of specialized skills, products, and services" in which nearly

everyone-men, women, and children-worked to a greater or lesser degree with their hands in what amounted to a household economy. At the same time, this reciprocal, small-scale, and localistic kind of work resisted the pervasive threat of market failure through reliance upon community resources, including local governmental institutions and protectionist debtor-creditor laws.[9]

The chief market agents distinguishable from this "producer economy" were large merchants and corporations. Exploiting speculative credit opportunities not available to smaller proprietors, larger-scale merchants exercised increasing power over producers, gradually moving from "horizontal integration of households, to an early form of vertical or hierarchical integration of artisans."[10] Eventually such merchants, either privately or through banks, provided much of the capital that made possible forms of corporate industrial enterprise which included manufacturing firms and transportation facilities, especially the railroads. For the purposes of this study, the point is that these merchant and corporate capitalists possessed financial advantages attained through risk, economies of scale, and political and legal influence which smaller-scale producers generally lacked. The threat to producer independence that these market and political advantages represented, moreover, seemed very great. So great that it was understandably difficult for average producers to conceive that they had the same economic opportunity as the corporate or mercantile capitalists. It was this abiding fear that politicians articulated in their public discourse.

Antebellum political economists recognized how strong these social and market cleavages separating capitalists and producers were. Indeed, the differences were powerful enough that economic commentators assumed that large merchant and corporate capitalists were a class apart, separated from the producers by a privileged legal and market position. The very nature of such privilege was that the opportunity it represented seemed closed to most individuals. Thus for Carey and other American political economists, average producers did not share the same capitalist values with those they feared insofar as those values were defined in terms of corporations and mercantile speculation.[11]

The followers of Adam Smith in America recognized the distinctiveness of the capitalist and producer classes. Smith himself distinguished between "productive and unproductive" classes. The capi-

talists, especially those whose capital was invested in larger-scale manufacturing, were "devils" occupying the unproductive category. This was so because "owners of capital" competed with each other, and competition invariably reduced profits. Thus it was in the self-interest of capitalist investors to seek "monopolistic advantages" that further insulated them from the growth-generating productive classes. In America the "old" Jeffersonian Republican John Taylor made his own distinction between capitalists and the producing classes in which he included banks among the "devils."

Daniel Raymond was a spokesman for economic ideas that were eventually identified with the Whigs. He rejected many of Taylor's theories, but the hero of both was the small, independent, unincorporated enterpriser. Unlike Taylor, Raymond particularly favored tariff protectionism and internal improvements, central to what became Henry Clay's "American system." Still, Raymond distrusted speculation, moneylending, and wealth accumulation for its own sake as generally parasitic. Neither Taylor nor Raymond liked "private" corporations. But Raymond countenanced those "public" corporations employed as internal improvements as long as they were regulated. Thus in contrast with Taylor, Raymond favored extensive government intervention in the economy in order to protect the modest-sized producer from the parasitic corporate and commercial capitalists who enjoyed the advantage of special privilege.

The Jacksonian Democrats' antimonopoly crusade also drew upon the ideas of political economists. Paul Conkin and others have noted the complexities and diversity of thought associated with the economic ideas identified under the rubric of Jacksonian Democracy. In part they looked backward to Taylor's "old republicanism," while at the same time espousing a popular attachment to laissez-faire which resembled the ideas dominating the period after the Civil War. In addition, particularly regarding the welter of social and political values and interests touched by the bank issue, there are profoundly difficult analytical problems arising from the Jacksonian belief in individualism. Yet again for purposes of this study, what deserves attention is that notwithstanding many ideological intricacies, there were powerful stands within Jacksonian political economy which assumed the dominant social and market importance of "independence" and the producer values it represented. Indeed, the opportunistic accommodation of state banks that Jacksonian economic theorists William M.

Gouge and Condy Raguet made after Andrew Jackson vetoed the Bank of the United States should not obscure the degree to which even on the bank issue the antimonopoly crusade epitomized the antebellum political culture's preference for small-scale producers over corporate and mercantile capitalists.

This was the wider ideological significance of the more familiar anticapitalist rhetoric of William Leggett. As a journalistic popularizer of economic ideas in the New York *Post*'s attack on the "monster" Bank, Leggett presented formulations that were explicitly anticapitalist. The Bank symbolized "monopoly," "privilege," and "corruption" associated invariably with the "aristocratic" and "grasping monopolizing spirit of capricious capitalists" and their "rich . . . proud . . . privileged" allies who were driving America toward a "vast disparity of condition." Yet this growing "disparity" threatened the middling class of producers. The distinction was not simply between those who otherwise shared the same values, disagreeing only over the abuse of their application. Remove "a hundred ploughmen" from the "fields and a hundred merchants from their desks," said Leggett, "and what man, regarding the true dignity of his nature, could hesitate to give the award of superior excellence, in every main intellectual, physical, and moral respect, to the band of hearty rustics over that of the lank and sallow accountants, worn out with the sordid anxieties of traffic and calculations of gain?"[12]

By the Civil War the political economist who synthesized these ideas was Henry Carey. He theorized that small traders, artisans, manufacturers, yeoman farmers, and the growing class of industrial workers were all potentially "capitalists" sharing a "harmony of interests." Carey's use of "capitalist," however, did not necessarily include large incorporated or mercantile enterprise. Social, cultural, and market realities set the latter group apart. Under the influence of Stephen Colwell, an iron and steel manufacturer with close ties to the Presbyterian church and Princeton Theological Seminary, Carey attacked "selfish, non-Christian individualism and competition under a socially irresponsible form of 'capitalism.'"[13]

The form of enterprise Carey favored was locally oriented, unincorporated, and small in scale. Banks or transport corporations serving a cluster of local communities, for example, were "good." But Carey resisted incorporation of banks or railroads to serve the national market. Similarly, he praised mining and manufacturing enterprisers like

his friend Colwell whose businesses were generally not incorporated and earnestly pursued responsible, cooperative, and Christian practices toward employees, consumers, and society as a whole. Also, his ideal economic order functioned principally within local or regional markets at the center of which were small towns. Carey's vision did not assume as strong a distinction between class groups as the earlier political economists. Yet his resort to Christian principles that separated economic groups on the basis of moral grounds represented what to a considerable degree amounted to a divergent market consciousness. More significantly, perhaps, Carey's local market, smaller scale, and community-oriented society in many ways harkened back to the traditional producer economy. Moreover, it was a society sufficiently under threat from unChristian capitalist values to require protective government intervention on its behalf.[14]

Thus constitutional conflicts reflected deeper ideological divisions involving social-class struggle. The discourse of antebellum political leaders and publicists usually assumed that American society was separated into three classes or groups. Capitalists were above and dispossessed paupers occupied a place below the middling classes who more or less corresponded to the producers. This "middling sort" valued modest economic independence based on honest individual labor over the extremes of capitalist wealth or desperate pauperism. Eventually these producer values were amalgamated with evangelical Protestant moralism, providing a basis for the free-labor ideology that emerged prior to the Civil War.[15]

This conception of middle-class groups reflected pressures for ideological accommodation. The gradual process of cultural reconciliation centered on small-producer, republican values of personal independence. But this cultural accommodation also had to confront the exaltation of individual talent and personal endeavor to transcend simple independence, expressly identified with capitalist values. Even as Carey and others moved toward such an ideological amalgamation in the "harmony of interests," however, they remained distrustful of "artificial" embodiments of individualism in the form of corporations or commercial speculation. Accordingly, the antebellum culture's attachment to independence incorporated a producer consciousness and evangelical Protestant moralism to form the middle-class values that dominated society. Nevertheless, these values were regarded as distinct from capitalist values, at least insofar as capitalism was repre-

sented by corporations and the speculative finance of large mercantile enterprisers.

Reinforcing social conflict was the dual-market structure of the antebellum economic order. Even as late as 1860 a dual economy existed in which local and national market relations coincided. Although the modern American economy was clearly emerging by the Civil War, its "development had been uneven across different regions and industries. It was far from complete even in the most advanced sections of the country like New England, where many village blacksmiths and old-time shoemakers could still be found," observed James M. McPherson. "Many Americans still lived in a nearly self-sufficient, handicraft premarket economy not much different from what their grandparents had known." Even so, the characterization of premarket versus market economy was relative. None of those identifying themselves as producers, for example, could be said to be entirely removed from some sort of market relations. Rather, involvement in the market existed along a continuum ranging from those engaged in predominately local activity to those whose enterprise was more nationally oriented.[16]

These conflicts and the resistance to capitalist values that they reflected interacted with the constituent constitution. On the formal institutional level, the largest policy issues involved the scope and limits of federalism. Political parties, the federal and state governments generally, and the Supreme Court in particular were the primary institutional channels through which ideological and social conflicts shaped economic policy making. Throughout the period before the Civil War, the role and authority of these constituent institutions changed. Especially after 1815, the states displaced the federal government as the primary stimulators of economic development. The Supreme Court gradually acquired significant authority as the umpire of the federal system, but its rise to leadership ultimately accommodated and sustained the states' policy-making dominance. Political parties were the principal articulators of group interests and values. Even so, especially in the states local control was such a strong force that usually politicians could implement policies only by compromising their party's principles.[17]

At the same time, popular faith in basic constitutional values influenced ideological and social conflict. Fundamental to American constitutionalism was the ideal that all forms of public or private power

should be checked by and responsive to power outside of itself. The working or functional content of the ideal took different forms depending on the issue. In most controversies involving federalism, for example, the ideal acquired practical force as local control versus "consolidated" power. At the more abstract level of public discourse, the ideal blended attachment to local control and the core values of legitimacy and accountability. Especially regarding struggles over economic policies, both capitalist and producer interests appealed to these same constitutional values to justify their demands and conduct.[18]

Still, having the most to gain from the enforcement of these core constitutional values were middling-class producers. Both the labor theory of value and the Old Republican commitment to personal independence were vulnerable to the aggressive and exploitative individualism identified with corporate and mercantile capitalism. In addition, corporate and large mercantile capitalist enterprise tied principally to the national market threatened the locally oriented market relations of unincorporated, producer enterprisers. Finally, the specter of business failure and the corresponding loss of independence haunted producers and capitalist groups alike.

Offsetting the producer's market weakness, however, was his political influence. The central place that producers occupied in the public discourse of the period suggests the priority they were given as voters in the minds of elected public officials. At least insofar as this franchise democracy was an accurate measure of political clout, moreover, producers actually controlled juries and other local governmental institutions. None of this denies the obvious power that corporate and big mercantile capitalists possessed in American politics. On the contrary, the convergence of these large-scale capitalists' market and their political dominance compelled producers to employ a discourse which proclaimed the need to check both public and private power. As a result, producers appealed to the values of legitimacy and accountability inherent in the constitutional ideal. The practical form that this appeal took may have been simply attacks upon aristocracy, monopoly, and corporations. But the ideological force of such attacks derived from a popular faith that to be legitimate, power had to be accountable to external authority.

Producers' appeal to constitutional values coincided with the rise of evangelical Protestant moralism, which also distrusted capitalism. As-

suming that objectively identifiable and inviolable universal moral principles governed individual lives and society generally, the activist evangelical Protestant faith embraced self-reliance, self-discipline, and individual responsibility. Individuals whose lives expressed these traits did their duty, and a limited government was best suited for a society composed of such citizens. Protestant moralism was not inconsistent with individualism and private rights. But it resisted these doctrines when they took the form of exploitative corporate and commercially speculative capitalism because capitalist values eroded the sound character upon which depended personal responsibility and society's welfare. Because of the threat of moral corrosion, therefore, proponents of evangelical Protestantism formed common ground with producers in the concern for the preservation of personal independence.[19] To contain the threat that corporate and large mercantile capitalist values posed, representatives of both groups defended and appealed to the constitutional values of legitimacy and accountability.

The persistence of locally oriented market relations fostered further appeals to constitutionalism. While nearly everyone throughout the nation's economic order to varying degrees relied on credit, the interpersonal bonds governing legal obligation were stronger in local markets. Small-scale, unincorporated, owner-operated agricultural, commercial, and industrial enterprises were more willing to prolong the time in which debtors had to pay their creditors than were larger, foreign mercantile and corporate creditors. Local personal bonds in part reflected market contingencies favoring long-term considerations. Yet these immediate economic concerns often blended with various social and cultural values and interests, creating associational relationships that transcended narrow market imperatives. These relationships were common enough to constitute what amounted to a locally oriented associational economy at odds with the demands of big corporate and mercantile enterprises tied more directly into the national market and identified with capitalism. Responding to national market pressures, the producers bound together within the associational economy naturally turned for protection to local governmental institutions and the constitutional values they represented.[20]

This study focuses on how antebellum constitutionalism responded to and shaped these appeals for protection. Placing the constitutional system's operation in the context of the nation's profound ideological and social conflicts, it suggests that because of the normative force of

constitutional values, protectionist policies often opposed the emerging corporate and mercantile capitalist consensus. It also suggests some possible consequences of these policies, at least in the short run, for the eventual triumph of American capitalism. The first chapter sets out a framework for understanding the social basis of constitutionalism and its policy-making impact. Four subsequent chapters employ this framework in the setting of four mid-Atlantic states: Delaware, Maryland, New Jersey, and Pennsylvania. The study focuses on four principal policy areas: debtor-creditor relations, taxation, eminent domain, and railroad accidents. This mid-Atlantic region is intended to serve as a federal system in miniature, offering opportunities for comparative analysis.

# 1

## Constitutionalism, Capitalism, and Antebellum Society

During the first half of the nineteenth century, capitalism and the meaning of the Constitution grew together. The Constitution framed in 1787 and ratified the next year began operation in a mercantilist economy where state governments controlled market relations.[1] After the coincident end of the War of 1812 and the Napoleonic Wars in 1815, the states' and to a lesser degree the federal government's role in the economy became increasingly promotional.[2] More than ever before liberal capitalist values associated with free-market economic growth gained dominance over locally oriented markets of small enterprisers.[3] Encouraging these changes, the Supreme Court and the federal judiciary under chief justices John Marshall and Roger B. Taney interpreted constitutional provisions to strengthen contract and property rights. One strand of constitutional meaning thus sanctioned an emergent capitalist order. Meanwhile, from the 1830s on the struggle between free and slave labor steadily redefined the relationship of the Constitution to rising capitalism. By the 1850s the Republican party employed a free-labor constitutional interpretation to repudiate the *Dred Scott* decision, thereby overshadowing the Court's accommodation of past constitutional constructions to an expanding national

market economy.[4] Also, critics increasingly challenged gender and racial discrimination, but its grip on American life persisted.[5]

Before the Civil War, however, constitutional interpretation did not sanction unrestrained capitalism alone. James Madison, Alexis de Tocqueville, and others emphasized how original was the federal system that the Constitution established.[6] The periodic political party struggles that gradually determined the boundary between state and federal power involved a fundamental constitutional ideal: all public and private power should be checked by power external to itself.[7] Throughout the antebellum period various social groups also appealed to this constitutional ideal in order to contain emergent capitalism. Debtors belonging to locally oriented markets resisted foreign, big-city merchants, and smaller property holders and unincorporated enterprisers shifted tax burdens to large merchants and corporations; these groups also won regulation of corporations in order to protect themselves and their communities. None of this diminished the exploitation of women and African-Americans.[8] Still, larger political party confrontations were symptomatic of underlying constitutional values of legitimacy and accountability that many smaller and weaker market interests could and did turn against mercantile and corporate capitalists.

As these social and political conflicts defined federalism, predominately local and capitalist market relations coincided. The tariff, the Bank of the United States, and public land policy to the contrary notwithstanding, the federal government influenced the nation's economic order less directly than the states. Especially after 1815 the dominant political party coalitions of first Jeffersonian and then Jacksonian Democrats professed primary support for states' rights. Despite important opinions favoring national power, the overall thrust of the Supreme Court's and the federal judiciary's decision making also sustained the states' broad police power.[9] Accordingly, modest-sized enterprisers and property holders involved principally in local markets often were protected by state legislatures, courts, and local legal institutions. The same constitutional ideal that sanctioned greater state than federal promotional intervention in the economic order fostered protectionist policies benefiting locally oriented market relations. By facilitating market diversity, federalism thereby encouraged interest groups that both supported and opposed capitalist values.[10]

Strengthening the interconnection of federalism, market diversity,

and the constitutional ideal was social-class fragmentation. To a greater or lesser extent, the public rhetoric of all major political parties from Jeffersonian and Jacksonian Democrats to Whigs and Republicans endorsed a tripartite social structure. Social commentators recognized these same class distinctions. Manipulative finance capitalists were above and dispossessed paupers were below a moderately prosperous middling class of independent producers. Throughout the period those perceived as belonging to the middling classes changed, culminating finally in the Republican party's advocacy of free labor producerism, including manual industrial workers, yeoman farmers, and small, unincorporated, owner-operator artisan, trader, and manufacturing enterprisers. But the composition of the two classes threatening the "middling sort" remained basically the same. Since it was from the middling producer groups (however defined) that all political parties drew support, the tripartite class rhetoric possessed ideologically normative force.[11] The same groups espousing this ideology, moreover, appealed to the constitutional ideal to win protectionist policies from state and local public officials. Thus within the federal system the interpenetration of locally oriented market relations and the politically enfranchised yet threatened middling producers facilitated protectionism.

The convergence of protectionism and the constitutional ideal sustained associational market relations. Antebellum America's specie scarce economy depended upon credit.[12] The interconnection between credit and the persistence of local markets supported business relationships in which individual accountability was of primary importance. At the same time, an omnipresent threat of business failure pervaded local communities of market interests who to varying degrees were indebted to nonresident or out-of-state big, urban merchants or banks. The tension between personally accountable yet economically vulnerable unincorporated smaller enterprisers on the one hand and large-scale mercantile and corporate capitalists on the other helped to define a locally oriented, associational economic order. Those engaged principally in this economy appealed to state and local authorities on the basis of the constitutional ideal for protection from foreign capitalist enterprise. The evolving interpretation of federalism often sanctioned protectionist policies and thereby perpetuated an associational economy.

The federal judiciary's role in this dual-market economy was ambiv-

alent. Through interpretation of the Constitution's commerce, contract, judicial, and other clauses, federal judges led by the Supreme Court could and did defend emerging capitalist interests engaged in national markets from state and local protectionism. Countervailing institutional pressures engendered by political parties and the federal system itself, however, forced the federal judiciary generally to act indirectly.[13] Federal judges employed a textualist interpretive technique which neutralized attacks upon their own power. The federal judicial establishment and the Supreme Court in particular were nonetheless unable to defend capitalist values unequivocally. Indeed, the overall trend of decision making under both the Marshall and Taney Courts was toward constitutional interpretations that generally sanctioned a broad police power, thereby encouraging many protectionist policies. As the Court accommodated the tension between local and national markets and producer and capitalist values, it also reconciled republican and liberal constitutional ideologies that were consistent with the popular faith in American singularity.[14]

These institutional and ideological factors acquired distinctive focus in a four-state mid-Atlantic region. In Pennsylvania, Maryland, New Jersey, and Delaware relatively small-sized, modestly capitalized, unincorporated enterprisers were the norm. These owner-operator proprietorships and yeoman farmers coexisted with major mercantile and corporate capitalists located primarily in Philadelphia and Baltimore. Although steadily declining, slavery also existed in Maryland and Delaware. Represented by one of the nation's foremost economists—Henry Carey—political and social commentators in the region espoused small-scale producerism over corporate and large mercantile capitalist values. The political rhetoric of the competing party organizations throughout the period generally supported the same preference. A prominent group of constitutional commentators from the region argued for the reconciliation of republican and liberal ideologies. Meanwhile, many of the Supreme Court's leading decisions interpreting the contract, commerce, judicial, and other clauses arose from the region. Women and free African-Americans generally remained comparatively subordinate within the region's diverse economic order. Taken together, these factors constituted a working federal system in miniature which encouraged, on the basis of appeals to the constitutional ideal, the protection of independent producers united by associational market relations.

### The Social Basis of the Constitutional Ideal

Societal discourse about the limits of private and public power appealed to a constitutional ideal. Fundamental to the constitutional order created in 1787 was the popular faith that all power should be responsive to and checked by power outside of itself. Known more generally as "checks and balances," the meaning of this constitutional ideal was not static. Political party struggles over the Virginia and Kentucky Resolutions, nullification, slavery, and secession did not involve the functional operation of the federal system alone. Contemporaneously, political rhetoric and Supreme Court decisions set forth conflicting ideological formulations regarding the appropriate bounds of the states' and the national government's legitimate authority. A similar discourse pertaining to such private interests as corporations, monopolies, or "aristocracy" embodied equivalent concerns about constitutional legitimacy and accountability. Thus legislative and judicial controversies possessed a symbolic as well as an operational content. The political and market interests behind these confrontations, moreover, grew out of a fragmented social-class structure.[15]

As a symbolic and working entity, the Constitution's meaning during the antebellum years was unsettled. By melding together the traditions of local or state and national sovereignty, the Constitution embodied a new theory. The resulting institution was nonetheless, Tocqueville observed, anomalous in that it required "not only that the federal government should dictate the laws but that it should itself see to their execution." Yet as a practical matter the nature of this federal power "rested almost entirely on legal fictions." Through "good sense and practical intelligence" the Americans by the 1830s had managed to "avoid the innumerable difficulties deriving from their federal Constitution." Even so, "clearly here we have not a federal government but an incomplete national government. Hence a form of government has been found which is neither precisely national nor federal; but things have halted there, and the new word to express this new thing does not yet exist."[16]

The symbolic content of the Constitution emerged between 1789 and 1860, said Michael Kammen, "haltingly and incompletely." Eventually a consensus revering the Constitution appeared, but it was a consensus shaped by conflict. Soon after ratification, to be sure, the Anti-Federalists and Federalists agreed that for the nation's posterity

the document drafted in 1787 made "prosperity inevitable." Still, what sort of prosperity, for whom, and how it might be embodied in constitutional symbolism were subject to recurring conflict. In the wake of Jefferson's Revolution of 1800, Philadelphia's Benjamin Rush doubted whether love for the Constitution was strong enough to unify the nation. What "shall we fight for? For the Constitution? I cannot meet with a man who loves it," he observed. "It is considered as too weak by one half of our citizens and too strong by the other half." Forty-seven years later Frederick Douglass repudiated his former agreement with William Lloyd Garrison that the Constitution was a "Covenant with Death." Defending the Liberty party's platform, he denied that the Constitution was "a pro-slavery instrument" and affirmed it as a symbol of abolitionism.[17]

Thus throughout the period, Kammen concluded, the cultural and institutional Constitution was dual dimensional. "Americans . . . acquired the capacity to view their Constitution with a vision that was occasionally clouded and frequently bifocal: bifocal in the sense that the Constitution as a cultural symbol, rationalized in various ways, could be seen on a separate plane—or literally through a discrete lens—from the Constitution as a 'practical system.'" This bifocal vision manifested itself at both the state and national levels of government in the platforms of political parties, including Jefferson's Democratic Republicans, the Whigs and the Jacksonian Democrats, and finally Abraham Lincoln's Republicans. It found expression in the decisions of the Supreme Court under Chief Justice John Marshall and his successor Roger B. Taney. And it was the subject of ongoing popular and professional commentaries. Even so, the vision's emerging symbolic content interacted with the routine operation of formal governmental institutions and the intermittent struggle to sustain a societal discourse possessing significant normative force.[18]

At one level, Willard Hurst argued, this societal discourse crystallized as an abstract ideal of constitutionalism. In generalized form the ideal was that "in a humane society, there should be no centers of unchecked practical or legal power of some people over others. Every center of legal or practical power should be subject in material degree to checks exercised from outside itself, regarding the ends it pursued and the means by which it pursued them." In practical terms this fundamental ideal of constitutionalism shaped and was shaped by the market and governmental policies that allocated resources and ad-

justed competing interests within the American social order. The scope and scale of this interaction was as wide as antebellum society itself. Within such broad limits the ideal embodied a principle of legitimacy, according to which "powerholders choose at least their intermediate goals by reasoned examination of relevant facts and values, and chose means reasonably calculated to reach their goals." At the same time, and more profoundly, legitimacy required that power holders demonstrate a "humane regard for the worth and dignity of individuals living within the power system" at least insofar as this included the politically enfranchised.[19]

But even among the enfranchised, determining the working application of the ideal was subject to conflict. The new "federal" character of America's constitutional order that was described by Tocqueville engendered inevitable struggles involving the limits of the legitimate exercise of governmental power. Establishing the boundaries separating federal and state authority was a well-known source of controversy. James Madison's *Federalist* No. 51 explored the relationship between the constitutional ideal and federalism by emphasizing that with the two coexisting sovereignties checking each other's power, the people's rights were protected. "In the compound republic of America, the power surrendered by the people is first divided between two distinct governments, and then the portion allotted to each subdivided among distinct and separate departments," he said. "Hence a double security arises to the rights of the people. The different governments will control each other at the same time that each will be controlled by itself."[20]

The interplay between federalism and the constitutional ideal involved political parties. The clash over the Alien and Sedition Acts that spawned Madison's and Jefferson's Virginia and Kentucky Resolutions before the 1800 election, Andrew Jackson's confrontation with South Carolina over the 1828 tariff leading to the nullification crisis, Georgia's dispossession of the Cherokee Indians, and the clash over fugitive slaves and the status of slavery in the territories that resulted in secession were conspicuous political party struggles concerning federalism. Clashes of such significant proportions inevitably had broad-based impact on the way social tensions were defined and contained within the party structure. As such, their cultural and institutional implications reached beyond the immediate participants. Citizens throughout the nation were acquainted with the symbolic

meaning and working content of the constitutional ideal. Thus to a certain extent the social basis of constitutionalism reflected the political party structure as defined by periodic crisis.[21]

Such struggles also raised problems of legitimacy more explicitly related to the market. Conflicts involving banking (either banks within the states alone or clashes between those banks and the Bank of the United States) engendered social concerns about legitimacy within the market. The spread of transportation corporations aroused similar sorts of market and social-class tensions. In either case the problem of legitimacy had major social ramifications because it touched the issue of taxation. The states' grant of the power of eminent domain to canals and railroads and the railroads' liability for accidents aroused further questions of legitimacy and accountability. The legal relationship between debtors and creditors concerning the transferability of credit through negotiable contracts and the status of contract obligations under bankruptcy and insolvency laws were other vital market issues. Thus, not unlike the political party crises, each of these issues touched social groups who possessed an independent stake in determining the appropriate boundary of state and federal constitutional authority and its relation to local and national markets.[22]

As the national economy evolved, the federal system increased the costs of economic development. Several factors fostered uncertainty in the federal system. First, there was little or no uniformity in the local law of the states governing rights and obligations arising out of private transactions. This lack of uniformity was pronounced enough that many times the local law included different rules on similar or even identical issues. In addition, state courts and legislatures changed these rules periodically, so that there was often considerable doubt as to what the law on many subjects was at any given time. Furthermore, interstate rivalry and local distrust of outsiders generated state laws and regulations that frankly discriminated against out-of-state business. This uncertainty in many of the "rules of the game" governing interstate enterprise thus constituted a barrier to economic development.[23]

In general, states sought to discriminate against nonresidents, especially out-of-state creditors who had in-state debtors. State legislatures at times even went to such extremes as closing the courts to prevent adjudication of debtor-creditor controversies, making depreciated paper legal tender for debts, allowing extensions of time to

debtors through stay laws (which were virtual moratoriums), and even passing private acts to overturn court decisions. Debtor-creditor laws were a major example of the ways in which state legislatures could use their power to protect local debtors from out-of-state creditors. Massachusetts and New York, commented Congressman Elijah H. Mills in 1818, carried on a kind of "border war," in which each state used its laws to favor locals at the expense of businessmen from the neighboring state. During the distress of the panic of 1819–22, Kentucky, Ohio, North Carolina, Indiana, Mississippi, Alabama, Tennessee, and Maryland passed laws similar to those of New York and Massachusetts in an effort to alleviate the financial burden on state residents, many of whom were indebted to creditors in other states. During the 1830s Alabama attempted to close its borders to corporations chartered in other states by passing a law which virtually denied the validity of contracts negotiated between locals and out-of-state corporations. But surely the most extreme example was Kentucky, which created a whole new judicial system to protect its debtors; while the old Kentucky judiciary continued to function at the same time that state-based defiance involving debtor-creditor relations and corporations remained important. While increasingly by the 1840s such issues were overshadowed by slavery controversies, in practical terms they continued to be important.[24]

The federal judiciary worked to reduce these tensions, but its general impact on the states was indirect. "Federal judges almost always alone decide those questions," Tocqueville wrote, "that touch the government of the country most closely." Yet during the antebellum years the states rather than the federal government, he said, exercised "real power." Nevertheless, Americans accepted that "it was almost impossible that the execution of a new law should not injure some private interest." The Constitution's "makers" relied on that "private interest to attack the legislative measure of which the Union might have complained," and it was that interest to which the federal courts "offer[ed] protection." Thus while "federal justice" and "state sovereignty" were "at odds," the federal courts "attack[ed] only indirectly . . . strik[ing] at the consequences of the law, not at its principle; it does not abolish but enervates it." The courts "intervened," Tocqueville concluded, "in public affairs only by chance, but the chance recurs daily." The overriding constitutional command that federal judges protect individuals—particularly residents of different states—thus

compelled repeated consideration and interpretation of the limits and meaning of state and federal law and the Constitution itself.[25]

A vital institutional link between social groups and constitutionalism was the jury. The jury was "above all," observed Tocqueville, "a political institution." The "jury system as it is understood in America appears to me to be as direct and as extreme a consequence of the sovereignty of the people as universal suffrage." Jury lists including 144 names from Philadelphia during the 1840s reveal the social-class ramifications of this assessment. The great majority (49%) of those serving as jurors were identified as artisan-mechanics, such as carpenters, bricklayers, and plumbers. Merchants or small wholesalers made up 25% and farmers 10% of those appearing on the lists. Among the remaining 16%, seven men were laborers, six were service people or professionals, and just three were identified as "gentlemen." In rural areas jurors were drawn from the ranks of small as well as large farmers and small-town artisans.[26]

The democratic composition of juries was linked also to the increasingly elected character of local courts. In the small towns and rural areas where the great majority of Americans lived, single law firms made up of a few lawyers were known to have considerable influence over local judges and juries. The fact that most state judges, from the local level to the highest court, were increasingly elected further strengthened the ties between local social imperatives and democratic politics. Federal judges, by contrast, possessed authority that reduced the independence of juries through instructions and other procedures. Too, federal juries were drawn from a much wider area than juries in many local trial courts. Throughout the first half of the nineteenth century, these sorts of institutional changes gradually strengthened the judge's control over the jury in state courts. Nevertheless, by the Civil War state courts at both the trial and appellate level remained comparatively more responsive to popular local interest and values than their federal counterparts.[27]

Underlying social-class tensions worked through the local legal system, aggravating business interests. Whether or not state judges succeeded in limiting the jury's authority over law, leaving to it responsibility for the facts, commercial litigants complained of bias. As late as 1856 the "frequent inability of jurors to agree in commercial cases" was "a matter to be regretted," wrote a critic in *Hunt's Merchants' Magazine*. He was undoubtedly aware that the preponderance of ur-

ban jurors came from the ranks of artisans and small traders. Those same groups tended to be of ethnic immigrant stock. As a result, he perceived a "foreign" threat. "We think there is great reason to suspect that in this system there has crept some foreign element, which thrives only upon the virtues it destroys, and is destructive of the very ends for which the system was designed," the critic warned.[28]

The interplay between social-class tensions and local legal institutions altered the role of lawyers. Tocqueville and other commentators, as well as later historians, noted how antebellum lawyers constituted a bulwark of conservatism.[29] Notwithstanding the correctness of this assertion, it underestimates the growing diversity of the market for legal services that was emerging before the Civil War. The democratized social basis of state and local legal institutions provided opportunities for lawyers who were defending the constitutional ideal. The most conspicuous instance of such appeals was the rise of contingent fees in railroad accident cases, whereby lawyers received payment only if the jury verdict favored the plaintiff. Letters from railroad managers and corporate reports emphasized the impact the contingent fee had on encouraging the firms' public accountability and even, on occasion, humanity.

The link between the constitutional ideal and the market for legal services was evident elsewhere. In debtor-creditor relations, property assessments resulting from eminent domain proceedings, the administration of charter provisions regulating banking and transportation corporations, and other areas of legal dispute there were always at least two sides. In such instances, propublic appeals derived from popular respect for the ideal of constitutionalism benefited debtors, modest-sized property holders, and other weaker groups at odds with large mercantile creditors and corporations. Lawyers representing this side of legal controversy argued, moreover, that they stood for the public interest. By empowering weaker groups before democratized local legal institutions more attuned to their interests, lawyers gave normative force to the constitutional ideal.

The interplay of federalism, social groups, and the constitutional ideal also involved social-class structure. As Stuart M. Blumin has urged, a discernible middle class, distinct from procapitalist elites and manual workers, existed in America by the middle of the nineteenth century. Possessing identifiable personal and social experience evidenced by "work, consumption, residential location, formal and infor-

mal voluntary association, and family organization and strategy," this class embodied an emerging "way of life." For Blumin this process of social-class development represented neither (in Marxist terms) an "inessential or transitory" class nor one whose formation was less significant and enduring than the "process of class polarization" between the bourgeois and proletariat. Blumin's formulation suggests that like artisan-mechanics and farmers and large corporations and merchants a category which included manufacturers and major urban wholesalers, "middling-class" groups possessed socially coherent and distinct values and interests.[30]

This characterization of social-class structure suggests the social forces shaping the influence of constitutionalism. The arguments of politicians, lawyers, and publicists supporting the constitutional ideal recognized three social-class divisions: the poor, capitalists, and the "middling" classes. Fostering the identity and cohesion of the middling classes was the paradoxical convergence of market vulnerability and political power. Throughout the antebellum period a cycle of depression and prosperity generated uncertainty throughout the credit system upon which the market economy depended. This instability, combined with the considerable market power of large merchant creditors and corporations, threatened the welfare of modest-sized agricultural and commercial enterprisers. At the same time, the dispossessed represented a danger because of potential social unrest and costs associated with administering the poor laws. Meanwhile, the middling classes were an important political constituency. Appealing to the constitutional ideal through political parties and local legal institutions, the middling classes sought and won policies that protected it from those above and below.[31]

Blumin's social-class categorization suggests that the working and symbolic content of constitutionalism emerged from social fragmentation. Accordingly, struggles over the operational boundaries of federalism and appeals to the constitutional ideal involved more than intra-class conflict within a capitalist consensus. Vested interests, sanctity of contract, and property rights were not only not absolute, they were significantly circumscribed in the name of republican government and popular sovereignty. Essentially, such limitations rested upon the traditional principle of federalism: the states' police power. Where capitalist values and the police power clashed, policies often resulted that

protected the interests of weaker social-classes. Offsetting doctrines such as contributory negligence, for instance, did not undermine doctrines that sustained the prevalence of the contingent fee in railroad accident cases. This was so partially because antebellum railroad managers acceded to the constraints of moral accountability implicit in the constitutional ideal. Employees generally did not benefit from the railroads' deference to humane concerns. Still, most of those maimed or killed were members of the middling classes whose social status and political clout railroads ignored at their peril.

Social-class influence also shaped policies governing debtor-creditor relations. Despite certain United States Supreme Court decisions, most state insolvency and bankruptcy laws favored debtors, who generally were small or modest-sized traders. Also, the policies aided this same group at the expense of large merchant wholesalers who resided within a state or were out-of-state mercantile competitors. Similarly, legal rules governing the transferability and circulation of credit under commercial contracts benefited not only big merchants but the multitude of small enterprisers as well. Taken together, both categories of debtor-creditor policies facilitated the entry of marginal groups into the business order and protected smaller debtors from large creditors within or outside of a single state. In either case the significant beneficiaries of the policies were the weaker participants in the market. Antebellum commercial periodicals and other popular publications distinguished this middling class of traders from both the big capitalist and the poor.[32]

Various social groups benefited from policies regulating corporations, but none more than the middling classes. Clearly, state legislatures conferred important privileges upon corporate capitalists. They did so, however, subject to tax policies requiring banks and transportation companies to fund public education, particularly in major cities, and the general operational expenses of government. The resulting income paid for the education of industrial workers' children, especially in leading urban centers. It also significantly reduced or removed altogether the need for farmers and merchants (including small traders) to pay property or income taxes. State-imposed rates on railroads and canals, moreover, favored the interests of the farmers and merchants of certain communities over others. The general outcome was nonetheless that those classes in more rather than fewer localities

benefited. Meanwhile, smaller urban and rural property holders gained from the value assessment procedures imposed by the process of eminent domain.

These tensions reflected the social basis of antebellum American constitutionalism. The "new" federal system created checks on public and private power centers to which social-class groups, market interests, and political parties could appeal in the name of constitutional legitimacy and accountability. The substantive content of such appeals embodied both working and symbolic realities that evolved over time. Even so, the core of the constitutional ideal was that all centers of power were to be accountable to and legitimated by external formal checks. While a variety of market, social-class, and political interests professed loyalty to this constitutional ideal, its multidimensional character facilitated a public discourse which smaller, weaker debtor and property groups used against mercantile and corporate capitalists. As a result, when local and state legal institutions and policy makers clashed with capitalist interests and the federal judiciary, local control often prevailed. To the extent this was so, the enforcement of the constitutional ideal was thus consistent with social fragmentation.

## Federalism, Institutional Legitimacy, and Social Conflict

The interconnection between federalism and the constitutional ideal was fundamental if often obscure. In the great political party battles such as the confrontation involving the Virginia and Kentucky Resolutions, the nullification controversy, or secession, the significance of the two principles was obvious. Less conspicuous but not unimportant were many mundane instances in which the ideal shaped policy making as a result of the federal structure more narrowly.[33] The United States Congress passed few important regulations of interstate commerce before 1860 because southerners feared that use of the power eventually might facilitate regulation of slavery. Accordingly, proponents of expanded or limited federal commerce power usually talked in terms of constitutional checks and balances rather than specifically mentioning the "peculiar institution." Similarly, slavery was a primary reason why the Supreme Court decided no major commerce clause case until *Gibbons* v. *Ogden* (1824), and it explained why the clause remained so contentious for the Court thereafter. In these and other

cases party leaders and the federal judiciary supported or opposed a loose or strict interpretation of federal or state power based on appeals to the constitutional ideal. The multifaced character of the symbol, however, clouded the substantive realities engendering its application.[34]

The ideal also shaped policy where its influence may have been still more indirect. Throughout the long period from 1800 to 1860, constitutional crises as well as court cases involving constitutional interpretation were intermittent. State legislatures and courts, by contrast, more or less continuously confronted social and political pressures requiring immediate response. If, as in the case of the commerce power, congressional action was limited and the Supreme Court's decisions were episodic, state officials operated within a power vacuum requiring that they define the parameters of legitimate authority themselves. In such cases a policy's scope and content were determined by the national government's relative constitutional silence. The degree of silence varied from case to case and over time as Congress enacted a law or the federal judiciary settled litigation. Yet in accord with Tocqueville's observation regarding the open-ended character of American federalism that compelled repeated resort to "legal fictions," the range of uncertainty within which state and local officials freely operated was extensive.

The states' liberal application of the constitutional ideal coincided with attacks upon the Supreme Court. Drawing upon constitutionalism's multisided and emerging character, critics attacked the Court as partisan and consolidationist. The partisan issue reflected partially Thomas Jefferson's famous assertion that under John Marshall the Federalists had retreated to the judicial branch. Andrew Jackson embraced the same principle in defending his appointment of politically correct Democrats in order to check such conservatives as Joseph Story. Less well known yet perhaps of greater significance in light of its bearing on secession, the Republicans ironically echoed Jackson's rationale when they advocated appointment of judges who would overturn *Dred Scott* and respect states' rights represented by the personal liberty laws. The broader struggle nonetheless involved the code word "discretion." The content of this principle concerned the freedom of federal judges to interpret constitutional and legal texts. The critics charged that the federal judiciary not only interpreted these texts but did so according to a particular party's politics.[35]

The code word for the familiar clash between states' rights and national authority was "consolidation." The Marshall Court was the most well known object of the criticism that the federal judiciary fostered centralizing federal authority. Yet amidst the struggle over the personal liberty laws and enforcement of the federal fugitive slave law, antislavery groups and abolitionists used the "consolidationist" argument against Chief Justice Roger B. Taney and the federal courts. The underlying issue involving the consolidationist rhetoric was whether the federal judiciary's jurisdiction was to be coterminous with the power of Congress. Thus critics claimed not just that the Court was an umpire playing for the national government's side. The critics attacked such decisions as *McCulloch* v. *Maryland* (1819), *Gibbons* v. *Ogden* (1824), or *Ableman* v. *Booth* (1859) also because by sustaining a constitutional interpretation which extended congressional power to charter a bank, regulate commerce, or implement the fugitive slave code, the Court was enlarging the federal judiciary's authority over the litigation that would inevitably result. This outcome, the critics argued, obscured the threat that the federal courts posed for states' rights, enabling the Court to claim that it was merely carrying out the Constitution's grant of jurisdiction over national laws.[36]

Led by the Supreme Court, the federal judiciary successfully fended off the critics. From the 1790s on there were repeated attempts in Congress to curtail the federal judiciary's jurisdiction, particularly by abolishing section 25 of the Judiciary Act of 1789, which enabled the Supreme Court to review the decisions of each state's highest tribunal. Since Congress possesses almost complete control over federal jurisdiction, it is potentially vulnerable to these political pressures. Except for the Eleventh Amendment, however, no such effort succeeded before the Civil War. The Marshall Court deflected the threat by giving such code words as "commerce," "contract," or "union" purportedly neutral meanings that deflected the critics' assertions regarding consolidation and discretion. The Taney Court followed the same strategy, adjusting its predecessor's precedents to changing political and market conditions. The Taney Court, moreover, actually extended federal judicial power in the fields of admiralty and commercial credit. Meanwhile, the Jacksonian-dominated Court obscured its accommodation of the Marshall Court's jurisprudence by using states' rights code phrases. The general proposition that the Court of both the Marshall and Taney eras established concerning the text embodying

these code words was that the Court merely found and declared law; it did not make law.[37]

The Court prevailed by making a three-pronged response to the critics' attacks. First, the Court employed a linguistic analysis of the constitutional or legal text embodying such terms as "contract" or "commerce," extracting from the words a purportedly neutral principle which would be used in turn to pack the word with an extratextual meaning. The principle drawn from the commerce clause in *Gibbons*, for example, was intercourse, resulting in an interpretation of the commerce power which extended beyond trade alone to include the regulation of steamboats. The Taney Court employed this technique in commerce clause cases to define the boundary of state regulation of commercial activity (including slavery) as long as Congress remained silent. Similarly, the Marshall Court extended the contract clause to include not only private contracts between individuals but also state-chartered corporations. Beginning with the *Charles River Bridge* decision, the Taney Court altered the contract clause further by enlarging the states' regulatory authority. A second prong was to adapt this technique to nonconstitutional doctrines of the common law, recasting their content to apply to new situations. The most notable example was the Taney Court's creation of the general commercial law in *Swift v. Tyson* (1842). Finally, both the Marshall and Taney Courts shielded their deliberations from significant public scrutiny through institutionalized secrecy.[38]

This three-pronged response was, in turn, anchored in larger cultural currents. Beginning around 1815 the basic material conditions driving cultural change were rapid population growth, territorial expansion, and the transportation revolution. While these forces transformed American life, social-class stratification and local autonomy persisted. Accordingly, popular values found, for instance, in James Fenimore Cooper's literary works embodied tensions encapsulated in an amalgam of republican and liberal ideologies. An Americanized version of republican ideology persisted until the 1830s; eroding and eventually supplanting it was a liberal, egalitarian individualism which by 1860 possessed ideological force within a free-labor paradigm.[39]

These popular values interacted with and gave content to the constitutional ideal. The contentiousness involving the scope and limits of federal/state relations and the power of the Supreme Court acquired

meaning through several central cultural presumptions. America was a new republican society liberated from the corrupting influence of English feudal institutions. This society possessed a novel form of government in which sovereignty rested with the people and the abuse of power resulting in tyranny was limited by constitutional checks and balances. God, moreover, had given Americans a virgin continent and abundant resources. Taken together, these assumptions sustained the hope that Americans were exceptional in that they might break the cycle of growth and decay characteristic of earlier republics and thereby realize a future destiny. Thus the American republic might be truly free: free from corruption associated with aristocratic hierarchy, free to pursue individual opportunity liberated from monopolistic regulations, and above all free from historical laws which determined that republics eventually decayed and died. The triumph of American exceptionalism depended, then, on whether Americans could control the relationship between the past and the future.[40]

The Court's three-pronged response to this challenge adapted the Constitution and the common law to change while denying that a court made law. Thus the Court presented its alteration of constitutional language or common-law doctrine as the clarification or reassertion of settled principles. It explicitly denied that it was creating anything new. This technique succeeded primarily because it employed the constitutional ideal to permit a reconciliation of the past and the future which was central to the ideological tensions associated with American exceptionalism and escape from the historical cycle of growth and decay. In addition, the Court's particular recasting of "commerce," "contract," and other code words of constitutional and legal texts facilitated the adjustment of republican ideology to the rising influence of liberalism and the free-labor paradigm. Finally, at least until the *Dred Scott* decision, the response deflected the charges of critics regarding partisanship and "consolidation" by sustaining the Court's and the federal judiciary's neutrality in defense of federalism and independence from corruption and tyranny.[41]

Facilitating this textual-packing, interpretive technique was the evolving and restricted attention given "original intent." For years after 1787 the use of intention as a tool for interpreting constitutional or legal texts was unsettled. During the framing and ratification era virtually no respect was given to what the framers of the Constitution might have said was their intention in drafting the document. Prac-

tically this was so because for decades after 1787 the participants in the Philadelphia convention kept an oath not to discuss their activity publicly. Not until 1821 were the convention notes taken by Robert Yates of New York published. The much more extensive material prepared by James Madison during the convention appeared posthumously in 1840. More significantly, the original meaning of original intent was open to dispute. Influential cultural traditions rooted in the Enlightenment and British Protestantism adhered to such rigorous textual rationalism and literalism that any purported interpretation was suspect. A competing tradition drew upon the legalistic devices found in the common law. Thus at the time of the ratification conventions of 1787–88 the tension between these cultural traditions undercut the assertion that some unequivocal intention existed.[42]

With the rise of the Jeffersonian Democrats another interpretive tradition involving intent emerged. To counter the consolidationist policies of the Federalists, the Jeffersonians developed an intentionalist theory which ignored the Philadelphia framers and most of the expectations of the participants in the ratification conventions. The focus of the Jeffersonian intentionalism was the sovereign states. The relevant intent was that involving "consideration of what rights and powers sovereign polities could delegate to a common agent without destroying their own essential autonomy. Thus, the original intentionalism was in fact a form of structural interpretation."[43]

By 1840 consolidationist and states' rights advocates converged on a final intentionalist theory. The Senate's Daniel Webster and the Court's Joseph Story rejected all state sovereignty principles. For them the constitutional text construed and established by the precedents of the Supreme Court provided the Constitution's ultimate meaning. Even so, the Court looked to the "intent" of the Philadelphia framers to legitimate the Court's decisions. A new states' rights school led by John C. Calhoun argued, by contrast, that the states possessed final authority to interpret the Constitution. Like his opponents, Calhoun resorted to the intent of the Philadelphia framers to justify his interpretive theory. At the outbreak of the Civil War both Unionists and Secessionists defended their cause by turning to "the Constitution formed by our fathers" and "their well-known intent."[44]

Ironically, James Madison himself rejected this intentionalist theory. "As a guide in expounding and applying the provisions of the Constitution," the man known to posterity as the Father of the Constitution

wrote in 1821, "the debates and incidental decisions of the Convention can have no authoritative character." The "legitimate meaning of the Instrument must be derived from the text itself; or if a key is to be sought elsewhere, it must be not in the opinions or intentions of the Body which planned and proposed the Constitution, but in the sense attached to it by the people in their respective State Conventions where it rec[eived] all the authority which it possesses."[45]

The intentionalist controversy converged with the textualist packing technique to promote the states' interpretive role. Both the republican and the liberal ideological faith that adherence to the constitutional ideal would save America's future from the threat of decay was consistent with active state policy making. As the embodiment of the people's will, and because the potential for abuse of its power was circumscribed by constitutional checks and balances, a state's right to make law was ideologically legitimated. In addition, the policy vacuum or silences resulting from congressional inaction also fostered an activist approach to extracting power from constitutional and legal texts. The Marshall and Taney Courts construed constitutional provisions to prescribe the limits of the states' police powers. Ultimately, however, the Supreme Court did more to sanction than restrict this power. As far as the issue of legitimacy involved "original intent," moreover, the Jeffersonian theory sustained state authority. Even after an intentionalist theory based on the Philadelphia framers prevailed, the struggle between Unionists and states' rights advocates left the question unsettled before 1860; thus ideological tensions facilitated the states' role as the interpreter of their own authority.

Ultimately, the Supreme Court, too, affirmed the broad interpretive authority of the states. Thanks to the Jeffersonian repeal of the sweeping Federalist Judiciary Act of 1801, only a comparatively few though nonetheless important cases were held to come within federal jurisdiction, and in many of these cases state law bound federal judges. Even Chief Justice John Marshall's nationalism sought to curb rather than destroy states' rights.[46] In spite of his ringing defense of the federal commerce power in *Gibbons* v. *Ogden* (1824), for instance, Marshall recognized that a state's police power constituted "a portion of that immense mass of legislation which embraces everything within the territory of a state, not surrendered to the general government; all of which can be most advantageously exercised by the states themselves." By the late 1820s, this principle gained increasing influence.[47]

In construing the contract clause, Article I, section 10, in *Dartmouth College* v. *Woodward* (1819), the Marshall Court struck down the legislature's interference with a corporate charter. Especially from the mid-1820s on, however, the Court sanctioned the states' right to regulate and repeal such grants. Under this principle states exercised considerable regulatory authority over corporations they chartered for purposes of economic development.[48] Marshall did, of course, defend nationalist principles in such cases as *McCulloch* v. *Maryland*. But even here states' rights prevailed due to Jackson's veto of the Bank of the United States.[49]

The Supreme Court under Chief Justice Taney further extended the states' influence in the economy. The Taney Court went beyond Marshall in holding that under the commerce power the states possessed the authority to regulate the local economy as long as Congress had not acted. Because Congress failed to exercise its authority, state power superseded national power in issues involving the commerce clause. In its contract clause decisions the Court further encouraged state action; the states used this power to promote economic development.[50] In the famous *Charles River Bridge* case Taney held that a Massachusetts law authorizing the construction of a new bridge which would compete with an older one did not violate the contract clause. This decision encouraged the states to foster new enterprises vital to their "well being and prosperity." Even such nationalistic opinions as *Swift* v. *Tyson* (1842), which declared that federal courts were free to ignore state law in cases involving commercial credit, affirmed a duty to follow local law whenever it applied.[51]

Given these realities, the frequent laments of the commercial press were understandable. "In a country like ours," cried *Hunt's* in 1846, "composed of a federal government and some 29 distinct and independent sovereignties . . . it is a source of no little regret that there should be discordance in the fundamental laws of the several states, by which the rights and obligations of the citizens of a commercial country are defined." Another *Hunt's* article reiterated a common complaint: The "merchant, trading with 29 state and territorial legislatures [needs] to understand the laws by which his debts may be enforced or their obligations discharged." Further, that merchant "is not only to understand the rules today, but to understand them tomorrow, as they may be changed by the fluctuations of caprice and experiment." And with "the increase of commerce . . . this evil is becoming more felt. May we

not hope that the day is not far distant when it shall cease! And . . . that the private rights of the American citizen, of whatever state in the Union, may be defined and constructed by the same general laws."[52]

Ideological tensions interacting with state and federal power politics gave the constitutional ideal substance and force. Treatise writers centered in Philadelphia, Boston, Charleston, and elsewhere, as well as legal articles appearing in such prominent periodicals as *Niles' Register*, *Hunt's Merchants' Magazine*, *National Review*, and *DeBow's Review*, translated the popular values reflected in such popular fiction as James Fenimore Cooper's works into legal commentary that informed the jurisprudence of the federal judiciary and the Supreme Court, state legal institutions, and practicing lawyers.[53] The ideal that all power should be responsive to and limited by power beyond itself emanated from the Constitution as three principles: an anticorruption principle, embodied in the separation of the legislature, executive, and judiciary; an antityranny principle, embodied in the idea of a written constitution; and the federalism principle, embodied in the creation of two sovereign entities, state and federal, checking each other. Applying these principles, the Supreme Court and the federal judiciary it led, as well as state courts, legislatures, and local authorities, shaped the nation's ability to avoid republican decay. In so doing they helped to achieve the promise of American exceptionalism.

Meanwhile, the winners and losers were clear in some cases but not in others. Jurisprudential assumptions by which the Court filled constitutional or legal texts with extralegal meaning would have been well suited to the adaptation of natural-law principles favoring the defense of exploited Indians, slaves, free blacks, white laborers, and women. A few decisions and other official policies benefited disadvantaged individuals, but most of the results favored white, male property holders. Some free blacks, slaves, and fugitive slaves received protection from due-process guarantees, culminating in the personal liberty laws. Married women's property laws and feme sole trader statutes also enlarged the rights of women. Still, overall, the constitutional ideal undercut neither white racial supremacy nor the separate spheres imposed by patriarchy.[54] All the more surprising, then, was the degree to which the ideal influenced certain state policies protecting debtors over creditors and smaller enterprisers from large corporate or mercantile capitalists. Thus, whereas the constitutional line distinguishing liberty and op-

pression was fairly apparent involving race and gender, it was much less so regarding the majority of white males within and without the business order.

### Capitalist Accountability, "Middling" Classes, and the Associational Economy

Resort to the constitutional ideal reinforced the survival and influence of anticapitalist values. Political parties and public officials justified the states' policies protecting debtors, small property holders, and modest enterprisers generally by appealing to the values of limited and accountable private or public power. Jeffersonian and Jacksonian Democrats used constitutional values to attack corporate monopolies and "paper aristocracy." When it suited their interests Whigs and Republicans drew upon the same rhetoric. The point was not that political opportunism enervated the power of ideology. Quite the contrary, until the end of the period there were always enough social, market, and political interests which felt threatened by unrestrained capitalism that resort to constitutional prescriptions helped to sustain anticapitalist ideological presumptions identified with associational market relations.[55]

The tension between the constitutional ideal and aggressive capitalistic acquisitiveness partially reflected uneven market development. What "most astonished" Tocqueville about the early American economic order was "not so much the marvelous grandeur of some undertakings as the innumerable multitude of small ones." This modest scale of enterprise may be understood in two senses. First, it involved those workers and smaller enterprisers existing within the growing national and international markets who were on the defensive from increasingly dominant liberal capitalist values. Second, it concerned those groups who remained more involved in local markets where capitalist enterprise did not yet prevail. In either case the smaller scale and market position of the modest-sized enterprisers fostered the sort of vulnerability that encouraged appeals to the constitutional ideal. The individual's, group's, or community's support for the ideal thus included Americans who were "slow to adopt to economic change, slow to receive many of the products of mass production (as against hand craftsmanship)," and who possessed "psycho-

logical and cultural resistance to mechanization, and the cheapness of labor and services," all of which "made for continuation of established means and norms. The motivation to remain with the circular flow . . . [was] notably stronger [and] the incentives to innovate [were] corresponding weaker."[56]

The interpenetration between local and national or international markets generated further tensions. During the first half of the nineteenth century the typical American did not live in an ideal competitive world guided by Adam Smith's invisible hand. Most traders were self-employed shopkeepers operating within local markets dominated by a few businesses. At the grassroots level industry developed along streams in small rural communities where modestly capitalized, unincorporated workshops, mills, and factories served a single locality. To be sure, certain articles such as British textiles and other quality imports were distributed nationally, and cotton, of course, dominated the nation's foreign exchange. The market for most manufactured goods and foodstuffs, however, usually did not extend beyond regional limits. Since owner-operated firms bought and sold chiefly within these markets, they strongly identified with the home community and adhered tenaciously to local control. Geographic divisions within and among states often corresponded to local markets and heightened a sense of autonomy, independence, and rivalry, as well as encouraging the demand for local protection.[57]

Thus by the mid-nineteenth century the forms of individual enterprise clearly diverged. Large merchant and corporate capitalists oriented to the national market were increasingly dominant. The leading enterprisers remained, however, the unincorporated, modestly capitalized producers who served the local or regional market. In the antebellum North, though major landed interests certainly existed, most farmers labored on small to medium-sized plots. In the South the great slave holding planters and merchants were conspicuous, but the vast majority of southerners were small-scale farmers who owned few or no slaves. Similarly, before the Treaty of Ghent a few big urban merchants dominated the nation's commercial order. But after 1815 they lost influence to a growing number of specialized middlemen trading within growing local and national markets. New York and New England had noteworthy large, incorporated factories and mills, but the great majority of industrial firms in both the rural and urban United States remained small, nonincorporated, owner-operated en-

terprises. Urban America also had an artisan elite. Even so, though the number may have been steadily shrinking, the majority of working people were small, independent proprietors.[58]

Fostering the group consciousness of these small, locally oriented enterprises was the specter of market failure. Peter J. Coleman has estimated that "in the early nineteenth century, one householder in every five would, during his working lifetime, fail outright rather than merely default on a particular debt. The incidence of difficulty probably rose as the century advanced."[59] To be sure, failure was as much a realty for large merchants and corporations as it was for small enterprise. But the producer's distrust of the "heavy capitalists" convinced him that they were in fact the cause of recurring depressions and business failures. In addition, economic collapse resulted in the proliferation of paupers that increased social welfare costs. At the same time, these pressures fostered a common feeling of vulnerability and shared experience among small enterprisers themselves. Knowing that failure could force them into the ranks of the dependent and propertyless, the modest-sized producers displayed sympathy for the unlucky, deserving poor and increasing antagonism toward the capitalist speculators and the pauper class they spawned.

Yet smaller producers shared more than fears. They hoped for the modest prosperity that economic development made possible, believed fervently in private property, defended individual rights (for adult white males), loved equality, and despised inequality. All of these they wanted on their own terms, subject to their control.[60] Profits should be limited and "longer accumulating" profits so that they would be "more certain"; property and fortunes should be "equalized" to favor the great mass of small enterprisers. The principle that private property was sacrosanct did not preclude its taking through taxation and other assessments; but taxes upon luxury items, corporations, and "paper capital" were preferable since they "fall upon the rich." Similarly, the protection of individual rights was vital as long as it preserved the independence of the individual and did not benefit the "moneyed class."[61]

These fears and hopes found material expression in the pervasive reliance upon credit. Jeffersonian and Jacksonian Democratic rhetoric lauded the benefits of specie over credit. This opposition principle applied generally, however, not to the ordinary credit transactions upon which small enterprisers in local markets depended. Rather, the

criticism extended to bank credit, especially that of the Bank of the United States. After all, given the chronic scarcity of specie characterizing the American economy from 1800 to 1860, no one—not Thomas Jefferson, Andrew Jackson, Abraham Lincoln or the constituents supporting their party organizations—could have survived without extensive credit. Thus the political rhetoric of each of the nation's parties was flexible enough to recognize and condone the value of honest as opposed to speculative credit. This reliance, moreover, helped to explain why, anticapitalist rhetoric to the contrary notwithstanding, even mainstream Democrats throughout the period supported state banks.[62]

Still, the qualified political rhetoric obscured the interpersonal associational bonds that credit dependency created, especially in local markets. An intricate web of contractual rights and obligations bound together local and nonresident traders and producers, making them at once debtors and creditors. Most of these contracts involved bills of exchange and promissory notes (called commercial paper), upon which specialized legal rules conferred the right of transferability known as negotiability. Small as well as big, farm as well as mercantile, artisan as well as industrial enterprise depended on credit exchange sanctioned by the principle of negotiability. Without this principle neither local, national, nor international markets could have functioned effectively in antebellum America. At the same time, the prevalence of locally oriented markets engendered on the state level protectionist debtor/creditor policies that conflicted with the interests of big nonresident merchants and banks. As a result, credit sanctioned by state law encouraged interpersonal or associational market relations favorable to local debtors and unfavorable to out-of-state creditors.[63]

The interdependency between locally oriented credit transactions and state protectionism facilitated an associational economic order. Associational market relations favored extending rather than limiting the debtor's credit. While these relationships did not ignore the rights of foreign creditors, they represented the primacy of local over national or international markets. In addition, the interpersonal bonds resulting from this legally sanctioned priority extended the rights and opportunities of the smallest, weakest enterprising individuals as well as facilitating their entry into the business order. Often these associational relationships softened the consequences of insolvency or bankruptcy by carrying an individual until better times returned.[64]

The associational bonds reflected by local credit networks and sanctioned by state authorities fostered a producer identity. Embracing a labor theory of value, the producer consciousness divided society into three groups. Although those constituting the "middling" classes varied over time and according to political party affiliation, the composition of the top and bottom classes remained fairly constant throughout the antebellum period. A sense of threat helped to define the identity of "middling" producers. The chief enemy was the "paper aristocracy," including banks and other corporations, capitalist speculators, and those with inherited wealth. As one dedicated Jacksonian exclaimed, "A few heavy capitalists, who live on the interest of their mortgages and lands, and grow rich by accumulating *compound interest*," menaced the "great *mass of the industrious classes*." Vigilance was essential to fend off the "brokers, shavers, stockholders, merchants, and *gentlemen*" who "cajole the weak, allure the avaricious, impose on the credulous, and entice the timid, to enter into a destructive speculation in the stock, which is only kept from sinking to its intrinsic value, by means of the most false devices, and disreputable arts."[65]

The "paper aristocracy" spawned the other group threatening producers: the propertyless pauper. Few Americans doubted that "inequality of fortune" was "natural to society, because talent as well as physical power" was "unequally distributed to mankind." But even fewer believed that inequality or diversity of faculties necessarily led to pauperism. It was a "first principle that no man can become rich without making another one poor, and that all accumulation of great fortunes, necessarily begets pauperism." It was "apparent" that while not every man could become rich, it was possible to "produce enough to make all comfortable, and happy." Yet when "some . . . acquire immense portions from the mass of labor, it must leave others without any." The dispossessed then became a burden on society, supported at community expense in "alms-houses." No one denied that society had a duty to provide for those caught in "meritorious poverty"—those suffering due to no fault of their own—but capitalist accumulation encouraged exploiters, the "hardened and confirmed vice, little superior to felons," who were nonetheless "pampered at the public cost." The "middling" producer was called upon to pay the bill.[66]

This rhetoric was identified most commonly with mainstream Jacksonian Democrats, but it was not unique to them. The Jeffersonians' "middling sort" included primarily self-sufficient yeoman farmers and

certain artisans. They embraced traditional landed property because it provided independence and protection from "artificial" market pressures generated by corrupt financial manipulation. Independence also protected the producer's freedom from corrupted political power linked to this same market manipulation. Even so, the enemy was the "speculating," "aristocratic," "monarchical," "bloodsucking," "parasitical" corporate and mercantile capitalists and their lawyer allies.[67] The Whigs and Republicans defined a middling group which united modest-sized enterprisers and laborers in what economist Henry Carey called "perfect harmony," each "deriv[ing] advantage from every measure that tends to facilitate . . . [economic] growth." Again, however, the middling class composed of a harmony of interests between those involved in trade and others doing hand labor was threatened from below by the dispossessed (particularly ethnic) poor and from above by the corrupting influence of artificial, usually corporate or inherited, wealth.[68]

Ideological tensions reflected social-class fragmentation. Although many social groups and political interests gradually moved toward adopting liberal capitalist tenets, those who rejected such tenets generated conflict that thereby impeded ideological consensus. Jacksonian Democratic rhetoric more than that of the Whigs, having "minimized the difference in innate capabilities among white males, accordingly minimized the likelihood of great economic discrepancies developing in a truly open and competitive society, one free of the 'special privileges' that blocked equal opportunity." Yet during the 1840s and 1850s spokesmen for constituencies supporting Whigs and later Republicans attacked "aristocratic" and corporate capitalists as a threat to the harmony of interests among the middling class of free labor. In addition, the northeastern agricultural press and certain "master and journeymen mechanics" who had avoided struggle "embraced as a harmonizing theme the notion that hard-working, virtuous, and comfortable economic independence was as preferable to great wealth as it was to desperate poverty."[69] Finally, within the Democratic party itself could be found social groups espousing "agrarian, pre-capitalist," genuine working class, and liberal capitalist values.[70]

Nevertheless, reflecting the influence of associational market relations, ideologically fragmented groups could unite behind the constitutional ideal. At least in certain states, small enterprisers throughout the mainstream political parties benefited from the extended credit

that prodebtor policies established. Regardless of party affiliation, those favoring protectionism turned the threat from capitalistic financial manipulation and pauperism into a defense of individual rights. Similarly, the moral responsibility upon which local credit relationships depended was consistent with regulatory policies holding corporations to standards of constitutional accountability. The interblending of protectionism and moral as well as legal accountability gave normative force to the constitutional faith that public and private concentrations of power were not legitimate unless checked by formal external constraints.[71]

These ideological and social tensions encouraged ambiguous attitudes toward economic development on the state level. Internal improvements like roads, canals, and railroads were good if they benefited the local community and its producers, enhancing the autonomy of both. But such development should be resisted if it aided one community at the expense of another, or if its motive was merely capitalist speculation. In marked contrast with Europe, American artisans often embraced new technologies in order to increase productivity; because of the pull of producer values, however, this acceptance was often "hesitant and equivocal."[72] Under certain circumstances even banks were legitimate as long as they were subject to community control and served the producers' interests. Tensions between local and national markets, big and small enterprise, and individual and community interests fostered conflicts within and among state-based political parties. In particular the cycle of boom and bust, the pervasiveness of failure, and the dual threat of corporate privilege and pauperism fostered anxiety and the demand for protection. Lawmakers resolved these tensions through a process of bargaining and compromise between the urge for unqualified capitalist accumulation and the more limited promise of producer independence, community control, and modest but sufficient prosperity.[73]

The interaction between these tensions and the constitutional ideal aided only somewhat the rights of women and African-Americans. Changing markets and emergent capitalism strengthened separation between the public patriarchal and feminine domestic spheres. Paradoxically, the security and new family relationships resulting from separate spheres provided many middle-class women opportunities to become involved in reform efforts outside the home, efforts that ultimately were subsumed in the abolitionist crusade. Increased activ-

ism, in turn, strengthened a feminist movement for equal rights identified with the Seneca Falls Convention of 1848, which demanded
gender equality based partially at least upon appeals to the constitutional ideal. Although the large program met defeat, the activism
never faltered, encouraging passage of laws sanctioning greater property rights for women. This effort converged with already existing
feme sole trader laws that granted married and widowed women
extensive rights to participate in the market economy. These laws
reflected the vigor of federalism that was at the center of the antebellum constitutional ideal. Similarly, as Frederick Douglass's switch
from Garrisonian opposition to abolitionist support of the Constitution suggests, the North's resort to the constitutional ideal to attack
slavery benefited African-Americans. Nevertheless, these changes
were modest indeed compared to the degree of dispossession each
group faced.[74]

Still, the marketplace itself encouraged legislative and judicial compromises based upon appeals to the constitutional ideal. Greed, unrestrained exploitation, and unbridled individualism indisputably were
to be found in the market. But it was more than a "Hobbesian war of all
against all." The market also rewarded individuals who were disciplined in their pursuit of happiness. At the same time, those corporations or individuals whose reckless conduct violated accepted norms
were often distrusted. Two fundamental features of the nineteenth-
century marketplace encouraged restraint: the reliance upon personal
accountability and the insecurity associated with the pervasiveness of
failure. After all, throughout the nineteenth century the lifeblood of the
American economy was credit. The capitalist corporate and mercantile
speculators certainly exploited the credit system, but many businessmen could not afford such behavior since it destroyed the reputation
essential to acquiring loans. Credit dependency heightened the risks of
failure, but individuals considered personally accountable were more
likely to receive temperate treatment from creditors than were unprincipled entrepreneurs, especially in local communities. In such a market
modest-sized, unincorporated disciplined enterprisers shared common ground with all producers, for whom credit was also indispens-
able. Both had reason to resort to constitutional legitimacy and demand
legal rules that favored debtors and regulation of corporations. When
state lawmakers in the name of constitutional accountability responded
favorably to this pressure, they deflected class tensions.[75]

Evangelical Protestantism heightened faith in the constitutional ideal and the concern for individual accountability. This activist Christian faith fostered a belief in universal moral principles that were as objectively identifiable and inviolable as the laws of Newtonian physics. Adherence to this moral absolutism instilled trust in self-reliance, self-discipline, and individual obligation. Those who possessed such traits of character could be relied upon to do their duty. A society made up of such citizens was best suited to limited government in which individual liberty and community welfare were interdependent. Though not inconsistent with individualism and private rights, Protestant moralism questioned these principles because they undermined the sound character upon which depended society's well-being and personal responsibility. During the early nineteenth century perhaps only an elite shared these moral precepts, but by the 1830s they not only pervaded the consciousness of genteel and working-class urban society but also penetrated small rural communities and blended with producer values. This Christian activism was consistent with the principles of legitimacy, accountability, and restraint of power inherent in the constitutional ideal.[76]

The interplay of these institutions and values encouraged associational relationships. The nation's abundant resources unquestionably fostered exploitative capitalist schemes and developmental projects. But the persistence of local markets, the need for credit, the prevalence of failure, and locally oriented popular government also supported a countervailing reliance upon reciprocity. Strains within Protestant and producer values that were also consistent with the constitutional ideal favored the interdependence of individual accountability and community welfare facilitating associational over exploitative market relations. In part these bonds emerged from kinship, friendship, and personal trust; they could have also reflected more opportunistic motivations whereby businessmen merely subordinated immediate gratification to long-term considerations. In either case state and local resort to protectionism in the name of the constitutional ideal gave formal sanction to associational market relationships.[77]

Politics and the legal profession also tapped the constitutional ideal and facilitated associational relationships. Of course, politicians gained votes by supporting capitalist enterprise. But another compelling political force was the demand from producers and local communities for protection; and whenever this depended upon enforcing a

reciprocity of interests, associational values could triumph. Similarly, attorneys did not serve corporations and capitalist promoters alone. Often country lawyers represented local clients and benefited from the local judge's and jury's distrust of outsiders, especially those identified with monopoly and the "moneyed power." To contain these "foreign" evils, appeals to strands within the constitutional ideal were common. Moreover, local lawyers, judges, and elected officials using such appeals often shared political and social bonds with one another, the community, and their delegation in the legislature that could offset the influence of the developers. This associational political economy often made it possible for debtors to win over creditors, workers to gain concessions from corporations, isolated communities to acquire transportation and the credit facilities similar to those of larger urban areas, and small enterprisers to defeat big capitalists.[78]

Ultimately it was the state rather than the federal government that grappled most with this conflict. President James Madison's veto of national funding of internal improvements in 1817 was a turning point. Following the veto, the extensive federal role in the economy that Alexander Hamilton had worked to establish steadily diminished (although he, too, had believed that federally financed internal improvements were unconstitutional without a constitutional amendment). By Jackson's election in 1828 two national parties struggled over how best to develop the nation's vast resources. The group that eventually became the Whig party embraced Henry Clay's American System, advocating federal economic promotion. Until the 1860s, however, it was Jackson's Democratic party that generally determined the national government's course. The Democrats emphasized the compatibility of limited federal action, individual liberty, and states' rights; the federal government provided a framework for territorial expansion within which citizens and states pursued the fruits of liberty.[79] To be sure, federal authority continued to control western settlement. Especially in the Pre-emption Act of 1841 Congress gave legal sanction to the right of squatters to settle on portions of unsurveyed public land and to purchase at the minimum price when it was formally put up for sale. But the nullification crisis and Jackson's veto of the "monster" Bank significantly retarded what Hamilton considered two of the most important elements of federal economic leadership, the tariff and a national bank.[80] The federal judiciary was, of course, also vital to

national economic development, but as Tocqueville observed, its influence was circumscribed.[81]

As the federal role in the economy diminished, the states became the primary stimulators of economic development and individual opportunity. Exercising power authorized by state constitutions and sanctioned by Supreme Court decisions, courts and legislatures promoted banking and monetary policies that increased the credit available for individual enterprise (including weaker producer groups on the margins of the business system), supported enlarged transportation facilities, and sanctioned the rights of debtors and creditors. The states also developed rules favoring free labor in the North and slavery in the South, broadened somewhat the property and contract rights of women, and fought over the rights of fugitive slaves. Consistent with constitutional accountability, tax laws favored independent producers, placing the heaviest fiscal burden on big merchant capitalists and corporations. The states also fostered manufacturing and technological invention. In pursuing this promotional role, states protected the interests of individual producers and their communities in the name of the constitutional ideal, often discriminating against foreigners and nonresidents in favor of associational market relations.[82]

### The Mid-Atlantic Region

The predominance of modest-sized, unincorporated enterprise in four mid-Atlantic states presented a contrast to other regions. Throughout much of New York and New England between 1800 and 1860 large factories organized as corporations were beginning to dominate the economy. In the South the slave plantations had long before established their dominance. The middle Atlantic states of Maryland, New Jersey, Pennsylvania, and Delaware represented yet another pattern of development in which relatively small-scale, modestly capitalized, unincorporated proprietorships were the norm. These locally oriented enterprisers coincided with the emerging capitalist economic order. Philadelphia and Baltimore were behind only New York City as the nation's foremost urban, commercial, and financial centers. Even with regard to railroads—the earliest form of big business in the United States—two of three leading trunk lines were located in Pennsylvania and Maryland: the Pennsylvania Railroad and the Baltimore and Ohio

Railroad. The region included two slave states; but in Maryland slavery was "declining," and Delaware was "a slave state in name only." The free black population in Maryland was the largest in the United States and probably outnumbered the state's slaves.[83] Since this mid-Atlantic region included a preponderance of independent producers as well as the extremes of large mercantile and corporate enterprise and slavery, it provides insights into the formative era of American capitalism.

The four mid-Atlantic states included a producer economy. Although the United States was the world's second ranking industrial nation by 1860, less than 10 percent of the employment in mid-Atlantic urban areas was in industrial pursuits. In a few cities like Philadelphia, Baltimore, and Newark, industrial activities occupied a more significant place. But even in the Quaker City (the nation's leading industrial center), the figure was just 17.5 percent. Newark's roughly 70 percent of employment in industry was thus exceptional indeed. Manufacturing was the wave of the future in these communities, but even here the scale of enterprises was mixed rather than totally dominated by large factories. In Philadelphia there were large, highly mechanized factories; medium-sized, relatively nonmechanized enterprises; sweatshops, private residences that housed domestic outwork; and neighborhood shops run by artisans. Each of these enterprises operated with a different market orientation and had differing degrees of market autonomy or dependency. Within each type of enterprise workers maintained different levels of control; employer-employee relations also varied.[84]

In other industrial pursuits the pattern was similar. According to Alfred Chandler anthracite coal from Pennsylvania fields was the principal energy source for industrial development in nineteenth-century America. Between 1827 and 1857 more than half of the total anthracite coal mined in the United States was produced in Pennsylvania's Schuylkill region by unincorporated, independent owner-operators and their employees. A similar structure existed in textiles. In the mid-Atlantic states textile mills were small to medium in size; employees typically numbered about sixty, and they often worked under the supervision of a proprietor-owner. These mills, like those examined in Anthony F. C. Wallace's classic study *Rockdale*, usually were located in rural areas, and they were rarely incorporated. Du Pont's

famous gunpowder works and the flour mills along the Brandywine in New Castle county, Delaware, fit the same mold.[85]

Agriculture and commerce remained the leading pursuits. In Pennsylvania, Maryland, New Jersey, and Delaware the production of staple grains declined because of competition from midwestern staples. Dairying and other livestock pursuits, the supplying of brewing and distilling industries, and orchard crops and truck gardening became major agricultural enterprises as urban demand grew. Improved transportation lowered the costs of reaching growing urban markets, which in turn reduced the extent of marginal agriculture. But the decline of the marginal farm as the principal supplier of the urban food supply occurred slowly between 1820 and 1860. Another transformation took place after 1815 in the mercantile order. In Philadelphia, Baltimore, and elsewhere general merchants lost their influence and leadership to the new group of specialized middlemen doing a volume business in new markets.[86]

The region enjoyed uneven prosperity. Although relatively limited, occupational mobility was present, providing the promise of increased opportunity for some. Perhaps of greater significance was the number of business, professional, and political leaders in urban areas who had risen from humble origins. A few others were always able to become independent producers by accumulating enough resources to buy a farm in the West. The diffusion of class consciousness was aided by the uneven and gradual rate at which the transfer from artisan to skilled or unskilled mill or factory worker took place. During this transfer wage rates for those at the bottom of urban populations may have increased by as much as 82 percent from 1820 to 1856 (though, of course, those in the upper groups did substantially better). Especially after 1840, when agricultural and industrial output increased, food and household goods became cheaper compared to growing wages. Thus the means for acquiring possessions and sustenance were fairly widespread, even if upward mobility was not. In spite of such conditions failure remained a perennial danger, and losing a proprietorship was perhaps as easy as the establishment of it.[87]

Uneven population distribution and development further shaped the economic order. The split between urban and rural areas was conspicuous, particularly in Pennsylvania and Maryland. The division between commercially backward, often isolated areas and those en-

gaged in a larger market economy was also significant. Underpopu-
lated counties in northern Pennsylvania, on the Eastern Shore in
Maryland, in the pines of southeastern New Jersey, and in the southern part of Delaware were often at odds with growth centers elsewhere in each state. Also pronounced was urban competition within a
single state, like that between Philadelphia and Pittsburgh, or across
state lines, such as that among Philadelphia, Baltimore, and (outside
the region) New York. Such rivalries within and among states perpetuated a tenacious attachment to local control, determined winners and
losers, and fostered appeals to the constitutional ideal.

Consistent with this protectionist political economy, politicians
from the region exhibited a self-conscious middling-class identity.
Suggesting the dual threat from capitalists and paupers, Pennsylvania
Republican Thaddeus Stevens praised the "middling classes who own
the soil, and work it with their own hands." They were the "main
support of every free government." Similarly, Pennsylvania Republican congressman Samuel Blair said that the "manufacturing industry
of this country must look to men of moderate means for its development—the men of enterprise being, as a class, in such circumstances."
Stevens and Blair articulated middle-class, producer-oriented values
that were set off against corporate capitalism. Fellow Republicans
warned that the "money capitalists" were becoming "too much centralized . . . [in] a comparatively small number of people." The chief
danger moreover, was the "system of corporations," which was
"nothing more nor less than a moneyed feudalism. . . . It concentrates
masses of wealth, it places immense power in a few hands."[88]

The Republican party's attack on corporate capitalism reflected
older ideological strains within Whig, Democratic, and Jeffersonian
party rhetoric. Such "artificial" modes of wealth traditionally were
opposed by modest-sized farmers, self-employed artisans, and small
traders. Corporations engendered economic anxieties because they
"change[d] the relation of man to wealth. When a man has his property in his own hands, and manages it himself, he is responsible for
the manner in which he does it. . . . But when the management of
property is put into the hands of corporations, the many delegate the
power of managing it to the few." Thus the dissolution of personal
responsibility inherent in owner-operator producerism inevitably
threatened the constitutional accountability upon which depended
individual liberty and republican self-government. Corporate capital-

ism "aggregate[d] power, of course, and necessarily all the property of the commonwealth, included in these corporations, must be put into the hands of a few men. . . . Hence, the agent of a corporation of any kind, has absolute control over all persons connected with that corporation." Such rhetoric rang true to a wide range of producers in the four mid-Atlantic states where small-scale, unincorporated enterprise was the norm.[89]

Neither associational nor capitalist market relations disrupted gender and racial discrimination. Throughout the region women benefited from feme sole trader and married women's property laws, operating mercantile and agricultural enterprises ranging from small to large. Similarly, free African-Americans, particularly in Maryland, were involved in the region's economic order. In both cases, however, the number of enterprisers was comparatively small so that legal equality facilitating participation in either the associational or the capitalist marketplace did not fundamentally diminish the dominance of patriarchy and white supremacy.[90]

No one articulated more clearly an ideology consistent with the region's political economy than Henry C. Carey. Recognized as perhaps the foremost economist of mid-nineteenth century America, Carey lived and worked in small towns near Philadelphia in Pennsylvania and New Jersey. A well-known proponent of protective tariffs, he was the author of *Principles of Political Economy* (1837), adjudged the "most important economics treatise" published in the United States before the Civil War. Carey rejected the economic pessimism of Englishman Thomas R. Malthus, who said that population eventually would overwhelm the ability of the land to support it. He argued that land was so abundant in America that overpopulation posed little danger. The key to the nation's economic growth was therefore the encouragement of investment and the removal of any "artificial restraints" limiting it.[91]

Carey's vision of the good society was consistent with the political economy of the region in which he lived. He supported the Whig and Republican tenet that industrialization increased the opportunity of all, including the manual laborer. Hence his faith in the "harmony of interests." Indeed, he supported protective tariffs because they fostered a diversified economy beneficial to workers. Where "all are farmers," he said, "there can be no competition for the purchase of labor." Even so, the end result of market diversification was a society

built upon "little towns and cities" serving as a local manufacturing center and supplying the surrounding countryside. Long-range transportation facilities were thus unnecessary. *"The nearer* the grist-mill is to the farm," he wrote, "the less will be the labor required for converting wheat into flour, . . . the *nearer* [the farmer] can bring the hatter, the shoemaker, and the tailor, the maker of ploughs and harrows, the less will be the loss in labor in exchanging his wheat for their commodities."[92] Significantly, Carey's vision seemed fulfilled in the small mills of Rockdale or Du Pont's powder works along the Brandywine.[93]

Carey's repudiation of large-scale industry based in big cities included opposition to corporate capitalism. The small enterprises of his "little towns and cities" ideally should be unincorporated. Corporations were a type of "artificial" investment which ultimately retarded rather than facilitated the opportunity consistent with the "harmony of interests."[94] True to this faith, Carey at one point embarked upon a personal crusade against one of the region's most powerful corporations, the Camden and Amboy Railroad. He succeeded to the point that the New Jersey state government actually imposed upon the railroad greater legal accountability, which led to payment of higher toll taxes into the state treasury.

Carey's defense of accountability was sanctioned by and appealed to associational market relations and the constitutional ideal. While Carey moved against the Camden and Amboy Railroad out of regard for his economic theory, his campaign gave instrumental content to the accountability principle inherent in the constitutional ideal. His contention that the railroad was not paying its proper share of taxes appealed to the popular assumption that the company's charter conferred obligations as well as rights. The unfulfilled obligation raised the specter of unchecked power, and constitutionalism thus legitimated Carey's campaign. At the same time, the popular conception of obligation and legitimacy was rooted in the associational market relations pervading the small-scale, unincorporated owner-operator enterprise that characterized the region. The locally oriented credit relationships of Carey's "little towns" fostered a faith in interpersonal responsibility which corporate capitalism threatened.[95]

Also inherent in the values of constitutional accountability and legitimacy were moralistic assumptions that justified protectionism. Carey's opposition to special privilege sustained by artificial constraints led to a defense of government action to preserve an open

market. The faith in government intervention was consistent with a distrust of the corruption that undermined the moral foundations of the harmony of interests. Like most American economic theorists, Carey followed the teachings of Scottish Realist Protestant Adam Smith. Smith entwined concepts of value, supply, demand, desire, and scarcity to create a theory which blended moral and economic assumptions. His theory postulated that individuals had an absolute, natural right to the fruits of their own labor which the state should not disrupt. In addition, the labor required to produce something, rather than consumer demand, determined value. These ideas in turn supported the view that the free market produced a "natural" price, and the inalienable rights of contract and property governed this price rather than that which might be arrived at solely through voluntary bargaining. In Britain the utilitarianism of Jeremy Bentham and John Stuart Mill displaced Smith's natural-law assumptions. The positivistic norms established by the sovereign excised from British economic thought explicit moralistic concerns.[96]

American economic theorists like Carey, however, remained committed to Smith's moralistic principles. Thus most Americans rejected utilitarianism because it placed the goal of maximizing human desires above considerations of morals, a result many viewed as "atheistic." It was at this point that the corrupting influence of special privilege identified with corporate capitalism threatened constitutional accountability and legitimacy. The danger, in turn, justified government intervention to restore or maintain individual liberty. The blend of moral and constitutional ideals tapped a residual republicanism which assumed that true liberty was impossible unless the individual remained economically independent and free to participate in public affairs, which in turn fostered the good of the commonwealth and public virtue. In public discourse the ideological linkage between virtue and commonwealth did not persist beyond the 1830s. That economic dependency resulted in the corruption of free government, however, was a distinct republican presumption influencing nineteenth-century American economic theorists such as Carey.[97]

The congruence between the region's market relations and Carey's political economy suggested the factors shaping public policy. Laws that favored debtors in locally oriented markets, imposed taxes upon large merchants, banks, and transportation corporations, and regulated corporations generally supported the producer and associational

values prevailing in the anticapitalist public discourse of the region's Jeffersonian and Jacksonian Democrats, Whigs, and Republicans. Similarly, while certain tenets of Carey's "harmony of interests" clashed with elements of the Democratic party's ideology, both defended small-scale artisan, agricultural, and manufacturing enterprise against capitalist hegemony. A convergence also existed in the preference for middling-class prosperity as opposed to the extremes of acquisitive capitalist wealth or pauperism. Finally, these ideological and policy unities shared an underlying acceptance of the accountability and legitimacy principles inherent in the constitutional ideal.

The interplay of the law, market, and ideologies also fostered multiple demands for legal services. Many of the nation's foremost lawyers were members of the Pennsylvania and Maryland bars, and certain of those from New Jersey and Delaware ranked only a little behind. A small group of these lawyers were in turn a disproportionate number of the elite bar of Supreme Court and the federal courts of the Third and Fourth circuits, which included the region's four states. The attorneys practicing in state or federal courts and serving as counselors and political lobbyists served the interests of all groups, inevitably reflecting social fragmentation rather than the dominance of a single capitalist class. In addition, from the 1820s on Philadelphia was the center of prominent constitutional commentators. This "Philadelphia group" included Thomas Sergeant, William Rawle, Peter S. DuPonceau, and others; they advocated theories of federalism and legal change that generally sought a middle path between the extremes of nationalism and states' rights.[98]

The convergence between a more open legal culture and distinctive constitutional commentary reflected the region's political economy. Accommodating increasingly diverse class interests, Baltimore's David Hoffman at the University of Maryland and Peter DuPonceau at the Law Academy of Philadelphia taught that law "should be adaptive to local conditions, grounded on fundamental principles, universal in scope, and systematically organized." Law was "moreover . . . inseparable from political economy and moral philosophy, so that the fundamental principles that lay at the root of its doctrines were indistinguishable from the organizing principles of republican government and the necessities of commercial exchange." This teaching coincided with the principles advocated by the constitutional commentators, to explain how the declaratory theory of law was consistent with the

change required to ensure the broad-based economic prosperity identified with American exceptionalism. As a result, America could avoid the decay that republics were prone to because of corruption. Adherence to the constitutional ideal in particular would save America's future from the past.[99]

Lawyers could use these jurisprudential principles, like Carey's economic theory, to defend protectionism from federal courts. Under the Constitution and acts of Congress the federal judiciary had jurisdiction over suits in both law and equity. Many litigants used diversity jurisdiction in order to gain the benefit of equitable doctrines and procedures. A Pennsylvania lawyer stated explicitly why this was so: "Actions . . . between merchants which form the appropriate subjects for a court of equity . . . are in Pennsylvania spun out to an interminable length, and often without the hope . . . of any redress at all." Therefore, it was common practice, the lawyer continued, for "most of these cases . . . to be carried into the circuit court of the United States, when the parties, by any contrivance whatever, can bring themselves within its jurisdiction, and which may be affected in most cases by crossing the Delaware." When nonresidents attempted to enforce the United States Supreme Court's procreditor *Bronson* decision of 1843, however, the chief justice of Pennsylvania's highest court, John Bannister Gibson, balked. Repudiating the broadly inclusive spirit of *Bronson*, Gibson sustained the state's prodebtor temporary stay law.[100] "To hold that a State Legislature is incompetent to relieve the public from the pressure of sudden distress by arresting a general sacrifice of property, by the machinery of law, would invalidate many statutes whose constitutionality has hitherto been unsuspected," he said.[101]

Thus federalism created a dual market for legal services which could sustain protectionism against capitalist values. The enforcement of the *Bronson* precedent in Pennsylvania and Maryland pitted nonresident creditors against local debtors. The creditors generally were nonresident, big-city merchants, and as such they personified what the people of the period called capitalists. The laws that Gibson defended protected in-state debtors, who included not only Philadelphia or Baltimore merchants but also the far more numerous small traders and farmers involved in the locally oriented associational economy. Accordingly, on one level the clash between federal and state authority was intraclass, pitting urban mercantile capitalists against each other. Yet at a second level the majority of debtors receiving protection were

small traders or farmers who possessed closer interpersonal and market relations with producers than they did with the mercantile capitalists. In this sense, then, it was an interclass struggle, and the debtors won.[102]

Cases involving corporate contract obligations raised similar conflicts. The Taney Court's *Bronson* opinion followed contract clause principles that the Marshall Court established in *Sturges* (1819) and *Saunders* (1827) prescribing the boundaries of a state's power over private contracts. A second class of contract clause cases concerned a state's authority to regulate the corporations it chartered. In *Dartmouth College* (1819) and other decisions the Marshall Court, of course, strengthened the rights of corporations. But in each of these cases the Court also sanctioned a reserved regulatory power. The Taney Court accommodated these dual principles while enlarging a state's authority to regulate corporations. The region's four states fervently applied the regulatory principles, thereby favoring wide-ranging social-class interests. The Marshall Court, for example, repudiated New Jersey's attempt to reclaim the right to tax former Indian land it had given up under a corporate charter. New Jersey nonetheless did not comply with the Court's decision and imposed the tax anyway.[103] Meanwhile, all four states enacted bank tax policies and regulated the tolls of transportation companies in order to pay for social services, including education and the operating expenses of government. At least until 1861 the control of transport rates also protected the competitive local market advantage of many small communities.

Like the private side of contract clause issues, these public contract controversies had social-class implications. New Jersey's outright defiance of the Supreme Court was not unusual. Still, it indicated a political determination rooted in the majority of small enterprisers and property holders to shift public service costs onto corporate capitalists. The bank taxes and toll rates imposed on canals and railroads aided various modest-sized producers involved in more locally oriented associational market relations, including those in smaller, more isolated communities. Regarding the taxes supporting education, moreover, the beneficiaries were primarily workers' children. Thus the states' implementation of the tax power that the Court reserved to them in the contract clause decisions reflected underlying social-class tensions in which weaker groups prevailed. Much the same was true concerning corporate liability in railroad accidents.

The evolution of the commerce clause followed a similar course. Many of the Court's leading commerce clause decisions involved litigants from the mid-Atlantic region. In *Gibbons* v. *Ogden* (1825) a New Jersey steamboat operator (employing none other than the young Cornelius Vanderbilt) defeated New York's steamboat monopoly. *Cooley* v. *Board of Wardens* (1852), which through the doctrine of selective exclusiveness formalized the dormant commerce power principle implicit in *Gibbons*, upheld a state's regulatory power over markets touching interstate or international trade. The Marshall Court, moreover, facilitated state policies in *Brown* v. *Maryland* (1827) and *Willson* v. *The Blackbird Creek Co.* (1829) which helped small retailers and property holders in locally oriented associational markets. In these cases mercantile and propertied capitalists also benefited, but not to the exclusion of the weaker groups.[104] Similarly, in the lengthy *Wheeling Bridge* litigation of the 1850s the Court upheld the interests of Pittsburgh's local steamboat operators against the Pennsylvania Railroad. Although Congress undercut the decision, the long-term policy ultimately balanced the interests of steamboats and railroads, protecting the former. Thus while these cases raised issues that were partially intraclass in nature, the fundamental defense of the states' protectionist authority also aided weaker classes.[105]

The growth of the federal judiciary's authority also coincided with the region's protectionism. In the famous decision of *McCulloch* v. *Maryland* (1819), the Court upheld the Bank of the United States over the state's defense of local banks, which included tax policies favorable to the associational economy. Jackson's veto of the Bank did not diminish the Court's defense of congressional authority over the national credit market. The end of the BUS, however, strengthened the competitive advantage of state banks within local as well as national markets, which in turn facilitated the protectionist credit policies favorable to small as well as large debtors and enterprisers involved in both markets. Similarly, the emergence of the federal judiciary's general commercial law culminating in *Swift* v. *Tyson* (1842) did not destroy local control of credit. On the contrary, it created a dual credit market in which the federal courts aided interstate credit transactions while the state legal institutions were free to and did protect locally oriented associational market relations. Finally, the Taney Court used its authority to uphold New Jersey's power to protect from competitors oyster fisheries in its public waterways.[106] These judicial contro-

versies thus suggested the degree to which the mid-Atlantic region epitomized the national struggle to reconcile constitutionalism and capitalism.

Before 1860 the interplay between market and constitutional institutions in the mid-Atlantic region reflected the nation's diversity. In the antebellum United States locally oriented markets sustaining smaller independent trading, industrial, and agricultural workers coincided with national markets in which mercantile and corporate capitalist enterprise increasingly dominated. Inequities associated with free and slave labor and gender and racial discrimination also characterized the nation's society. Market diversity encouraged middling-class producers to resist capitalist exploitation and dependency arising from economic failure. Appealing to values of legitimacy and accountability inherent in the constitutional ideal, these producers often won protectionist policies from state and local authorities. Federalism facilitated protectionism. Despite decisions that favored property and contract rights, the Supreme Court and the federal judiciary ultimately sanctioned the states' vigorous police power upon which such policies depended. Henry Carey's economic theories and constitutional and legal commentary suggested that the four states of the mid-Atlantic region epitomized constitutionalism's role in the conflict between modest-scale producers and emergent capitalism.

# 2

## Constitutionalism and the

## Associational Economy

Constitutionalism as a symbol and a working system interacted with divergent market relations, fostering a diverse economic order. While virtually everyone depended on credit, this reliance had different ramifications within local or larger markets. Between 1800 and 1860 the federal government enacted only two significant, short-lived bankruptcy or insolvency laws prescribing the obligations of debtors and creditors.[1] State action and the federal judiciary's interpretation of its limits filled the policy "silences" resulting from this federal power vacuum. The Supreme Court's leading decisions establishing the status of state debtor-creditor laws under the Constitution's contract clause and other provisions were intermittent enough to permit the four mid-Atlantic states ample opportunity to protect debtors. The lower federal courts more or less continuously decided commercial contract cases under diversity jurisdiction, gradually formulating a general commercial law.[2] The main result of coexisting federal and state jurisdictions was, however, a dual demand for legal services which corresponded to the coincidence of local and interstate contractual obligations. The constitutional ideal in turn legitimated the shift-

ing interplay between federal and state policies, sustaining both local and more extensive market spheres.[3]

Early American social and market relations thus were bound together by credit within the constitutional system. Although gold and silver were the official national currency, the stock of specie was so small that it could never satisfy the needs of a growing people. To compound the problem, community banks issued their own notes, which significantly depreciated beyond local limits. For practical purposes, then, the principal medium of exchange locally and throughout the nation was credit. Moreover, because credit was so vital, Andrew Jackson's veto of the "monster" Bank of the United States seemed to be a useful measure of American character and interests. It represented, as well, a triumph of the constitutional ideal. Yet the BUS and state banks were only one dimension of the credit system. Molded by the constitutional dynamics of federalism, legal rules governing the rights and obligations of debtors and creditors were at the heart of the economy; and few issues tested the nation's institutions and values more than the legal disputes arising from the enforcement of these rules.[4] To be sure, large, nationally oriented mercantile interests and corporations gained in these conflicts. Nevertheless, the law fashioned by state courts, juries, and legislative politics and responsive to the demands of locally oriented markets also protected debtors within an associational economy.

The constitutional and economic parameters of associational market relations reflected social-class tensions. Governmental policy regulating commercial contracts and market failure in the mid-Atlantic states arose from a locally oriented, credit-dependent, small-scale, unincorporated economic order. Development was, of course, a central goal of government action. Producer and Protestant moral values, however, intermingled with capitalistic motivations to shape the lawmakers' efforts to achieve prosperity and growth. Moreover, judges and legislators could not ignore the majority's assumptions regarding constitutional legitimacy and accountability and the interdependency of individual and community interests. These factors created pressures upon government to spread the costs and benefits of credit transactions among various social groups. At the same time, virtually everyone, regardless of class, either experienced or was vulnerable to failure. Thus faith in the constitutional ideal, values favoring the ambiguities of individual enterprise, the belief that risks were broadly

shared, and the assumption that producer enterprise was the heart of American prosperity and society deflected class tensions arising from social fragmentation and a persistent inequality of wealth.

### Constitutionalism and Associational Market Relations

Constitutional principles shaped the rules governing credit, sustaining associational market relations. The federal government's limited intervention in debtor-creditor issues, the Supreme Court's intermittent contract clause decisions, and the circumscribed impact of the federal judiciary's diversity jurisdiction aided the interests of the mid-Atlantic states' locally oriented debtors. Federal and state court decisions enlarged the reach of the principle of negotiability upon which extensive credit depended. Negotiability benefited major urban wholesalers who were the principal creditors of smaller traders. Yet the same principle was also vital to a majority of modest-scale enterprisers capitalized at $4,000 or less. The pervasive reliance on credit, combined with inadequate reporting methods and slowness of communications, exacerbated everyone's vulnerability to failure. The prevalence of local control encouraged policy preferences that protected debtors, including those involved in locally oriented markets. The interconnection between these local debtor-creditor relations and the modest scale of enterprise, as well as the economy's susceptibility to failure, fostered associational bonds of individual accountability and obligation enabling smaller enterprisers to resist the control of mercantile capitalists.[5]

The basic principle governing credit transactions was negotiability. Private written contractual agreements serving as a money substitute were the medium of exchange for most antebellum business transactions. By regulating the rights and obligations of parties to these contracts, the law allocated the credit upon which the nation's economy depended. Commercial contracts, especially bills of exchange and promissory notes, were negotiable, which meant they were legally transferable from one person to another like money. The public confidence that sustained this transferability arose from the law's scrupulous enforcement of the rights of holders of negotiable paper. Negotiability was, observed *Hunt's Merchants' Magazine*, "an indulgence to commerce; it is a . . . compliment to the utility of a credit

system." Given the nation's persistent scarcity of specie and confused currency, the credit represented by innumerable transactions of nego-tiable paper significantly influenced the degree of individual oppor-tunity and risk in the antebellum economy.[6]

Constitutionalism influenced negotiability and the credit system as a whole, facilitating state control. The principles of legitimacy and accountability inherent in the constitutional ideal were central to fed-eralism, which left most governmental control of commercial credit to the states. The Supreme Court's interpretation of the contract clause bounded a state's authority over the commercial contracts upon which negotiability depended. Marshall and Taney Court decisions upheld state regulation of contracts made after protective debtor laws were passed. Such regulations, moreover, technically could not reach the substance of the contractual obligation. But the cumulative impact of these decisions also sanctioned wide-ranging remedial measures that delayed recovery and in other ways protected debtor rights. It requires emphasis, furthermore, that the Court decided the leading cases over many years, the most important ones being in 1819, 1827, and 1843. During the interim, states enacted laws affecting even the substance of contractual obligations. Finally, consistent with the spirit of federalism at least in the mid-Atlantic states, state courts often successfully re-sisted the Supreme Court's decisions.[7]

The constitutional independence of the lower federal courts also influenced the states' protectionist policies. The coexistence of state and federal authority nonetheless reinforced a dual market for legal services. Apart from contract clause issues that arose episodically, the federal courts exercised little direct control over the states' local laws. Federal judges were, however, capable of formulating a fairly uniform standard within their own jurisdiction. Because nonresidents pre-ferred to sue in federal court, and because many of these suits in-volved interstate commercial credit contracts, the lower federal tri-bunals had ample opportunity to develop a uniform commercial law. In the mid-Atlantic states, meanwhile, legislatures and courts re-sponded to in-state interests, defending local debtors from out-of-state creditors. State and local authorities thus were sensitive to locally oriented associational credit relations. The federal courts' potential for establishing uniformity rested upon the relative constitutional inde-pendence of such procedural forms as jury instructions, equity, and the right of appeal. Through such devices the federal judiciary ex-

ercised a unifying and nationalizing influence over the commercial credit linking big-city mercantile capitalists and the local associational economy. Nevertheless, federalism ensured that both markets persisted.[8]

State policy making dominating the interplay of the negotiability principle and debt default thus shaped credit transactions. Throughout the nineteenth century failure due to indebtedness, of course, haunted individuals and families. The pervasive occurrence of failure continually threatened to disrupt the chain of credit relations created by the negotiation of commercial contracts. Since negotiable bills or notes drawn to pay one party ordinarily were transferred by endorsement through several other parties before finally becoming due, the insolvency of the drawer or any of the endorsees affected the credit of not only one but many. As the paper was endorsed from party to party, each subsequent endorsee acquired the right of recovery protected by the principle of negotiability. But when one of the parties in the chain failed, the question arose as to who became legally bound to cover the note. Because credit, negotiability, and failure were so entwined, whether lawmakers chose to favor debtors or creditors in such cases was a critical issue.[9]

Tension between the demands of local and foreign markets contributed further to the problematic nature of credit relations. After the coincident termination of the War of 1812 and the Napoleonic Wars in 1815, the nation's mercantile order underwent significant change as the new group of specialized middlemen displaced general merchants who had controlled the economy since colonial times. These developments encouraged the new middlemen to invest in manufacturing and transportation facilities, which produced the nation's first big business—the railroad. In spite of the emergence of this large corporate enterprise, however, the dominant economic influence on the new business order remained the local market. Within this market most traders were from the producer class, whose members did not organize themselves into corporations but chose instead to work alone or in partnership in small to medium-sized firms. But the local producers' reliance upon large, urban wholesalers for credit, combined with default in payment due to failure and other uncertainties, bred federal and state legal disputes.[10]

Distance and poor communications strengthened the influence of local markets. An indication of such problems was the length of time

necessary to convey President Jackson's State of the Union address to several leading cities in 1830. Through a system of relay "expresses," the message—in what was then regarded as "amazing speed"—took a record-breaking 15½ hours to go from Washington to New York, more than 31 hours to reach Boston, just under 3 days to arrive in Charleston, and about 6 days to reach New Orleans.[11]

Even after the coming of the telegraph in the 1840s, the slowness and uncertainty of the mails posed serious problems for interstate business. This was especially true for the determination of the credit standing of those with whom a big urban merchant traded. During the years before the Civil War, traders relied on personal connections and other informal methods to establish the credit of others. For such a system to work, a middleman had to carry on extensive correspondence with those with whom he traded in order to remain informed about changing business conditions in distant places. This system was, of course, no better than the mails, but despite this handicap some large merchants attempted to improve and regularize their informal credit-reporting methods in the 1830s and 1840s. Of these, Lewis Tappan, whose firm in later years evolved into R. G. Dun & Co., was the most successful. He established the first true credit-reporting agency in 1841.[12]

Although the efforts of Tappan and others were important, they never succeeded in securing the confidence of the majority of middlemen who could have relied on their services before the Civil War. Several factors explained this. The reliance upon local lawyers and merchants as correspondents through whom to determine the credit standing of their neighbors was a source of friction and uncertainty. Tappan commonly paid for the investigatory services of local lawyers by promising them that they would handle any litigation arising from failures they discovered while evaluating the solvency of persons in that area. Although these relations were usually honest, the opportunity for error and the interplay of self-interest were nonetheless present.[13] At the same time, other lawyers could counter the influence of out-of-state creditors by appealing to the constitutional ideal. Moreover, the slowness of communications and the dependence upon personal connections strengthened the bonds among producers and their local creditors. These same factors also worked to the advantage of marginal enterprisers and debtors generally because they encouraged the extension of long-term credit. There was good reason, then,

for producers to favor the status quo and to resist developments that might weaken local control.

The law's treatment of debtor-creditor rights also had a significant bearing on class relationships. Failure was as pronounced a reality for the modestly capitalized, nonincorporated mercantile, mining, farming, and manufacturing producer interests as it was for artisans and journeymen. Particularly in the grassroots industrial towns where the bulk of the nation's industrial enterprises were located, local store-keepers extended credit to workers during strikes and other hard times. This support grew in part out of the daily contact between small shopkeepers and workers who provided the stores with much of their trade. It also developed because many local producers often had risen from wage-earning backgrounds by acquiring modest credit and thus identified with their customers' condition. Similarly, most local shops began business and continued to trade on marginal resources, which meant that the loss of a proprietorship often was about as easy as establishing it. When failure occurred, the individual would likely return to the lower social stratum from whence he had come. Because negotiability controlled the availability of credit, it significantly influenced the ability of enterprising individuals to enter this local business order.[14] The rules controlling debt default governed the debtor's loss of economic independence and the means of reestablishing it. Thus the interplay of law, individual opportunity, and failure shaped sentiments of class solidarity and values regarding individual enterprise.[15]

The federal and intensely democratized character of antebellum government further influenced the rules of negotiability and debt default. Unlike the more centralized and hierarchical regimens of England and Europe, and true to the principles of federalism and constitutional legitimacy and accountability, the United States tenaciously adhered to a belief in local control. Moreover, this value blended with Americans' fierce attachment to republican liberty and the constitutional ideal, which in turn sustained the conviction that individual and community interests were not only compatible but interdependent.[16] Furthermore, local courts and juries and the country lawyers who made their living before these institutions often were more sensitive to community interests than the attorneys serving nonresident corporations and big-city merchants. These institutions and assumptions weakened the dominance of national market interests.[17]

The relationship between negotiability and credit was therefore complex for technical reasons. The law could sanction transfers of credit as payments for existing obligations or it could hold that the purpose of such an exchange was to secure further advances of credit. These two results might seem easily separated; in fact, however, it was often difficult to determine whether the parties negotiated a contract in order to liquidate indebtedness or because they wanted to extend credit. A letter from Philadelphia wholesaler Samuel Troth to a New York firm suggested the intricacy of credit negotiations: "In case you have drawn on me for the above amount [stated in the letter], then please hand this check [also included in the letter] over to Brooklyn White Lead Co. . . . to be placed to my credit on their books."[18]

These technical factors, however, operated within an institutional and market context having wider social-class implications. Negotiable paper passed from hand to hand as various parties became bound by the contract. These parties included banks and other commercial and financial agents. As the paper circulated, it was discounted, collected upon, or its date of payment was extended through some accommodation.[19] Moreover, as a sampling of credit reports of the predecessor of R. G. Dun & Co. showed, most of the parties using negotiable paper as a money substitute were small to medium-sized, unincorporated producers who either worked alone, with family members, or with one partner. The estimated total worth of 51 percent of these enterprises was $4,000 or less; nearly 27 percent were assessed at between $4,000 and $10,000, while the overall value of 22 percent was more than $10,000. Over three-quarters of the proprietors held real estate, which in a credit-based economy was a desirable security. In most instances, however, personal property constituted the bulk of the firms' assets. The flexible transactions that negotiability made possible thus encouraged a generous use of credit. Big urban wholesalers like Samuel Troth of Philadelphia clearly benefited from the principle, but it also increased the opportunity of modest-sized enterprisers.[20]

Debt defaults within a predominantly local market were also features of these credit relations. The antebellum credit structure was built in large part upon numerous, comparatively modest debts, generally contracted within one locality or region. In an area including the District of Columbia and several Maryland counties, a group of insolvent debtors revealed how this system worked. The total debt of one merchant was $15,908, but the individual amounts comprising the

whole ranged from $20 to $700. More typical was a shipbuilder whose debts ran from $42 to $250, totaling $3,475; an actor whose average debt was $5, totaling $683; and a contractor for railroads and canals whose debts ran between $5 and $50, totaling $495. A shoe salesman, a few blacksmiths, several clerks, and a dealer in china, glass, and queensware were still other representative members of this group.[21] Among such groups debt default was pervasive. Credit reports showed that in several Pennsylvania, Maryland, and New Jersey counties between the 1840s and 1850s approximately 40 percent of the firms examined failed. Moreover, state laws often made debt default not too difficult.[22] Correspondence involving a Baltimore merchant, James Partridge, who was indebted to a member of the Du Pont family, suggests how the system worked. "I believe he is in quite an embarrassed situation. There is little difficulty in getting discharged by our insolvent law, and it is more than probable after Mr. Partridge has made settlements he will at last have to avail himself of the insolvent law." As a result, the letter writer concluded, "Mr. Du Pont had best make a settlement with him by getting what he can from him in order to close an unfortunate business."[23]

The law regulating this web of credit transfers and defaults fostered locally oriented, associational market relations. The experience of two producers, Phillip and Jacob Kierschner, reveals the stakes, opportunities, and tensions inherent in this process.[24] Phillip was a farmer of German descent living in Chambersburg, Pennsylvania; his son Jacob was an aspiring blacksmith whose shop and residence were located on a farm in Hagerstown, Maryland. Following family custom, the elder Kierschner rented the Hagerstown property—called First Snow—to Jacob; upon the father's death the son would acquire full ownership. The young man started renting the land in 1813. Simultaneously, to build the blacksmith shop, he began, through the medium of negotiable paper, borrowing from numerous individuals in the community small sums amounting to between $2 and $9. Unfortunately Jacob's business did not prosper and his creditors repeatedly called upon the justice of the peace to recover on the overdue paper. Probably to gain time until funds came in from other sources, the young smithy usually paid his creditors only after an official protest from the authorities. Assisting Jacob in these efforts were several local associates, including a sheriff.

The panic of 1819 disrupted the Kierschners' credit relationships.

Sometime in 1819 Phillip began sending his son monthly pleas for overdue rent on the First Snow farm. By October 1821 he wrote in German (which was later translated when the letters became legal documents): "As to what concerns me, I am not quite well already these eight days, and thou writest, that thy Family are not well; but I am in want of my money so much, that I can hardly wait. I wish thou wouldst send it to me as quickly as possible. If thou canst send it to me next week, I am satisfied; but settle the interest on the money that remained behind from 1820." After the payment of one installment the father wrote his son that he was "pretty well" but hoped that "thou wouldest send me the remainder as quickly as possible. I am in debt, and the people would like to get it." Phillip noted that Jacob had pleaded that the rent was "too high"; the father replied that he did not "know how soon a change may take place . . . [i]f times do not get better, I shall not be too hard with thee." Finally, the senior Kierschner filed suit in the Maryland federal circuit court in 1825 for recovery of several years of partially delinquent rent and interest. In 1827 the court decided that Jacob and three partners owed Phillip $10,000, which the son agreed to pay.

State law thus facilitated locally oriented associational market relationships that counterbalanced exploitive capitalist values. Father and son Kierschner faced market pressures that threatened and ultimately disrupted the familial bonds embodied in the father's gift of land to his son. Throughout five years of economic depression, however, those associational relations endured. During those years federalism reinforced the associational bonds in that the two Kierschners resided in different states subject to competing protectionist debtor-creditor laws. These laws, along with the expansive state regard for the principle of negotiability that aided debtors as well as creditors, created a legal environment encouraging delay in the recovery of debts. In the case of Jacob's shaky blacksmith enterprise, the benefit of local legal institutions also included the support of a sheriff. Eventually the elder Kierschner sought and won recovery against Jacob in federal court, but only after the return of better economic conditions. Until that point the values of legitimacy and accountability inherent in the constitutional ideal and maintained by federalism sustained associational market imperatives over capitalist ones.

The interplay of legal rules grounded in constitutionalism and the credit system also shaped the associational market relations of Bernard

Schlesinger.[25] In 1836 Schlesinger, a German immigrant, arrived in Baltimore with a "very small" amount of capital totaling $150. He could understand and speak English reasonably well but was unable to write the language; he could also make rudimentary accounting calculations. With these meager resources Schlesinger began "selling old clothes." After six months he entered into a partnership with B. Greensfelder, who sold dry goods and clothing; within a year the newcomer accumulated $700 for himself and soon dissolved the partnership. In another four months Schlesigner's resources amounted to $1,000, while through relatives in Baltimore his wife acquired another $300 worth of goods on credit.

Then a flood destroyed Schlesinger's gains. He lost approximately $2,400 in capital and goods and owed debts of about $1,800. The small-time producer settled with several of his creditors at fifty cents on the dollar. But during the same period— because he had "acted honestly with them"—several creditors extended the debtor "small credit for dry goods, which he tried to sell at wholesale." These and other debts were contracted for time periods ranging from six, to twelve, to as long as twenty-four months, giving Schlesinger time to pay.

To mid-1841 Schlesinger's business involved no more than $300. By then he tried to sell some inventory through Weaver and Cannon, a Baltimore auctioneering firm; after several sales he asked the partners for authority to draw upon their credit via the medium of negotiable paper in order to make larger purchases. Schlesinger hoped to buy goods on credit in Philadelphia so that he could auction them off at better prices in Baltimore. Weaver and Cannon authorized him to draw on them at sight for fifty cents on the dollar. But there could be no extension of credit until the partners actually gained possession of the goods. Probably because of this support Schlesinger acquired $2,700 worth of consignments in Philadelphia. Unfortunately, the auctioneers were able to sell the stock only at prices lower than their hopeful agent had paid. Facing dwindling resources and overdue accounts, he "begged very hard" for a small loan. Although Weaver opposed the idea, Cannon decided that "we will lend it to him anyhow." Through such assistance Schlesinger held on until 1843 when he finally failed. Characterizing himself "a merchant," he petitioned the federal district court to be classified an insolvent debtor under the short-lived national law of 1841. The petition listed his total debts as $4,093 and total credits as $1,291.

But Bernard Schlesinger did not quit. The insolvent debtor attempted to form a partnership with a member of his wife's family; the relative, however, refused. Then, several months later, Schlesinger did "buy out" a tavern stand for $80. He paid $5 to the individual who had given him the information that the stand was for sale. To get the purchase price, Schlesinger borrowed $30 from "a tailor residing in his house" and took over the debt that "a former tenant" owed the landlord of the boardinghouse in which they lived, which added another $42 to his capital. As he reimbursed the landlord "from time to time," Schlesinger accumulated another $6 "elsewhere," which he paid off as he was "enabled to do it," and finally got $2 from his wife. With this he was back in business.

His wife's relatives and even his own creditors manifested associational sentiments that enabled Bernard Schlesinger to rise after repeated failure. No doubt, particularly with the creditors, narrow economic considerations influenced the willingness to help the immigrant; keeping him afloat with small loans at least created the possibility that Schlesinger might be able to pay when times improved. Cannon's decision, despite his partner's opposition, to extend Schlesinger another loan because he had "begged very hard" suggests, however, that less capitalistic sentiments could intermingle with more explicit cost-benefit considerations to determine business judgments.

Thus federalism and the other constitutional values sustained locally oriented associational market relations. The states' protectionist policies facilitated distinct local markets in which the principle of negotiability bound together an intricate, interlocking network of debtors and creditors. The comparative ease with which individuals like Jacob Kierschner and Bernard Schlesinger could build up capital through numerous modest loans, along with generally increasing wages, spurred the proliferation of small-scale, unincorporated, independent proprietorships. Even so, when he filed for bankruptcy, Schlesinger's net worth was $4,093, equivalent to the smallest proprietors listed in the credit reports of the period.

The interplay of federalism and market tensions nonetheless deflected social conflict. Supreme Court contract clause decisions to the contrary notwithstanding, the mid-Atlantic states' implementation of the constitutional ideal fostered legal rules that sustained faith in producer enterprise and limited upward social mobility. Ironically, however, if easy credit increased opportunities for entry into the busi-

ness system, the ultimately unstable character of such capital also heightened the possibility of failure. But since so many Americans went broke, a bond of shared experience existed which mitigated the class tensions inherent in the ever-growing inequality of wealth. The law governing negotiability and debt default encouraged associational sentiments that interacted with the capitalist impulse to spread risks and gains throughout society. The interplay of these values and interests ameliorated class conflict, diluted concerns about an unequal distribution of wealth, put off the day of reckoning for those operating on marginal resources, and encouraged the belief that individual enterprise and interpersonal cooperation were compatible with constitutional accountability and legitimacy.

### The Associational Economy at Work

Closer examination clarifies the associational and market dimensions of the constitutional and economic interrelationships. The weak private and public mechanisms governing commercial credit contracts facilitated associational market relationships even among prominent capitalists such as gunpowder manufacturer E. I. Du Pont. With long time associates and in isolated local markets where vigorous pursuit of defaulting customers would have been particularly counterproductive, Du Pont and his agents were quite lenient. In other instances his capitalist aggressiveness was straightforward. In the credit reports, moreover there were numerous examples of modest-sized enterprisers who operated principally within local markets adhering to the same associational values rather than capitalist ones. Local debtors and creditors treated one another much more cooperatively than foreign creditors treated them. In addition, local enterprisers and their worker customers shared close bonds. These interpersonal relations to some extent embraced even women and blacks, while ethnic discrimination against Jews was pronounced. Nevertheless, suggesting how pervasive social fragmentation was is the fact that the ardent capitalists were most distrusted.

Americans undeniably valued economic independence based on individual enterprise, yet the realities of the credit system nonetheless often fostered a dependency upon reciprocal social relations. Market pressures, human emotions, and moral presumptions encouraged interaction between independence and dependency. A wealthy credi-

tor like Du Pont revealed the strength of this relationship in his deal-ings with an old friend and business agent, Samuel Briscoe. During the panic of 1819 Du Pont loaned Briscoe credit through the medium of negotiable paper at no interest so that his firm could stave off failure.[26] When the collapse came anyway, Du Pont continued to assist his friend: "For all your goodness to me and the firm I have nothing to offer but gratitude," was the agent's response. The failure also un-leashed more traditional capitalist instincts, as when a debtor of one of Briscoe's partners wrote Du Pont, "I am truly sorry to find that . . . [he is] so largely in your debt and it will afford me much pleasure to be the means of making him pay."[27] But the undoubted strength of such motivations did not entirely eradicate associational sentiments from the marketplace.

Local interests were also endemic to the associational economy. Briscoe noted in 1818 that a merchant in Baltimore County named Jamison sold a competitor's powder to local grocers at a price consider-ably lower than Du Pont charged. Briscoe pointed out that such a "bad policy" could result in "no advantage to the grocers" and furthermore would encourage other merchants to reduce their prices so that the merchant would have to go still lower until he made no profit at all. Jamison replied that he and his local competitors sold at the same price; he "could not sell higher," and when he "could no longer make a profit he would stop making it." Dismayed, Du Pont's agent departed with the observation that the merchant could only lose in the end. Perhaps because of such considerations, wealthy nonresident credi-tors like Du Pont extended the dates of payment on overdue notes, often without charging interest, rather than press local debtors. This was necessary on the relatively isolated Eastern Shore of Maryland where Briscoe made "little progress" in collecting Du Pont's outstand-ing debts because some debtors were "absent," others asked to be called upon at a later date, and some simply "refused to give either note or money."[28]

Confidential credit reports revealed that Du Pont's associational relationships were not atypical. For more than thirty years before the Civil War, William Torbert ran a general store in Elkton, Maryland. Due to his integrity and high standing in the community, Torbert received generous loans from "foreign" creditors. Conversely, social ties resulting from his position as a "leading Methodist" and overly generous sentiments toward his customers led the venerable mer-

chant by the 1850s to extend credit in amounts that proved to be too liberal. Playing on Torbert's generosity, many customers pleaded for and received ever lengthening periods of extended credit. The store-keeper "weathered the storm" for some time but ultimately, because of the "wretched neglect of his customers," could no longer honor his own debts. In 1861, acting with "strictest integrity," Torbert closed down his business and with his son serving as trustee settled with his creditors. He left business, it was reported, with the community's total confidence.[29]

Consumer advantage could result from a small producer's willing-ness to accept limited profits. Dry goods dealer C. M. McCauley possessed the esteem and confidence of the residents of McCon-nellsburg, Pennsylvania, because he adhered to the motto "small profits, quick sales." Similarly, John Emmons, a stranger in Madison, New Jersey, in 1847, opened a general store in a remote area of Morris County and sold goods at "very small profits in order to draw cus-tomers." Because he "trusted out too much" by generously extending the due dates of payments, Emmons continued for some four years to make little money. Eventually, however, he built up a net worth of two to three thousand dollars, sold out, and moved to New York State.[30]

Such pricing practices were not unusual in the credit reports.[31] Low prices and easy credit were the costs that producers bore to build up trade and to cultivate a favorable reputation in local communities. Customers undoubtedly gained from these exigencies, yet in most instances their deferring to consumers also created social costs that hindered the achievement of anything more than a modest business for many individual proprietors. Of course in other cases, as with Torbert in Elkton, Maryland, these factors might also lead to failure. At the same time, however, they reinforced the larger conviction that modest, unincorporated producers were sensitive to the interests of the local community.

These factors mitigated strictly capitalistic motivations in other ways. Sometimes, as with Joseph H. Hunter of Burnt Cabins, Pennsyl-vania, creditors hounded debtors, forcing them into bankruptcy and their removal to the West. This was not always so, however. Creditors left alone Dr. Robert S. Hunter of Speersville, Pennsylvania, in part because they considered him honest and "disposed to pay when he could," but also because they knew that too much pressure would force him into insolvency. Finally, the doctor went to Iowa, and

through legal action the lenders attached what little property he left behind.[32] Though possessing similarly meager assets, such failed debtors nonetheless received different treatment at the hands of their respective creditors. The experience of the first was consistent with a stereotype of relentless capitalistic harassment; that of the second was, comparatively at least, more humane. Thus other factors intermingling with more explicit exploitative considerations often ameliorated the most unrelenting capitalist impulse, partially relieving some debtors of the burden of all that the market could bear.

Through associational relationships local producers also shared with debtors the costs of failure. Shopkeepers in Cape May, New Jersey, knew John Dougherty as an honest, "shrewd trading fellow." During the spring of 1854 he owed considerable debts on goods purchased the previous fall in Philadelphia. One of the creditors from the City of Brotherly Love became concerned, therefore, and sued. The storekeeper's local friends had enough faith in him, however, that they advanced him funds to pay off the judgment that the Philadelphia creditor won. Dougherty's associates were convinced that litigation would only force him to sacrifice his property and thereby ultimately delay payments; everyone was certain that once the bathing season brought an influx of customers to the coastal summer resort town, he would make enough to cover the debts. By summer's end matters had not improved; but when the sheriff began auctioning Dougherty's goods, his friends again advanced him funds so that the sale did not proceed. In the late fall the collapse finally came; after settling with his creditors Dougherty cleared $500 and moved to Philadelphia. Even though the failure resulted in their general financial loss, the storekeeper's friends apparently accepted this as the price to be paid for trusting their judgment as to the viability of a trading associate in his time of need.[33]

Bankruptcy was often the price Americans paid to achieve economic independence. Rochus Heinisch, a German immigrant, made shears in Newark, New Jersey; creditors considered him an honest, first-rate mechanic, though a poor manager of money. In 1838 he resorted to the state's bankruptcy law, but Heinisch purchased tools from a friend and with a patent on shears was doing a good business with local tailors by the 1840s. Because of his poor managerial skills, Heinisch often had overdue accounts that resulted in suits from creditors. By the early fifties the immigrant nonetheless had acquired

enough resources to expand his business into a small factory, purchase a house, and borrow all the credit he wanted. Then in 1856 he was broke again. But within a few years he overcame this setback and was considered worth about four to five thousand dollars and good for any "reasonable" amount of credit.[34]

Throughout the mid-Atlantic states this pattern of business was not uncommon.[35] Of course, most individuals who failed never achieved more than a modest status as independent producers, but for people like Rochus Heinisch even shaky independence was no doubt preferable to working for someone else.

And many times it was only through the assistance of others that failure was overcome. Another "hard working German," Thomas Beck, was a locally respected but modestly capitalized carpet weaver in Baltimore during the late 1840s. Lenders extended him reasonable amounts of credit without question in his hometown; but because he was not personally known, loans were more difficult to procure in New York. By the end of 1850 Beck was offering to pay his creditors fifty cents on the dollar over twelve, eighteen, and twenty-four months. Assured of Beck's trustworthiness and industriousness, the Baltimore creditors accepted these terms; the New Yorkers, however, would not. Only after his father-in-law agreed to secure the compromise with his own credit did the New Yorkers accept the settlement. Between 1851 and 1858, even though the carpet business was depressed, the German paid the installments regularly until his debts were liquidated. With the cooperation of a relative and those who trusted him in his home city, Beck overcame the narrowly pecuniary motivations of his foreign creditors and remained an independent producer.[36]

Marriage was another important associational bond in the credit system. Married women, prior to and after the death of their husbands, operated enterprises as independent proprietors. Moreover, a wife's signature on her husband's notes often provided valuable security for transactions that either increased the couple's capital or protected it from default. Husbands confronted with failure might also save some assets by assigning them to their spouses. Creditors recognized, too, that wives could be more responsible than their husbands for keeping a business going. This was the case with "hard drinking Irishman" Richard Casey, a grocer in Cape May, New Jersey. As the store endured good times and bad, local lenders ascribed its persistence to Casey's wife, who possessed "all the business qualities."[37]

The standing of African-Americans in the associational economy was ambivalent. Unquestionably the law and white society in general discriminated against free blacks. At the same time, individual blacks apparently could receive fair treatment and even gain the trust, respect, and credit of white lenders. Moses Lake, a "Negro" shopkeeper in Annapolis, Maryland, was such an individual. Between 1845 and 1850 Lake ran two bakeries and held some vaguely defined "situation" in the naval yard; he also owned two slaves. Due to speculation in California, Lake encountered financial difficulties in 1852; he was never sued, however, and maintained a sound credit rating with Annapolis lenders. Until 1860 he and his wife continued to do fairly well; but during the war his business declined considerably. Though creditors still looked upon him as honest and respectable, he could no longer acquire much credit. Moses Lake then became the barber for the Naval Academy, a position he retained until his death in 1871.[38]

Social prejudices could override objective market factors when debtors and creditors dealt with Jewish Americans. Regardless of how prosperous Jewish enterprisers appeared to be, lenders extended them credit "cautiously." A confidential credit report on M. Solomon of Baltimore was typical: though no one knew for sure, he was said to be rich and for an "Israelite" had a "good reputation;" but, the evaluation observed, it was always "difficult to rate this class." In other instances a disgruntled debtor might refer to his creditor as a "Jew broker." Ultimately, however, such reservations and values did not hinder the market effectiveness of Jewish businessmen like David Hissonger of Frederick, Maryland, whose financial worth in 1860 was estimated to be $20,000.[39] Jews thus often succeeded as individual enterprisers but not necessarily due to the assistance of the native business establishment.

Interestingly, community enterprisers could be most critical of pure capitalists. Levi Perry sold boots and shoes on retail in Baltimore. Even though he cultivated the image of a "Saint," traders in the city considered Perry a "slippery," "tricky fellow," a "wolf in sheep's clothing" who would do "almost anything . . . within the pale of legality." That such a "black-hearted rascal" nonetheless owned two stores and was making money merely proved that the "Devil takes care of his own." Perry had learned that maintaining the "garb of religion" was profitable, a goal he pursued with zeal of a "Fanatic." All this undermined the retailer's credit standing within the Baltimore mercantile commu-

nity; others encountered similar resistance when they pushed beyond accepted social mores in their quest for gain.[40]

Ties of kinship, friendship, and acquaintance facilitated negotiable paper credit transactions that spread the costs of indebtedness and default throughout society. Of course, this distribution was not equal, and large capitalist enterprisers undoubtedly benefited from the system. But more significantly from the point of view of perpetuating society's faith in producer values, community, and egalitarianism, the associational economy also helped sustain the majority of modest enterprisers capitalized at $4,000 or less.

Unquestionably, strict market factors influenced lender decisions: creditors could keep debtors afloat to "squeeze" them over the long haul rather than risk losing everything through failure. But social sentiments might also intermingle with market pressures to encourage more humane results. Debtors were left alone and given time to pay as they could without harassment, even though for creditors the likelihood of ultimate loss was great. Moreover, traders extended loans to local associates and family members, even as foreign creditors pressed these debtors to pay. Since the incidence of failure was high in spite of such aid, something more was involved in the decision to take risks in favor of community shopkeepers than merely the local creditor's greater awareness of local economic conditions. For both local and foreign lenders the uncertainties enshrouding a debtor's solvency were formidable; yet when confronted with the possibility of default, local creditors often accepted the risk of assisting a debtor while outsiders did not. In such cases imprecise but nonetheless potent social sentiments and character assessments not shared by outsiders doubtless shaped the local community's judgment.

The interplay of market and associational factors also facilitated explicit distinctions in the treatment of women, free blacks, Jewish Americans, other ethnic minorities, and unequivocal capitalists. Wives operated businesses in spite of their husband's deficiencies; they served, too, as guarantors of spouses' credit transactions, thus subjecting market decisions to the vicissitudes of the nuptial bond. Such practices no doubt in part resulted from debtors' and creditors' assessment of market expediency, but they also demonstrated that women were significant participants in the socially interdependent credit system. In other cases ethnic stereotypes shaped market judgments, as when credit was forthcoming for "hardworking Germans"

but extended only cautiously to Jews because this "class" was "hard to rate." Unlike Jewish Americans, the Irish and even free blacks could benefit from the associational character of the credit system. Interestingly, the blatant capitalist was as stigmatized as the Jew. In an economy in which the pervasiveness of failure fostered a sharing of risks and gains, the individual who rejected reciprocal obligations was inevitably distrusted to the extreme; outside the reciprocal bonds of the associational economy, he stood comparatively alone in the market place.

### Social Fragmentation and Constitutionalism

Tensions inherent in the associational economy found manifestation in public debate, which in turn reflected producer and Protestant moral values that interacted with legal rules and constitutionalism. One incisive observer summarized the factors governing debtor-creditor policy making. In 1826 Peter DuPonceau, a naturalized United States citizen from France who settled in Philadelphia, wrote Thomas Jefferson's former secretary of the treasury, Albert Gallatin. The émigré doubted whether local political rivalries and economic interests would permit extensive, federally supported national development in America on the scale pursued by France. Both distinctive moral values and comparatively weak republican government embodied in the constitutional ideal made this so. The "good and evil principles" were "found together" in the American character. "The problem," DuPonceau said, was "how to combine strict honesty with the spirit of enterprise. . . . And whether too strict regulation . . . [would] check that spirit in an inconvenient degree." Reflecting, moreover, a preference for the "middling" classes, he feared that centralized national regulation could place business in the "hands of rich capitalists, and paralyze the efforts of aspiring talents without fortune."[41]

Such sentiments were evident in the public press. As Americans became all too familiar with failure during recurring panics and depressions, considerable skepticism circumscribed the acceptance of unqualified profit making. To protect families, one group of policy makers exclaimed, the law should enable failed debtors to rise by their "own means, or by the aid of friends." Widows were among those whom the lawmakers looked upon as vital to familial stability, though more than altruism alone inspired this concern. The estates of "thou-

sands" of debtors were composed of personal property, a delegate to the Maryland constitutional convention of 1850 observed, which was "perhaps derived from the wife or accumulated from her savings and industry." It was better that the law "diminished" the claims of creditors—and here the delegate pronounced a central concern—than "that these widows and children should be thrown on society for maintenance and education."[42]

Even the vigorous advocate of mercantile pursuits, *Hunt's Merchants' Magazine*, perceived the threat in unrestrained capitalism. It would, *Hunt's* wrote, "greatly promote the general prosperity, if a far larger proportion of young men would become practical farmers." The existence of too many merchants resulted from the "insane and insatiable passion for accumulation . . . [and] an undue and idolatrous estimate of the value of property." Elsewhere *Hunt's* counseled not to "make too much haste to be rich—By this means nineteenth twentieths of our merchants fail."[43]

Moral accountability and credit were mutually reinforcing, sustaining associational relationships. Business was "a moral dispensation, and its highest end is moral." Credit, the lifeblood of the antebellum economic order, depended upon the "moral qualities of the [nation's] population"; similarly, "the origins" of credit was "man's moral nature." The emphasis upon morals grew out of the need for interpersonal confidence that was essential to stable debtor-creditor relations. It was "plain that self-interest cannot be a basis for perfect credit," *Hunt's* exclaimed, "nor can it take the place of the reliance upon good faith and substantial honesty, which alone will insure the execution of an agreement." The relentless pursuit of wealth that so easily verged into fraud and dishonesty "sap[ped] the foundations of mutual dependence," thereby weakening the security of credit itself. Only when "sound principles and morals" were dominant with "a people, informing their rules of action, over infidelity and fraud . . . [would] credit . . . be turned to profitable use."[44]

Social class, if not capitalist interest, influenced these values and support for constitutionalism. The rise of "colossal and very antirepublican fortunes" like those existing in the "banking houses of the countries of the old world" threatened, wrote *Hunt's*, the "middling" classes. The nation's institutions depended "upon the preservation of a general equality of outward condition among our citizens." But individuals who "pursued profits" through the "skillful use of capital

and credit" alone could easily defraud the "credulous and confiding public." Such practices destroyed "all confidence in any but the most positive and undoubted names . . . already famous for the possession of overgrown wealth." A "monopoly of credit" among these "names" resulted, which increased the "piling [of] gold upon the already towering mountain of their worldly goods."[45]

Moreover, widespread misery and business collapse were concomitant evils flowing from unrestrained capitalism. When the opportunity appeared to make more than "ordinary profits," *Hunt's* warned, Americans were too easily tempted to resort to "fictitious credit" extended "far beyond" their "real capital." When this happened, "the hazard of bankruptcy and ruin" for the individual was "great." But the overzealous capitalist not only risked his "own property, but that of . . . [his] creditors," which was "hardly reconcilable with honest principles." Thus when "any sudden change" occurred in the "commerce or currency" of the nation, "a revulsion" was "inevitable," which, due to the interdependent character of the credit-based economy, meant that "thousands" experienced "unexpected ruin."[46]

To check this menace *Hunt's* appealed to associational values, alert public opinion, and disciplined moral character rather than strong government. The "great danger we ought to fear as a republic," wrote *Hunt's*, was *"too great a thirst for money, and too little scruple how it is acquired."* By following "purer and higher motives," American businessmen could free themselves from "oppressive customs" and thereby limit the "fluctuations which rest like black and threatening clouds over our devoted country." Although profits were vital, their pursuit should not override the desire to "promote the public good." The individual's, the family's and the community's development and well-being depended not upon greed but on the enterpriser's willingness to pursue the "means of subsequent as well as of present enjoyment." When governed by such "foresight" and "affections," Americans would be "frugal as well as industrious." Consequently, the journal asserted that debtor-creditor laws could "offer inducement" for "honest conduct" and even limit overt criminal behavior, but they could not "mend [men's] hearts." Furthermore, even "wise" laws "avail but little against laxness of integrity and a debased moral feeling." The remedy, then, was "well-principled public opinion . . . the real sovereign in our country." Fortified with sound morals and republican sentiments, this

opinion would sustain and enforce the "eternal principles of right and wrong."[47]

Throughout the antebellum years these arguments were repeated in the debate over debtor-creditor rights evidencing an inherent faith in the constitutional ideal. An anonymous pamphleteer in 1810 presaged the concerns expressed in *Hunt's*. Credit was, of course, central to both individual enterprise and the well-being of the "commonwealth." The writer called for national laws to prevent the sort of private arrangements among local debtors and creditors that state legislation encouraged, which discriminated against nonresident creditors. But along with these immediate preoccupations were other general concerns and presumptions. Since "misfortune" often was unavoidable, laws governing credit needed to be "constructive" and consistent with "our republican institutions" to "promote the interest of the whole." At the same time, they must not foster "monopoly" and "avarice," which resulted from "loose transactions," an "enterprise *too keen*," and those who lacked "religion, morality, or honor." Such laws, moreover, would protect the producers in America from dangerous extremes: the "evil of wealth" and a "servility of spirit."[48]

In 1821 another anonymous pamphlet expressed similar views. The "aggregate" of usefully employed individuals fostered the "Public prosperity." To increase prosperity and avoid "discontent and suffering," wise debtor-creditor laws should "pursue a middle course" between "lenity and severity." Overly strict treatment of defaulted debtors was ill-advised in part because most were "children of misfortune." But the law must also prevent the "mass of accumulated and overgrown wealth" by those who were "dead to a sense of . . . moral and social duties." The writer criticized state laws which permitted private arrangements between local debtors and creditors at the expense of out-of-state creditors. This created a diversity of rights from state to state; national laws were therefore the answer. Neither national considerations nor altruism alone motivated these sentiments, however. The deeper concern was that a failure to administer debtor-creditor rights effectively represented a threat to social order. As growing numbers of voters fell under the "pressing hand of poverty," society's laws came under the influence of "drones and idlers," which was "dangerous to the peace of the community."[49]

More than a decade later these sentiments remained strong. An

observer noted that credit "superseded" specie "or any other medium of exchange." Law and individual character reinforced the role of credit, which in turn had a direct bearing on society's well-being and individual opportunity. Reliance upon gold or silver as the basis of business "would cause the great mass of capital, to be accumulated into the coffers of a minority." But because credit was "in great measure created by industry, skill, and integrity," its use averted such dangers. Consequently, "the poor honest man" might be trusted over the "wealthy rogue; and in a poor community, where morality is strict, and the laws rigid, more credit will be in operation, than in a rich community, *where vice prevails, and the laws are inefficient.*" Thus specie supported "idleness or pleasure," whereas credit made the individual "industrious; unless he be willing by employing it dishonestly, to incur the evils of legal punishment, of lost character, and of lost credit."[50]

By the eve of the Civil War such arguments had not abated. Another advocate of federal debtor-creditor legislation noted the problems arising from local control. In doing so, however, he expressed assumptions about law, the constitutional ideal, society, and credit that were at least half a century old. Laws that favored corporate capitalists facilitated the influence of "a few men, with a power more dangerous than the Emperor of Russia, and more liable to be exercised for other purposes than the public good." Moreover, law should not encourage "people who are born rich" because they were not the "class who produce, manufacture, or trade." Productive enterprise was, by contrast, "carried on by the industry of the middling classes of society, who have been the artificers of their own fortunes." The proper beneficiaries of the law and the constitutional ideal, then, were those who started in "a lower capacity" and "by energy and attention to business" raised themselves.[51]

The tension inherent in this clash of values and interests threatened producer independence and Protestant moral principles. The nation's abundant resources, noted one observer in 1820, made "enterprise" the "presiding genius of our people." But it was unclear whether this would "become the destroying demon, or beneficent deity." The preferable enterprise was that of farmers, artisans, and shopkeepers, another writer said in 1819, whereas the "establishment of a large class of foreign merchants, in an agricultural society, will always prove injurious to it." By the 1850s the big cities were beset with peril because "morals" were "exposed to . . . danger . . . which pervades the whole

realm of commerce." God was "forgotten" and Caesar reigned "supreme," the "multitudes have their eyes fixed not on heaven but on earth . . . [and] the motives which drive them on in the fierce race of competition." People must distinguish "right from wrong," yet it seemed that, at least in the cities, "PERSONAL RESPONSIBILITY" was waning.[52]

Representative government also contained tensions that jeopardized producer and Protestant moral values and trust in constitutionalism. The producer majority in America was honest, but, exclaimed a critic in 1855, a "large portion of our politicians are corrupt." These public officials were "low tricksters" operating a "political faro-bank" under the influence of "munificent stock speculators, . . . gamblers," and "foreigners" who had "corrupted elections." The axiom that a "good citizen" was a "good Christian" was being undermined by this "monster iniquity." A few capitalists like the "merchant princes" in Europe who held the poor in "their grip" thus were allied with that "dangerous destructive class who 'cut and shuffle' in politics."[53] Consequently, the specter arose of the "judge who perverts the moral influence of his station, or blemishes his ermine with the stain of faction; the ministerial officer who warps in the exercise of his functions to accommodate his private antipathies or attachments; [and] the juror who barters his verdict for a vote." The American republic, it seemed, was "at the mercy of its own instruments."[54]

Often the struggle centered on state-chartered banks. From the nation's earliest days banks were attacked. Yet at least in the mid-Atlantic states the need for banks in a capital-scarce economy was undeniable, as even many of their most adamant critics admitted. The dispute was not over banking per se but the extent to which a state should sanction and regulate it through incorporation charters. The same tensions inherent in the attachment to individual enterprise and constitutionalism ran through the bank charter debate. Opponents exclaimed that these institutions operated "upon the *labour of the producer*, for their income."[55] Despite such criticism, however, all four mid-Atlantic states chartered banks. The Democratic governor of Maryland offered an explanation in 1840. "The great body of people are tired of banks [because they were blamed for the panic and depression of 1837–40]," he said, "yet their representatives, many of them of our party, instead of reducing their number, content themselves with imposing restrictions upon their future operations. In this state we

now have the power to get rid of a portion of them by direct action of the Legislature. Yet I do not find a man in favour of this course."[56]

True to the constitutional ideal, many producers accepted that through regulation a state could keep incorporated banks accountable to the community interest. Several factors seemed to justify this faith. During the first half of the nineteenth century most localities relied upon storekeepers, merchants, and private, nonincorporated banks for credit. In 1830 there were only nineteen county and ten city banks chartered in Pennsylvania, and although the number certainly increased by the 1850s, state-incorporated banks did not displace private sources of credit before the Civil War.[57] Moreover, community rivalry for internal improvements encouraged bank incorporation in order to finance the enormous capital outlays that railroads and canals required. The initial beneficiaries of the credit that these banks made available were local builders, teamsters, and other small, unincorporated producer enterprises.[58] At the same time, the long-term credit that banks could extend in local communities enhanced producer opportunity; as one commentator observed, such credit "might not suit the extensive and complicated trade of a large commercial city, [but] it is well adapted to the limited transactions of a country bank." Additionally, states imposed taxes upon banks, which reduced or eliminated the tax burden on producers. As one contemporary observed, banks "saved State Government from taxation."[59] Finally, Jackson's identification of community interest and states' rights with opposition to the Bank of the United States undercut resistance to local banks chartered by the states.

Thus there were clear priorities in the media's discussion of credit-based prosperity. The general commitment to individual initiative did not undercut a preference for small-scale, nonincorporated, producer enterprise over unrestrained, capitalistic profit making. The faith in constitutionalism sustained—despite repeated criticism and the toleration of banks—an overriding commitment to local control and the values of legitimacy and accountability. The acceptance, as Tocqueville said, of the law as "King" did not diminish the conviction that disciplined character and enlightened public opinion were more effective than state-enforced sanctions. An infatuation with private property did not shake the presumption that its distribution should be widespread among the "middling" producer classes and protected from the threat of monopoly capitalists through constitutional restraints.

Because they yearned for prosperity, American publicists favored governmental support of development within the bounds of the constitutional ideal. But growth for whom and of what sort persisted as controversial public issues. In favoring "middling" producers over capitalist entrepreneurs, the law governing credit transactions and failed debtors—among antebellum America's most conspicuous losers—spread the cost of debtor-creditor relations and failure throughout society. Moral values, an associational economy, and localistic democratic politics encouraged appeals to constitutionalism, which in turn deflected concerns about an inequitable allocation of wealth and sustained the belief that relief from the risks of individual enterprise depended upon local control and enlightened public opinion. The preoccupation with morals and character, however, did not obscure an underlying concern about social order. In an environment charged with failure, marginal producers felt threatened from above and below. Consequently, their expectations of the law and constitutionalism were ambivalent. Public policy should allow easy entry into the business order through generous credit and should not be unduly hard on failed debtors; but it should also strictly limit sharp dealing and facilitate honest enterprise rather than capitalistic greed. Lawmakers in the mid-Atlantic states sought to resolve this conflict, keeping faith with the constitutional ideal.

### The Triumph of Local Control

Central to the struggle over credit was the issue of local control. No doubt the most famous instance of such a conflict was Jackson's veto of the Second Bank of the United States. The BUS seemed to threaten the availability of credit in local communities. Jackson's farewell address of 1836 no doubt reflected the anxiety many Americans felt during the crisis. The "monster" Bank "asserted (and . . . undoubtedly possessed) the power to make money plenty or scarce at its pleasure, at any time and in any quarter of the Union," he said. With this "unlimited dominion over the amount of the circulating medium," it could "regulate the value of property and the fruits of labor in every quarter of the Union, and . . . bestow prosperity or bring ruin upon any city or section of the country as might best comport with its own interest or policy." Jackson recalled the "distress and alarm which pervaded and agitated" the nation when the BUS "waged war upon the people in order to compel

them to submit. . . . The ruthless and unsparing temper with which whole cities and communities were oppressed, individuals impoverished and ruined, and a scene of cheerful prosperity suddenly changed into one of gloom and despondency ought to be indelibly impressed on the memory of the people of the United States." At least for Jackson and his party's supporters, then, the veto was a clear triumph for community control.[60]

Other confrontations raised the same issue. Among the most important uses of credit that negotiability made possible were long-term loans known as accommodations. Commercial credit extended through the medium of negotiable paper by a lender to a borrower purely to raise money or to obtain a further extension of credit was an accommodation loan. Such loans involved no actual exchange of any "valuable consideration"; they represented merely the borrower's use of the lender's name to bolster his credit standing so that he could borrow more from third parties than otherwise would have been possible. Many accommodations were exchanges between family members or longtime associates who knew each other well. In such cases the motivations for extending credit often were rooted in the social relationships of the associational economy. But it was also not uncommon for merchants and banks to make accommodation loans to strangers based solely on the word of others; here the motivation was more explicitly capitalistic since the borrower received credit only because the lender expected at some point to make a profit. *Hunt's Merchants' Magazine* described the distinction between the two forms of accommodation: one was "a matter of honor, of personal favor," whereas the other represented "a matter of business in a technical sense."[61]

As with other credit transactions, accommodation loans were the object of controversy. Many enterprisers, including producers, favored this form of credit because they enabled the individual holding accommodation paper to borrow more than was otherwise possible. But such uses of credit were also potentially objectionable, as one observer noted, because they were often "adopted by swindlers to defraud the public." Of course, what was in fact a fraud was not always clear. In either case, because of distance and the underdeveloped nature of credit reporting, nonresidents involved in accommodation loans were often least capable of judging the validity or worth of such transactions. This was especially true of large urban merchants

who had extended accommodation loans to numerous debtors in smaller communities.[62]

The federal judiciary proved more amenable to nonresident creditors, but its reach was limited. English courts gave the widest possible scope to the negotiability of accommodation paper. In the famous case of *Swift* v. *Tyson* (1842), the United States Supreme Court established the English principle for all cases coming under the jurisdiction of the federal tribunals. But even though many states accepted the principle of negotiability for certain forms of accommodation, few went as far as the Supreme Court. Moreover, various jurisdictional and doctrinal considerations further circumscribed the reach of federal precedent.[63]

State, not federal, tribunals heard and local lawyers argued the bulk of cases involving accommodation paper. In the mid-Atlantic states the status of accommodation paper was much litigated, and an interstate diversity in the negotiability rules governing these loans worked against the interests of large, urban merchants.[64] This inconsistency arose in part because of factors relating to lawyers and other considerations within the legal system itself. A writer for *Hunt's* noted that "in this country especially in our large cities, a large part of the legal business is of a commercial character. In these cities, the position of a sound commercial lawyer is enviable. It secures a lucrative practice and ultimate fame." Yet despite these rewards "many ludicrous mistakes have occurred by reason of the ignorance of judges and lawyers." Though appellate courts were often more sympathetic to nonresident merchants than trial courts and juries, the weak regard for precedent that characterized the antebellum era further undermined doctrinal uniformity. Even though a state supreme tribunal bound a lower court in a particular suit, other trial judges could find reasons to distinguish their case from those decided in the appellate courts. Moreover, especially outside the big cities, local judges and juries and the lawyers who practiced in the local community often favored debtors. *Hunt's* observed that "complaints are sometimes made by foreign [out-of-state] suitors . . . of the great delay and tardiness accompanying their proceedings." But a "hasty and erroneous proceeding" was "cause for regret." Delays were acceptable because they aided defendants, "one part . . . towards whom it has always been the disposition of the law to extend the greater lenity."[65]

But the link between negotiability and debt default further retarded

the national merchants' influence. What should the law do when one of the parties in the chain of negotiable paper transactions failed? From the point of view of nonresident urban creditors this was an especially critical question since they were farthest removed from the local market and thus most uncertain about the creditworthiness of local debtors. Moreover, as the publicists repeatedly exclaimed, state debtor-creditor laws discriminated against foreign lenders.[66]

By contrast national business interests governed English policy. In England, where creditors significantly influenced Parliament's approach to bankruptcy, only individuals whose pursuits the law recognized as mercantile could gain release from indebtedness through insolvency statutes. Furthermore, creditors could move against debtors without recourse to a judicial hearing, relying instead, at least after the 1830s, on a centralized administrative process. Before 1860 there were complaints that authorities were enforcing the payment of debts in a "summary and vindictive" manner with the result that "well meaning and honest customers" were hesitant to purchase on credit unless they "had the immediate power of payment.[67]

But if the law favored national creditors in England, such was not the case across the Atlantic. The republican tradition that favored weak government, an economy which depended on credit and in which so many economic activities intermingled with mercantile pursuits, democratic politics that gave debtors considerable clout over legislative policy, and the federal system that ultimately facilitated local control and producer values made it impossible for the United States to follow the English example. It was in response to this difficult problem that nationally oriented merchants pushed for federal laws. A measure of the strength of the locally oriented associational economy was that this effort failed.[68]

The controversial issue of preferring creditors revealed the social ramifications of the two nations' distinctive approaches. According to this practice—which grew in part out of the pervasiveness of accommodation loans—a debtor considering default would choose to pay one or several creditors, while leaving little or nothing to others. The debtor used a negotiable bill or note to assign the assets to the preferred business associates. Usually such a transaction was indistinguishable from an accommodation loan until, of course, the debtor formally defaulted and resorted to insolvency proceedings. Such preferences were unlawful in England. But even though in the United

States local law varied considerably, many legislatures and courts recognized the practice as legal at least in some form.[69]

Inconsistency prevailed largely because preferences were adaptable to sharp purposes. After the debtor gained a release under the insolvent law, for example, the preferred creditor would reassign part or all of the estate back to the debtor, giving the insolvent a stake with which to begin business again but also often leaving other creditors with nothing. Abijah Adams of Pennsylvania in 1820 charged that John D. Russell of Washington, D.C., had pursued such a course before his petition for insolvency. Russell had, Adams claimed, "directly or indirectly conveyed . . . some part of his property, rights and credits with intent to defraud his creditors . . . [having] assigned the greater part of his stock and trade to one Raphael Jones, one James Kearnan, and one Patrick Kearnan, and . . . others."[70]

In America the preferential creditor issue was continually debated. Those borrowers and lenders whose preferences were contingent upon associational relationships argued that the "near relation" ranked as the "highest confidence" based upon "the mutual dependence of man in society . . . forming the basis of all commercial faith and trust." Such interdependency and confidence compelled failed debtors, as a practice "customary among the brotherhoods of social labor," to prefer "confidential creditors" in the payment of debts. The opposition, of course, condemned such debtors as "swindlers." The creditors who received little or none of a failed debtor's assets because they had gone to a preferred associate no doubt held this point of view. More precisely, many critics were large urban wholesalers lending at long distances usually across state lines. When borrowers obtained credit from these mercantile firms only to favor local creditors when they became insolvent, the result was a genuine business loss. Wholesalers protected themselves as the credit reports revealed, by suing out-of-state debtors at the slightest hint of trouble, but the state court's acknowledged sympathy for local debtors could work against the nonresident creditor's interests.[71]

To end preferences the urban merchants promoted national uniform bankruptcy laws. From 1800 to the late 1850s, particularly following the panics of 1819, 1839, and 1857, there were repeated demands for congressional action. Although many debtors supported national regulation, the chief petitioners were mercantile creditors in major urban commercial centers such as Boston, New York City, Phila-

delphia, Nashville, and Charleston. Federal intervention was necessary, this group argued, because state laws favored local debtors in
general and encouraged preferring creditors in particular.[72] Even
states' rights champion Senator Robert Hayne of South Carolina urged
national legislation on behalf of creditors like his Charleston mercantile constituents. "UNJUST PREFERENCES" were not only morally repug-
nant, Hayne exclaimed, but they also facilitated "interstate competition" that destroyed "mutual confidence" in commercial relations. The
remedy for this "commercial gambling" that constituted a "moral
earthquake, which may shake this country to its centre," was national
law administered under the central jurisdiction of federal courts. Despite the fervency of such arguments, Congress passed national measures that lasted for only brief periods in 1800 and 1841.[73]

Localism helped defeat federal legislation. Opponents of national
bankruptcy opposed subjecting the administration of debtor-creditor
relations to centralized federal authority. Those favoring local authority claimed that the resort to the federal judiciary, like the unitary
administrative process that existed in England, facilitated "summary
proceedings," in many cases permitted action against debtors without
their consent, and, above all, discouraged the voluntarily negotiated
settlements between debtors and creditors that were fundamental to
the associational economy governed by the laws of the states. Such a
"foreign system" of national authorities with fixed salaries would lead
to an "army of commissioners" who could undercut the political advantages gained from local control. Moreover, the franchise itself encouraged prodebtor legislation in the states, since debtors also tended
to be voters. To achieve national legislation urban mercantile interests
thus had not only to overcome "interstate competition" but also the
majority of local debtors in their own states—difficulties that ultimately proved insurmountable.[74]

Constitutional values reinforced local control. American faith in
republican liberty, legitimacy, and accountability rested upon a belief
that government protection of private rights was consistent with the
interests of the community. Community interests and individual enterprise were viewed as interdependent. Supporters of national laws
argued in part that the denial of creditor rights violated the sanctity of
contract, thereby "destroying private property." Hence, the law
should encourage the individual to do "the best for himself, and
therefore for his country"; the law should "act for the removal of

inequality . . . [and of] impediments and restrictions," not for the creation of them.[75]

Opponents of federal authority accepted the reasoning that individual and group interests were entwined but stressed the primacy of the community interest and the need for state power to protect it. Government was founded upon an "express contract" which placed "all power in the people," against which even the right of property was not "inalienable." In light of such logic, a centralized federal bankruptcy system was a "monster" which sacrificed the "liberties of the people" and threatened the constitutional ideal of limited public and private power.[76] Both sides thus stood for republican liberty and constitutionalism, but ultimately the appeal that coincided with the power of the states won.

Defaulting debtors benefited from other state policies. Maryland and Pennsylvania legislatures, despite the prohibition in Article I, section 10 of the Constitution and the well-known cases of *Sturges* v. *Crowninshield* (1819), *Ogden* v. *Saunders* (1827), and *Bronson* v. *Kinzie* (1843), periodically passed stay laws that established for various lengths of time moratoriums on collection of debts; lawmakers also regularly enacted private or specialized bills benefiting particular indebted individuals or groups of debtors. Often the impetus behind such legislation involved urban-rural or commercial-agricultural conflicts that resulted from local political rivalries and social fragmentation. Neither New Jersey nor Delaware resorted to stay laws, but their rules fostered a variety of extralegal practices that favored debtors.[77]

State courts, too, were often not unfriendly to failed debtors. In certain instances local judges administered insolvency proceedings with such efficiency that hundreds of debtors gained release from their obligations within a day or two.[78] Moreover, when creditors challenged bankrupts in the appellate courts of the mid-Atlantic states, the debtor won in more than 60 percent of the cases. By contrast, out of concern for debtor rights, local courts handled the general run of debt collection cases with deliberation.[79]

Even imprisonment for debt was of uncertain value to creditors. Before about 1850 when the states finally abolished it, the debtor's prison received repeated criticism from reformers and creditors alike. Reformers attacked the institution for humanitarian reasons, whereas creditors opposed it because it benefited them only sporadically.[80] Their dissatisfaction was not surprising since in the mid-Atlantic ap-

pellate courts creditors won only a little more often than they lost in cases involving imprisonment for debt.[81] Unquestionably individuals suffered under the system, yet debt imprisonment probably survived as long as it did in part because it did not overly burden many debtors. At least by the 1820s state laws limited the incarceration of local residents to a few days; and if they met certain procedural requirements, local debtors could gain their freedom under state insolvency laws. Among the initial beneficiaries of these measures were female debtors—especially widows—but eventually they applied to virtually all defaulters until imprisonment for debt became an anachronism.[82]

Other factors undermined the effectiveness of the institution. The Gaol Calendar of the sheriff of West Chester, Pennsylvania, showed that of seventy-nine persons jailed for indebtedness over a three year period, the average length of incarceration was ten days, and nearly half were released within one to five days. One man escaped, and thirteen others gained liberty under the state's insolvency law. Debtors often were imprisoned at public expense, so local governments had a vested interest in expeditious release. Moreover, jailed debtors generally may have come from the ranks of middling property-holding producers who in most local communities constituted a voting majority. In West Chester imprisoned debtors belonged to the same class as a majority of the producers recorded in the credit reports whose business transactions were composed of numerous small to medium debts and credits. Defaults ranged in amount from 62½ cents to $70, the average debt was $17, and nearly half of the debts were for $8 or less.[83] Thus long before the disappearance of imprisonment for debt, the policy underlying the institution was solicitous of both the defaulting debtors and the modest, unincorporated enterprisers.

Consequently, the law governing failure was especially wary of nonresident creditors. Complaints about the state courts' treatment of debtors came primarily from foreign creditor plaintiffs. One reason for the complexity of state bankruptcy and insolvency laws was that legislators often formulated rules that treated local and nonresident creditors differently. The state statutes governing imprisonment for debt often favored local debtors over foreign residents. This discrimination arose in part because in-state creditors were simultaneously debtors of large, urban out-of-state wholesalers. Laws designed to protect in-state defaulting debtors from the nonresident creditors thus also protected the debtors of local creditors residing in the same com-

munity.[84] Furthermore, associational relationships and market factors facilitated local credit transactions like accommodation loans and preferential creditors that undercut the influence of big-city mercantile capitalists.[85] State appellate courts sometimes applied the principle of comity in favor of outsiders, but because the practice was erratic, it did not significantly alter either the legislatures' or the trial judges' general solicitude for local interests.[86]

Laws governing negotiability and failure opened up opportunity for and protected modest sized producers and reduced the consequences of default. Especially regarding accommodation loans and preferential creditors, the interplay of law and enterprise generated both risks and benefits. Big-city merchants suffered and gained from these same realities. Yet when urban creditors demanded federal laws in order to dominate debtor-creditor relations, local control and the associational interests it represented were jeopardized. State legislatures, courts, and local authorities defeated this challenge through legal rules regulating accommodations, preferences, and imprisonment for debt. And in such an environment small-town lawyers could defeat the counsel representing outsiders. Neither federal court jurisdiction nor *Swift* v. *Tyson* successfully displaced state and local action.

This triumph of local control indicated the persistence of the interplay between constitutionalism and associational market relations. The federal judiciary's interpretation of the contract clause and other provisions sanctioned national and local commercial credit transactions. Mercantile capitalists engaged in interstate trade benefited from the Court's procreditor decisions. The Court's coincident respect for federalism nonetheless enabled the four mid-Atlantic state governments to pursue protectionist policies favoring the interpersonal connections among small-scale debtor groups in locally oriented markets. The strength of debtor interests reflected the success of appeals to constitutional values of legitimacy and accountability that public officials embraced in order to reconcile conflicts between producer and capitalist enterprise. By deflecting social-class tensions, local and state authorities perpetuated faith in the constitutional ideal, thereby obscuring the growing dominance of capitalist values.

# 3

## Taxation and Capitalist

## Accountability

**A** significant measure of the relationship between constitutional values and corporate capitalism was taxation. The antimonopoly and antiaristocratic rhetoric of Jeffersonian and Jacksonian Democrats focused upon corporations in general and banks in particular as embodying the gravest threat to republican government, producer society, and constitutional accountability and legitimacy. Even Whigs and Republicans such as Henry Carey or fellow Pennsylvanian Thaddeus Stevens attacked corporations.[1] Yet at the same time public and private leaders rarely opposed corporations unequivocally, suggesting rather that there were good ones and bad ones. Good corporations were those legitimated by and held accountable to the public interest consistent with the constitutional ideal. A primary means of attaining both legitimacy and accountability was for the corporation to pay taxes. In the mid-Atlantic region public authorities successfully shifted the tax burden from the producer majority to corporations, thereby fostering faith in constitutionalism.

This tax policy involved more than mere political opportunism. By 1815 the states had superseded the federal government as the primary stimulators of development. Yet as the persistence of the credit-based

associational economy indicated, the majority of the states' citizens were small-scale producers continuously vulnerable to the threat or reality of market failure. Imposing a significant tax burden on these producers was thus economically risky and politically unwise. Better, then, at the time when the legislature granted or renewed a charter, to impose taxes in return for the many privileges that the corporation received.

In the mid-Atlantic states these taxes took different forms and had diverse outcomes. Before the transportation revolution beginning in 1815, the most common form was a bank tax which paid for public education, especially that of workers' children. Once the legislatures began chartering canals and railroads, another major source of revenue was tolls and fixed transit rates. Taxes on transportation companies had three broad policy outcomes. First, they altered trade flows so that communities or localities which otherwise would have been marginal could participate in major markets. Second, more so than even the banking fiscal policy, transport taxes funded social services, including education and the governments' operational expenses. Third, the combination of these results gave the majority of producers reason to believe that many corporations were giving something back to society in return for the privileges they received from the legislatures. Underlying the obvious mutual opportunism of this political trade-off was the popular faith in the constitutional ideal according to which the legitimate exercise of private power depended upon whether it remained accountable to public necessity.

Corporate taxation also had important implications for the tensions associated with enterprise promotion, protectionism, and emergent capitalism. Capitalist values increasingly attained dominance as state-chartered banks and transportation corporations facilitated the expansion of national and international markets. Yet the states' promotion of these institutions and values coincided with policies aimed at protecting local debtors and property holders from foreigners. States therefore often shielded local banks from out-of-state competitors. In return, banks not only paid social service taxes but also were required to pursue favorable lending policies toward producers. In addition, large mercantile capitalists paid taxes on inventory that benefited education and other social services in major urban centers. States nonetheless protected these same merchants from competitors in the big cities of other states through favorable debtor laws and, more importantly

perhaps, through transit rates that discriminated on their behalf. States also used this control of tolls and rates to protect the market position of local communities.

State protectionism fostered, then, the coincidence of locally oriented associational market relations and nationally emerging capitalist values. In-state banking and transportation corporations, as well as large urban merchants, were the primary agents of capitalism. In terms of size, market position, and the threat to traditional social and market relations, they were disruptive. Because of democratic politics, however, smaller enterprisers, property holders, and workers shifted taxes on to corporate and mercantile capitalists who in return received impressive privileges. The trade-off legitimated capitalist interests, but it also imposed upon them accountability that benefited society in various ways. While the mid-Atlantic states' protectionist policies did not forestall the triumph of capitalism, they nonetheless helped to perpetuate traditional associational market relations that were compatible with producerism. Accordingly, as late as the 1850s the free-labor ideology of Carey and others touted the superiority of modest-sized enterprisers and yeoman farmers against the evils of corporate and mercantile capitalists. Yet a "harmony of interests" could exist between the two forms of enterprise as long as capitalism was restrained by the constitutional ideal.[2]

The federal judiciary's interpretation of constitutional provisions imposed limits upon, but did not retard, the states' protectionism. While the Marshall Court's contract clause decisions strengthened corporate capitalism, they also sustained the regulatory power upon which tax policies rested. In addition, the Marshall Court did not overcome instances of outright defiance by certain local interests. Also, the *McCulloch* case upheld the BUS, but because of Jackson's veto state banks ultimately won. Similarly, in *Brown* v. *Maryland* (1827) the Court struck down as contrary to the commerce clause a license tax imposed upon import merchants. In the long run, however, the Taney Court applied the precedent to permit states to discriminate against out-of-state traders in favor of local enterprise. Beginning with the *Charles River Bridge* case of 1837 the Taney Court's contract clause decisions expanded the states' regulatory authority, particularly involving taxation of corporations. Despite the *Brown* precedent, the Court's application of the commerce clause also reinforced state protectionist policies. By contrast, the Taney Court went beyond its pre-

decessor in extending diversity jurisdiction in cases involving corporations, though the advantages were unclear before the Civil War.[3]

These constitutional and market conflicts reflected social fragmentation. As Edwin R. A. Seligman, the leading nineteenth-century writer of treatises on taxation, noted, "Where the differences in wealth become striking and the lower classes are politically powerless, the landed proprietors and the trades combine to throw the burden on the agricultural laborers and the urban artisans." However, where "aristocratic conditions prevail less strongly, as in America up to the present time, the laborer fares better, but the contest between the farmer and the city resident assumes a more acute form. The history of modern taxation is largely the history of these class antagonisms." Sensitive to this conflict, state legislatures and courts worked to deflect social-class tensions, encourage the faith that individual and community interests were interdependent, and perpetuate the belief that corporate accountability could be preserved through local governmental control and respect for the constitutional ideal. Although the state governments' tax policies were rarely equitable, they were usually effective enough to sustain these popular assumptions. Responding to diverse values and interests, lawmakers shifted the tax burden to larger mercantile enterprise and corporations. In return, of course, entrepreneurial capitalists received generous privileges. But to many producers the trade-off seemed justified as long as the taxation of capitalist enterprise benefited the local community and reduced the individual producer's taxes.[4]

### Taxation and Financial Capitalism

In the mid-Atlantic states the interplay between banks and constitutionalism deflected political attacks. As states responded to market pressures and created banks, opposition forces condemned the corporations as monopolies, agents of aristocracy, and evil generally. Defenders countered with arguments emphasizing the instrumental economic benefits. Politicians accommodated the two positions by submitting banks to taxation and other regulations that legitimated their privileges while maintaining their constitutional accountability. Even so conflicts over banks arose both within states and because of protectionist policies aimed at insulating local banks from foreign competition.[5] These confrontations led to Supreme Court cases involving

the contract and commerce clauses and other constitutional provisions. Ultimately, however, the Court sanctioned a state police power sufficiently wide to sustain the popular faith that producer and capitalist values were compatible.[6]

In the four-state region few denied altogether the value of corporations; disagreement arose, however, over how to hold them accountable to community welfare and producer values reflected in the constitutional ideal. Familiar objects of dispute were state-chartered banks. Debate in the Pennsylvania constitutional convention of 1837–38 suggests the terms of the controversy. Banks were, exclaimed one delegate, "the most dangerous monopolies that ever existed. They know no principle in moral or political economy. They are not only inimical to public safety, but to the very equality that should ever be the bulwark of a nation's security." Another delegate proclaimed, "You may set up your money King and place the crown of empire upon his head, but the people of Pennsylvania will not bow down to him nor worship . . . your Juggernaut." The people must always remain vigilant lest their leaders "sell them as slaves to this lordly money power—to corporate despots." Few described the threat more pungently than C. J. Ingersoll, who condemned state-incorporated banks as "a vast fungus grown upon government, upon property, upon liberty, and equality, by which the common welfare is thoroughly affected."[7]

Yet there were undeniable benefits arising from state-incorporated banks. These institutions, observed one delegate, "assisted much in developing the wealth and resources of this great state." Banks were "essentially instrumental in establishing and sustaining our useful manufactures. They have contributed largely by their loans to build our towns, to construct the turnpike roads and other public improvements which now distinguish our commonwealth." Such defenders of incorporation recognized the need for banks to serve the many groups that constituted society. "The man of small means, as well as the capitalist, may vest their money in . . . a corporation, so as to afford credit to a community. . . . The business and transactions of banks are for the accommodation of *all*."[8]

The Supreme Court's contract clause decisions established the constitutional parameters of conflict. Beginning with the *Dartmouth College* case of 1819, the Marshall Court interpreted the contract clause to include corporate charters as well as private contractual agreements. Although this extension of the contract clause was probably contrary

to the original intention of the Constitution's framers, it had enormous significance for the power that states exercised over the corporations they chartered. Potentially, corporations gained the same rights that individuals possessed under private contracts. In *Dartmouth College* and other decisions the Marshall Court itself, however, mitigated these principles by holding that states could formally reserve regulatory powers in the corporate charters they granted. It was this dual sanction of rights and regulatory authority which established the constitutional boundary for political clashes involving the trade-off between corporate privileges and obligations. Accordingly, from early on in the nineteenth century states included in bank charters the requirement that they pay taxes to support social services.[9]

True to the Jacksonian Democrats' antimonopoly tradition, the Taney Court enlarged the states' regulatory authority. Beginning with the *Charles River Bridge* decision of 1837, it expanded the limits of the "reserved" power. By the 1850s the Court attempted to strike a balance similar to that worked out with regard to private contracts under the contract clause. States were empowered to include wide-ranging taxes and other requirements at the time they granted corporate charters. But subsequent lawmakers, including state constitutional conventions, generally could not then alter or enlarge upon those obligations. Still, the main import of this course of decision making was to politicize the states' process of incorporation, particularly at the point when a charter was originally granted or came up for renewal. As a result, the traditional image of legislatures giving capitalist developers overflowing privileges was confirmed.[10] Less conspicuous yet no less important was the likelihood that the intensity of the bargaining process not only ensured that offsetting obligations were written into charters but that those provisions would be enforced.

The Taney Court further strengthened the states' authority to enact protectionist policies. In *Brown* v. *Maryland* Marshall attempted to limit the states' taxation of importers by establishing the "original package" doctrine. Under the doctrine state taxation of goods bought at wholesale was held to be contrary to the commerce clause. Only after the goods were distributed among retailers was taxation permissible. Initially, the principle benefited big wholesalers. Eventually, however, the Court's sanction of the expanded police power under the commerce clause enabled lawmakers to enact measures that protected retailers from out-of-state competition and in other ways benefited

smaller traders over large merchant capitalists.[11] Similarly, in the *Alabama Bank* case of 1839 the Court attempted to curb state protection of local banks from foreign competitors. The Court's regard for federalism and states' rights was sufficiently strong, nonetheless, that the principle of comity which the decision established limited states only if they consented to follow it. Accordingly, states in the mid-Atlantic region and elsewhere continued to defend local banks.[12]

Although the Taney Court extended federal jurisdiction over corporations, the benefits were mixed before the Civil War. In several cases the Court held that for purposes of diversity jurisdiction corporations were citizens of the incorporating state, thereby increasing the opportunity to sue in federal court. In addition, the *Swift* doctrine established the basis for a uniform commercial law which could reduce the costs that the states' multiplicity of legal rules created for corporations doing interstate business. Yet as a practical matter those principles were only beginning to benefit corporations before 1860. The Court's pro–police power interpretations of the contract and commerce clauses, as well as the voluntary nature of the comity rule, were strong barriers even if a corporation sued in federal court. In most cases a state's law was still controlling. The general commercial law being developed under the *Swift* doctrine, moreover, involved primarily bills and notes rather than substantive rules pertaining to corporate obligations beyond the limits protected by the contract or commerce clauses. Finally, the means of removing cases from state to federal court remained restricted until 1875.[13]

Within these constitutional boundaries the states sought to hold banking corporations accountable. State laws imposed limitations on capital and profits. Throughout the pre–Civil War years banking legislation in the mid-Atlantic states did not grant corporations full limited liability for debts. This increased their legal vulnerability. Moreover, lawmakers usually granted corporate privileges (which were generally quite generous) only in return for benefits favoring the state and the public welfare. Often banks were required to help underwrite economic development by purchasing stock in manufacturing and transportation companies. Laws also stipulated that a percentage of a bank's loans must provide farm mortgages at low interest for producers or generous terms of credit for small as well as large contractors constructing canals, railroads, and related improvements. State laws also protected local banks from foreign competition. In this way the

law lent some credence to the idea that corporate capitalism was responsive to local community interests, producer values, and the constitutional ideal.[14]

These ideological and political considerations converged on the issue of taxation. As the controversy over banks grew following the proliferation of bank charters during the early nineteenth century, the call for taxation also increased. Most citizens, especially farmers and the modest mercantile and industrial proprietors who comprised the bulk of the region's property holders, resisted taxes. The absence of any general tax levy between the end of the Revolution and the War of 1812 encouraged the belief that revenue needs could be met through special taxes. At the same time, there was growing popular demand for a public school system. Lawmakers responded to these pressures with a special tax on banks. Although the precise terms varied from state to state, even from charter to charter, there were continuities among the school tax provisions. During the period for which the charters were granted, the banks were required to pay an annual tax, usually based on a percentage of paid-in capital. Placed in a distinct and separate fund in the state treasury, the revenue was invested and credited to the counties for the purpose of establishing free schools. Banks paying the tax were often exempt from other kinds of taxation, and in addition their charters were extended for as long as twenty years.[15]

States were quite resourceful in developing the revenue potential of banks. After President Jackson defeated the recharter of the second Bank of the United States, its supporters turned to the legislature of Pennsylvania. Defenders and opponents of the charter hit upon a compromise. The legislature agreed to charter the BUS as a state bank, but only if it paid into the treasury a steady annual revenue. Throughout the state groups seized upon these funds as the means for satisfying various programs. "Eventually all the hobbies and local schemes in the State," William Graham Sumner observed, "clustered around this big carcass and fought with one another for slices of it." The charter required the bank to make an initial payment of $2 million to the state, another $500,000 shortly thereafter, and "the further sums of one hundred thousand dollars, on each succeeding first Monday of June, for nineteen years" thereafter, to support "common schools." Before the bank closed five years later, it had paid into the common school fund $3 million. Pennsylvania's dependency upon such special reve-

nues "for the benefit of the schools," noted another observer, "was quite in harmony with the policy of other states providing for free education out of non[-general] tax income." Indeed, Maryland, New Jersey, and Delaware did as well or better in providing a steady income for education through such special taxes.[16]

The bank tax was an important precedent in the states' development of fiscal policy. Though initially small, the tax was easily collected, and as time passed it provided a steady revenue. The income increased as the capital of established banks grew, or as the legislatures chartered new banks. The tax demonstrated the extent to which a legislature could use the process of granting corporate charters to distribute costs and benefits among different groups. Moreover, the allocation of the tax for such social services as education encouraged the idea that corporate privilege could aid the public. Of course, this diminished neither the politicians' practice of equating corporations with monopoly nor the citizens' receptivity to such appeals. But the public benefits gained from incorporation limited the effectiveness of such attacks and fostered faith in the constitutional ideal and the practical belief that through special taxes on corporate capitalists the producer and his fellow citizens could minimize or perhaps avoid altogether the costs of social services and development.

As a special tax, the bank levy was consistent with the legislatures' preference for indirect over general taxes. The system of indirect taxation depended significantly upon licenses paid by mercantile interests. The license fees were levied on small traders and after the 1827 *Brown* decision did not apply to certain imports. But by the 1830s, because the cost was adjusted according to the volume of stock on hand during the busiest trading season, the license levies hit hardest the large urban merchants or nonresident itinerant hawkers and peddlers. In Baltimore the rates ranged from $12 for stock worth less than $1,000 to $50 for stock worth over $20,000. Thus the larger the volume, the higher the fees the state collected. Because local markets were of such importance, the proscription of taxes on imports did not nullify the policy. And since the success of large wholesalers in cities like Baltimore and Philadelphia depended upon doing a volume business, these large urban merchants paid the highest proportion of the license fees. Also, because the Maryland legislature protected the competitive advantage of local traders, nonresident peddlers also paid a high fee. Similarly, proprietors of modest establishments such as ordinaries or

taverns paid only a low annual levy. For larger establishments, however, the Maryland law required the proprietor to pay in addition to the regular license a further 5 percent tax on any excess value above $500. Local officials were responsible for collecting the fees, and to encourage strict accounting the law granted them a percentage of each license they granted.[17]

Throughout the antebellum years taxes were periodically imposed on real and personal property. In most states, at least until about 1850, this was not a general tax but a county assessment collected by local officials. Not surprisingly in a society in which farmers constituted a significant proportion if not a majority of voters, the real estate assessments were usually low. Personalty, including property ranging from manufacturing establishments to coaches to livestock, was similarly assessed by local authorities with the same careful attention to the interests of local property holders. Each legislature merely set the state's tax rate, apportioned the tax among the counties, and fixed the mode of assessment. The county collectors were responsible for gathering the tax and turning it over to the state treasury. In each county, township assessors, with the assistance of declarations made by the taxpayers themselves, assessed the tax and apportioned the county's quota among the townships. Each township within the county also chose several commissions that met annually to hear and render judgment upon appeals in tax cases.[18]

Thus the enforcement of the system of indirect taxation depended upon local control. Collection of both the license fees and the county property levies was left to local authorities, subject to little or no direct supervision from each state's legislature. Similarly, the collection of the tax on incorporated banks was subject to local pressures. The legislative committees that drafted the banks' charters—including the tax provisions—were responsible for scrutinizing the ongoing operation of those institutions. The membership of these committees was often drawn from the representatives of the counties in which the banks were located. Since the bank tax was apportioned among the counties for the purpose of the school fund, local officials and each county's representatives in the legislature were interested in whether the tax was paid. Moreover, unlike property taxes, which were subject to the local assessor's low assessment, each bank's tax was based on the amount of capitalization that the legislature set in the original charter of incorporation. The legislature knew, therefore, how much

tax was due from each bank. Also, because banks were so often the object of political attack, they held the attention of the community, which through petitions or public demonstrations could in turn alert the legislature to a bank's objectionable conduct. Occasionally, in response to such pressures, legislatures closed banks down.[19]

State taxation of corporate capital sometimes met resistance. A New Jersey law of 1810 required several financial institutions in Newark, Trenton, and New Brunswick to pay annually "into the treasury of this state . . . this one half of one percent upon the whole amount of capital stock actually subscribed and paid in to such bank or company." The Trenton bank sent petitions to the legislature challenging the tax as "an encroachment on chartered rights and unequal in operation." No doubt the tax seemed "unequal" because corporations had to pay it whereas the great mass of property-holding citizens did not. Another petition exclaimed that the "revenue thence arising to the said state would, in the process of time, exonerate the good citizens of the state . . . from all taxes for supporting the government." Although the corporations joined together to oppose the tax, they failed.[20] Reports of the state treasurer showed that the bank stock tax generated approximately $23,000 annually for the school fund by 1837, rising to about $31,000 twenty years later.[21] Taken alone these amounts seemed modest; considered in conjunction with other corporate and mercantile taxes, however, their impact on the welfare of the producer majority was not insignificant. New Jersey's farmers and other independent producers, like those in other states, thus had good reason to condone the taxation of corporations.

Undoubtedly entrepreneurs and promoters gained from governmental efforts, but the bank tax demonstrated distributive pressures. Disparities in population and development, along with political and geographic divisions within each state, guaranteed that certain areas would pay more revenues than others. This was particularly true of cities like Baltimore, Philadelphia, Pittsburgh, New Brunswick, and Wilmington. These urban centers collected more revenue than such less populated or declining rural areas as Maryland's Eastern Shore, Pennsylvania's northern counties, the "Pinees" of southeastern New Jersey, and the isolated Sussex and Kent counties of Delaware.

The distribution of corporate tax revenues among the counties ensured that the financing of local educational opportunity was uneven. Some localities, particularly urban centers, were able to supplement

the state tax contribution with other revenues and thereby establish sound programs. More isolated rural areas generally lacked sufficient supplemental resources to provide for adequate free public education. In such instances county officials let interest on the appropriation accumulate in the state treasury until there was enough revenue to make a difference. Thus the state of Delaware managed its corporate tax fund so well that by 1843 the amount had reached $183,000, which was used to finance 182 schools with 6,148 pupils. In Maryland, however, although Baltimore possessed good common schools, elsewhere in the state schools were "in a state of most utter and hopeless prostration."[22]

Nevertheless the state tax and education policy was probably most significant in fostering social order. In Pennsylvania the legislature's enactment of laws providing for free public education closely paralleled the emergence of industrial labor strife. During the 1830s a coalition of evangelical Protestant reformers, capitalist manufacturers, and workers won legislative support for a system of free (but not compulsory) schools. Much of the funding came from bank taxes like those imposed on the state-incorporated BUS. The old free education system was based on the pauper law of 1809, which provided tuition payments to teachers for the education of children whose parents could not afford to send them to private schools. To be eligible under this system the child's parents had to formally declare indigent status before the local tax accessors, who then recorded the names on tax records. Although the child could then attend school free of charge, he carried the stigma of poverty. The parents who resorted to the pauper law had not been "poorhouse poor" but the working poor—respectable widows or journeyman mechanics and artisans. Although the motivations of those favoring reform varied, a central purpose of the new system was to increase the number of children eligible for free education while eliminating the criterion of poverty. Inevitably, reform meant that more than ever before children of workers in manufacturing centers would qualify, thereby removing one cause of labor unrest.[23]

The other mid-Atlantic states shared Pennsylvania's experience. Delaware's effective common school system developed in response to persistent criticism that it "favored" the poor. To meet this pressure the legislature enacted in 1829 a law making the schools free to all white young people between the ages of five and twenty-one. No

doubt the significant number of industrial laborers employed in New Castle County by Du Pont's gunpowder works and other manufacturers influenced passage of the measure. In Baltimore, the leading manufacturing center in Maryland, the need to improve the opportunities of workers probably contributed to that city's leadership in public education. In Newark and other growing industrial areas of New Jersey the number of workers employed in manufacturing increased significantly after the late 1820s. During the same period appropriations of the corporate tax for purposes of education steadily increased, with communities engaged in manufacturing usually receiving the largest allocation.[24] Thus the states spread the benefits of taxation through society; yet since manufacturing centers often received more revenues than rural areas, this attempt distributed justice unequally.

The constitutional and political status of banking and finance capitalism resulted from social conflict. Taunting the instrumental gains, bank interests won from legislatures corporate charters possessing significant privileges. Politicians representing the majority of smaller producers and unincorporated enterprisers could justify granting these privileges by pointing to tax and other obligations imposed upon banks. The Supreme Court's interpretation of the contract and commerce clauses and other provisions established boundaries to the states' police power that nonetheless sanctioned protectionist policies benefiting smaller producers and capitalists. The outcome of combined state and federal action was to sustain a popular faith that corporate and mercantile capitalism could be held constitutionally accountable to the majority of producers. This faith in turn deflected social-class tensions and obscured the increasing dominance of capitalist values.

### Capitalist Accountability and Transportation: New Jersey and Delaware

Transportation corporations also tested the popular faith in the constitutional ideal. The prosperity and increased opportunity that canals and railroads promised enticed producers and capitalist developers alike. The development of transportation facilities probably did more than banks or manufacturing corporations to weaken locally oriented associational market relations and to foster capitalist-dominated na-

tional markets. Nevertheless, in New Jersey, Delaware, Maryland, and Pennsylvania change was gradual and incremental. The Court's interpretation of the contract, commerce, and other clauses set the constitutional parameters of the states' policy making, permitting considerable local control.[25] The clash of local interests prompted varying degrees of state action. In New Jersey and Delaware state intervention in the development and regulation of transport corporations was minimal except for the enforcement of tax measures. These two states' tax policies reflected the persistent resourcefulness of producers in the use of the constitutional ideal to shift on to corporations the costs of social services. Supporting protectionist policies, producer groups also formed alliances with corporate capitalists thus encouraging the belief that a "harmony of interests" was possible.

The states' experience with incorporation and taxation shaped their role in the transportation revolution. From the end of the second war with Britain in 1815 to the 1850s the mid-Atlantic states, along with the rest of the nation, enjoyed tremendous growth. Simultaneously, there were significant economic recessions throughout the era, and during the late 1830s and early 1840s the nation experienced the worst depression of its first century. Improved transportation was essential to development. But the great cost combined with the uncertainties of the business cycle meant that the construction of transportation facilities was impossible without state assistance. Corporate charters provided a ready means to mobilize the necessary financial resources; their use, however, raised the issue of taxation. During the decades following the Treaty of Ghent governments grappled with the problems of transportation development and the means of paying for it. State aid forced lawmakers to fashion fiscal policies aimed at resolving not merely technical engineering questions but also the demands of competing political interests.[26] Inevitably, the interplay between fiscal necessity and the incorporation process tested the constitutional ideal.

In the mid-Atlantic states diverse local considerations encouraged the promotion of better transportation. Interstate and seaport competition for the produce of the rapidly growing west was a major influence, particularly in Maryland and Pennsylvania, for New York's canal and railroad system threatened the trading centers of Philadelphia and Baltimore, which were also commercial rivals of one another. At the same time, the nation's busiest commercial thoroughfare ran from New York City to Philadelphia, giving New Jersey a vital interest in

improving that transportation route. Similarly, across Morris County in northern New Jersey was the most direct route from Pennsylvania's rich coalfields to the New York City market. Delaware's New Castle County also was committed to internal improvements for particular reasons: leading manufacturers operating along the Brandywine River wanted better access to Philadelphia and Baltimore markets.[27] Such rivalries and interests intermingled to make transportation the most important local issue of the time.

Though corporate charters were the basis of each state's program, the level of government involvement differed. During the 1820s, as the Erie Canal revealed the promise that transportation held for the future, the New Jersey legislature debated what policy to pursue. No one questioned the need for some sort of governmental role. Three possibilities emerged: the state itself could construct the works as a public enterprise; it could contribute the major portion of the stock to corporations and establish a mixture of private and public enterprise; or it could simply grant privileges to a private company. The larger the government's financial contribution, the greater control the state would have over the enterprise.[28]

In New Jersey small, unincorporated enterprisers successfully opposed direct state involvement in transportation development. As one keen observer noted, for some time "no action was taken by the legislature since many feared that the cost would be too great for the State's resources. Moreover, a powerful opposition developed from teamsters, stage owners and innkeepers who feared that the . . . [proposed development] would injure their business." Similarly, farmers and small manufacturers in southeastern New Jersey resisted any enterprise which might benefit the northern or central portion of the state at their expense. The opposition also was concerned about preserving local control. Charters of incorporation invited foreign investment, which raised the specter of capitalist domination particularly from the nearby financial center of New York. As the legislature debated its course late in 1823, a local newspaper warned: "Let the people of this state carefully consider the matter and not be led away by designing men, who are endeavoring to allure us into a project which is evidently calculated for the benefit of the State of New York, which is now almost ready to swallow us up. Let us keep in our old, steady habits and take care of what we have got, and not be induced to ruin ourselves by the visionary schemes of a few designing speculators."[29]

Supporters of transportation development responded with appeals to local self-interest, especially the creation of a new source of tax revenue. During the recession of 1819–22 unemployment was a pressing problem which the building of internal improvements could alleviate. A newspaper summarized this view: "At a time when labor is unusually low, and the number of poor people out of employ unprecedented, the furthering of this important work ought to claim the attention of all those who are willing to ameliorate the condition of the poor, but industrious laborer." No doubt underlying this concern was the increased burden that such distress placed on tax-funded poor relief. Another argument, which drew upon the favorable experience of the bank tax, stressed the valuable contributions that corporations could make to public education. If the transportation companies were taxed in return for privileges, they would render a useful social service, "which would not only be sufficient to establish and maintain free schools in every part of the state, but endow the College of New Jersey with professorships and scholarships equal to any institution in the world." The most lucrative tax revenue would come from charging tolls on the extensive traffic that New Yorkers and Pennsylvanians shipped across the state. In this way, instead of Jerseymen being "forever tributary to the people of other states," exclaimed the New Brunswick *Times*, "we may as easily make them tributary to us."[30]

The interplay of local production, foreign competition, and reduced transit costs also strengthened the promoters' position. Orchard produce was vital to the state's agricultural economy. Yet persistent overproduction created a supply which begged the wider markets that only improved transportation facilities could tap. Without such improvements it was necessary to rely upon the distillation of orchard crops into alcoholic beverages, which were then barreled and transported to market in wagons. A state commission reported the remedy for these problems. The present system of "land carriage render[ed] it . . . necessary to have recourse to distilling as the only means of conveying the produce of our orchards to market." With better transportation "apples and cider would be exported instead of being converted into ardent spirits," which would profit "the farmer" and the "good morals of the community." A local newspaper, speaking through "Aristides," appealed to morals to make the economic point. "How much would we gain by the carriage of our cider to New York, instead of being obliged to distill it into poison; a poison which is now

beginning to be made so captiously at New Orleans that in a very few years we must be under sold and driven out of every market." This in turn would force New Jersey producers to "cut down half our orchards, or what is much worse, be obliged to drink all our whiskey ourselves."[31]

During the 1820s and 1830s these values and interests fired controversy over the legislature's granting of corporate charters. The representatives of Jersey "farmers" and "simple mechanics" remained "exceedingly cautious in matters involving [the state's] pecuniary responsibility." Meanwhile, lobbyists representing in-state and out-of-state special interests urged or opposed charters that created local advantage or disadvantage. The "insidious hostility" of Philadelphia, for instance, was counterbalanced by the merchants, coal miners, millers, distillers, farmers, and lumbermen of the upper Delaware River. The clash of in-state local interests also periodically brought to the "peace-loving and law reverencing people of Trenton," the state capital, a "large and tumultuous assemblage" of "men and boys, principally from another county." After the "flourish of trumpets, repeated loud huzzaings," and other "evidence of riotous patriotism," such mobs burned effigies of legislative delegates and the governor. Elsewhere in the state occurred other demonstrations of what newspapers called "a few made zealots." Such efforts were part of the promoters' and their opponents' general campaigns in commercial centers and counties to build pressure on the legislature. The politicians felt enough heat that sometimes they went about armed in public, although "free champagne suppers," which one lobbyist exclaimed was the surest way to get a vote, no doubt meliorated the danger.[32]

Ultimately the legislature exchanged generous corporate privileges for provisions guaranteeing the state significant tax revenues. In so doing, New Jersey promoted transportation primarily by creating private companies incorporated under special charters. Except for establishing procedures ensuring that the state received its money, the legislature turned over the control of canals and railroads to the enterprises themselves. Lawmakers established this policy through political compromises. To facilitate the commerce and development of the northern counties, the legislature chartered the Morris Canal, which did not have to pay transit duties, and the New Jersey Railroad, which was required to pay such duties. The Camden and Amboy Railroad

and the Delaware and Raritan Canal were combined to form one "joint company," possessing a lawful monopoly of the trade passing between Philadelphia and New York City. In return for the monopoly, the law required that the firm pay a transit duty or tax on all goods it shipped. The legislature's granting of the monopoly aroused enormous criticism. However, since the duties paid by out-of-state shippers, manufacturers, and merchants supported public services and alleviated the need for taxing New Jersey citizens, resistance was undercut.[33]

Yet the marriage of private interest and public gain entangled fiscal policy in perpetual political struggle. During the 1830s other corporate interests seeking to share the revenues from New Jersey's intercity trade attacked the joint company's monopoly. Recruiting such nationally prominent lawyers as Roger B. Taney, Chancellor James Kent, and Daniel Webster, the opposition challenged the constitutionality of the monopoly. The group paid printers to argue its cause in newspapers while lobbyists worked the legislature. In response, the monopoly gathered a cadre of prominent local lawyers who successfully rebutted the constitutional objection. The joint company also effectively mobilized tavern keepers, newspaper editors and legislative lobbies. According to one observer, it kept a room "adjacent to the state capital supplied with wines, liquors, cigars" for "thirsty, tired and it may be assured indecisive legislators."[34]

Throughout its campaign the monopoly appealed to local loyalty and interest. A newspaper supporting the company stressed the benefits that New Jersey's citizens received from the transit duties. "Let the people of New Jersey wake up. The hollow bowels of the state treasury, only a few years ago in the last stages of collapse, is now beginning to expand with wholesome food," the annual payments the joint companies paid to the state. The propaganda effort, emphasizing the meddling of outsiders like Taney, Kent, and Webster who were defending "foreign" corporations, also played upon local patriotism. "Why deprive our own native state . . . and extend the arms of . . . [a] new railroad." Moreover, how did these "pygmy trumpeters propose blowing out the brains of the old monster, monopoly?" They wanted to "beget a new one and call it half Pennsylvania and half New Jersey, or half sea serpent, and half alligator; thus creating a grand pair of monopolies that would drive over our citizens and their rights like . . . wildfire." In the end such arguments were persuasive: outspending its

opponents five to one, the joint company retained its monopoly. The state's policy seemed vindicated when during the depression of 1839–43 the treasury continued to receive ample revenues while other states—burdened with debt—teetered on the brink of repudiation.[35]

Political and economic considerations also limited the promotional role of government in Delaware. The Delaware and Chesapeake Canal was the line of demarcation between more metropolitan New Castle County and the "peninsular isolation" of Sussex and Kent, where a declining slave-based economy persisted. Before the 1830s the most significant transportation facility that the legislature aided was the D&C Canal, a "national" work supported by Maryland, Pennsylvania, Delaware, and the federal government. Yet Delaware contributed only minimally to the enterprise until Pennsylvania agreed to revise discriminatory quarantine laws in favor of New Castle County merchants. Moreover, although the state purchased stock in the canal, it did so in part to secure an income to finance its school fund. The legislature also closely scrutinized the canal tolls that determined the profitable return on the stock which funded education.[36]

While other states developed transportation facilities, Delaware lagged behind. The southern counties, where "apathy and innate financial conservatism prevailed," fostered a constricted government role. A local newspaper in 1838 articulated the concerns of promoters in New Castle County. The "chief reason why our lands sell for a nominal price, why enterprise is paralyzed among us, and monied men shun our county as a place of residence is, that we have no ready or pleasant means of communication with the rest of the world." Moreover, the supporters of development lamented, "we shall never emerge from our present condition until these means are supplied us." But the downstate residents remained unconvinced. As one close student of the area observed: "A farmer who had hardly ventured a dozen miles from home could not see the virtue of being able to venture to Philadelphia and return home between dawn and dusk. Furthermore the county merchants were afraid that he would do just that and then all local patronage would be lost to the big city stores."[37]

Given these pressures, internal improvements made comparatively little progress before the Civil War. The New Castle and Frenchtown Railroad was an important project built with state aid during late 1830s. In the 1850s it was consolidated with the Philadelphia, Wilmington, and Baltimore Railroad. New Castle County promoters were able to

procure a favorable charter for another railroad because it guaranteed the state tax revenues. But although this road eventually became part of the PW&B, it moved ahead slowly in part because the developers were divided among themselves. Moreover, the county's principal enterprisers, the Quaker millers of Wilmington, resisted the project.[38]

Nothing illustrates Delaware's mixed experience with transportation promotion better than the case of John R. Randel, Jr. Randel was a brilliant but eccentric engineer who had planned several of the more important transport programs in America. He was, one commentator observed, "strange and eccentric, and full of Utopian schemes and projects." Randel planned and helped construct the Delaware and Chesapeake Canal but was unfairly discharged by his supervisor, who described him as a "nincompoop." Driven by debt, pride, and the economic need to maintain his reputation, Randel went to court. As chief contractor Randel had used his own funds to construct one particularly difficult section of the canal. According to the terms of his employment contract, the company should have reimbursed him for these expenditures. Instead, due to misunderstandings and personality conflicts he was fired. After a decade of litigation the Delaware courts vindicated Randel, awarding him $226,885—the largest damage judgment won in America up to that time. The state legislature had to float a loan to enable the company to honor the decision.[39]

Randel's struggle revealed further how the era's general desire for development often could not overcome the political necessities governing local control. Boat captains paid tolls to ship goods on the Delaware and Chesapeake Canal. For years Randel used the local Delaware courts to attach these tolls as partial payment of his debt. The action hurt business, and the company tried to avoid the attachments by having the tolls collected in Maryland before the boats entered Delaware territory. Nevertheless the courts upheld Randel, forcing the boats to pay the toll twice. Moreover, the courts sustained the imprisonment of captains who refused or were unable to pay. The controversy resulted in litigation in Delaware, Maryland, and the United States Supreme Court; but because the canal's charter required the tolls be paid both in Delaware and in the other states, the courts decided every case in favor of Randel. More significant, perhaps, the company's effort to escape its charter obligations challenged a fundamental principle inherent in the constitutional ideal that corporations received privileges only in return for public benefits.[40]

Neither Delaware nor New Jersey supported transportation promotion unequivocally. The producers constituting a majority of voters in
both states resisted development unless it brought benefits to the local
community. In some instances local interests favored canals and railroads but did not want to pay for them; in other cases there was
opposition because one community or area might gain at the expense
of another. Fragmentation among capitalist developers, lawyers, and
political operatives opened up opportunities for compromises favoring local control. To be sure, corporations won vital privileges, but in
return they provided political patronage and jobs and, above all,
virtually eliminated the need for general taxes. Moreover, since this
fiscal policy contributed funds to education, poor relief, and the state
governments' general operating expenses, it also helped deflect social
class tension. Randel's triumph symbolized the individual's ability to
preserve corporate accountability and therefore maintain popular faith
in the constitutional ideal.

### Capitalist Accountability and Transportation: Maryland and Pennsylvania

Unlike New Jersey and Delaware, Maryland and Pennsylvania developed transportation programs that involved extensive state participation. In the two smaller states producers' ambiguous support for development and the resulting appeals to constitutionalism focused
primarily on the trade-off between taxation that would fund social
services and the grant of corporate privilege. In Pennsylvania and
Maryland these issues led to a larger struggle having international
financial implications. Following the panic of 1837, both state governments, like their counterparts in other regions, considered repudiating lawful debts. In his sonnet "To the Pennsylvanians," William
Wordsworth conveyed the consternation this action created for foreign creditors.

> All who revere the memory of Penn
> Grieve for the land on whose wild woods his name
> Was fondly grafted with a virtuous aim,
> Renounced, abandoned by degenerate Men
> For state-dishonour black as ever came
> To upper air from Mammon's loathsome den.[41]

Yet more than moral deficiency and greed contributed to the failure of Pennsylvania, Maryland, and other states. The states went into debt in order to promote community prosperity and individual opportunity through improved transportation facilities. But as construction costs outstripped public revenues, the need for increased taxes loomed large, engendering constitutional issues. Some states readily met the challenge; others like Pennsylvania and Maryland initially did not, thus creating economic dislocation at home and abroad. Central to the struggle over deficit spending, default, and taxation were the realities of democratic politics and the tension among local community interest, producers, and capitalist enterprise. In the more hierarchical and aristocratic regimes of Wordsworth's England or continental Europe, such factors were less significant than in America, where their influence was profound. Since the late eighteenth century the citizens of Great Britain and several continental nations had become familiar with income and other general taxes. Americans, however, generally avoided these until the early twentieth century.[42]

The repudiation crisis ended in the mid-Atlantic region by 1850. But its origins and consequences revealed the vital role that constitutionalism played in the struggle between producers and capitalists before the Civil War. As controversies over bank taxes suggested, capitalist developers overcame the producers' distrust of transportation corporations by linking privileges to obligations. The police power principle inherent in federalism, as well as the broader values of accountability and legitimacy underlying state policy making that the Supreme Court sustained, shaped this trade-off. The interplay between constitutional values and practical political and financial exigencies thus was inseparable from the instrumental concerns associated with satisfying as many interests as possible.[43]

Maryland began to launch significant internal improvements during the 1820s. Until then, deep local antagonism between northern and southern counties, the eastern and western shores, and Baltimore and rural areas had impeded action. New York's successful completion of the Erie Canal, which coincided with a period of general prosperity, temporarily lessened localistic tensions, and the legislature enacted a major transportation program in 1826. Using the same sort of techniques employed elsewhere, capitalist promoters achieved passage by mobilizing statewide support at the county level and in the legislature. The act of 1826 explicitly committed the use of the state's credit for

purposes of constructing a system of canals throughout Maryland. Yet in spite of the success of the promotional campaign, local resistance was so pronounced that the bill became law by only one vote. The city of Baltimore supported the act with reluctance. By 1828 the city and its allies in the northern and western counties had exploited this dissatisfaction to win from the legislature incorporation of the Baltimore and Ohio Railroad. Once this enterprise was underway, Maryland seemed well prepared to meet the challenge of interstate and internal rivalry.[44]

Between 1826 and 1840 the state financed its transportation program primarily through loans. The charters establishing canals and railroads made Maryland the primary investor in the companies' stock; the state also often underwrote the corporations' credit. By 1836 Maryland lawmakers established an unprecedented scale of indebtedness when they approved an appropriation of $8 million. The state attempted to ensure payment of its debt through strict charter provisions governing the interest earned from company investments and stock dividends. The corporations were required to pay these earnings into special state treasury budgets. Consistent with the trade-off inherent in the constitutional ideal, another significant revenue-producing measure was a tax upon passenger receipts of the railway running between Baltimore and Washington, D.C., which became a branch line of the B&O. Some other railroad charters included similar transit duties.[45]

The state resorted to deficit spending in order to satisfy distributional political pressures. The legislature framed the internal improvement laws, acknowledged one promoter, "upon the principle that . . . if the credit of the whole was to be used, for the purpose of improving one shore, the other was alike entitled to use the credit for kindred . . . improvements. On this just and broad basis that system was founded." Moreover, the developers' dependency upon public credit encouraged the companies to compromise rather than compete. A confrontation between the Baltimore and Ohio Railroad and the Chesapeake and Ohio Canal revealed the political dynamics of the state's promotional role. Appealing to the popular faith in constitutional legitimacy and accountability, each side condemned the other as a monopoly. Since the end of the eighteenth century developers had pushed for a canal to bring western trade to the Chesapeake. Amid the promotional enthusiasm of the 1820s the legislature granted a charter providing generous support for the project, but construction proceeded slowly. Mean-

while, Baltimore and its allies won legislative approval and funding for the incorporation of the B&O railway, whose route paralleled that of the canal. Eventually the two projects clashed over right of way, resulting in a suit in which the railroad claimed that its charter gave it precedence over the canal. The state's highest court, however, decided against the B&O. The decision threw the issue back to the legislature, which enacted an appropriation enabling both projects to proceed.[46]

The clash confirmed that the two corporations needed to cooperate in appeals for public credit. One promoter said explicitly that the court's decision had compelled cooperation. "I . . . would have regarded any other decision than that which was finally made by our Court of Appeals, as being truly disastrous to both works; for if the railroad company had prevailed at law, the result would have brought, in its train, a long series of defeats." Moreover, the court's decision legitimated both corporations, establishing an ongoing need to distribute the costs and benefits of development. Each company now required "repeated acts of grace at the hands of the legislature, and neither would obtain these, without a generous support from the friends of the other; in fine . . . united they would be strong, divided they would fall."[47] What went unsaid, however, was that this unity also brought mounting increases in the state's burden of debt.

To meet the swelling deficit state authorities resorted to financial machinations. Initially, the tax earnings from the newly chartered companies, instituted out of regard for constitutional accountability, provided what seemed an adequate revenue to finance the debt. But at the very time the state began marketing in Europe the bonds through which it expected to underwrite the $8 million appropriation, the panic of 1837 struck, and American public credit declined precipitously. Unable to dispose of its securities at a price even approaching that demanded by the magnitude of the deficit, the state resorted to a desperate expedient. Maryland entered into an agreement with the two companies, its two main transportation enterprises, by which they contracted to accept state bonds to an amount equal to their respective stock subscriptions. In addition, the companies agreed to pay the state a cash premium of 20 percent. To expect that the two corporations could do better than the state in procuring an acceptable rate on the bonds, especially during the depression, was shortsighted. Ultimately, both domestic and foreign markets refused to pay a satisfactory price for the state's securities. The B&O Railroad did work out a

temporary arrangement with Baring Brothers, but this proved inadequate in the long run. As the legislature grappled with this and other loans, the depression grew worse.[48]

Maryland's internal improvement loans ended abruptly in 1840. Up to this point, confident that increased growth resulting from development would save them, lawmakers had steadfastly refused to consider new taxes. A committee report of the House of Delegates expressed this view in 1837. "In anticipation of the future productiveness of our great works of improvement, it has been the policy of the state to rely on casual revenues to supply our annual deficiencies. As the day is almost at hand when these anticipations are to be realized or disappointed," the committee declared, it was "inexpedient to change that policy by a resort to a system of permanent taxation which might create an overflowing treasury." As late as 1839 the legislature held tenaciously to this conviction. "If, for the present, it [direct taxation] can be postponed it is the duty of the Legislature to do so." But by 1840 the situation was critical. In that year the interest on the state debt jumped from $291,888 to $585,819; simultaneously the receipts of interest and dividends earned from the various railroads and canals sharply declined. The tax on the receipts of the B&O's Washington branch provided a steady but inadequate revenue. All other sources, including the withdrawal of $120,000 from the school fund and temporary loans from banks, failed to meet the need. The legislature attempted to reimburse the school fund by diverting the transit duties there, but this merely exacerbated the debt. Maryland's revenues and credit were exhausted; the only available remedies were debt repudiation or taxation.[49]

For six years beginning in 1842 the state was unable to pay the interest on its debt. Maryland's public credit and the citizens' welfare were shaken. A dealer in Maryland securities writing from London in 1841 suggested the extremity of the situation: "I am called upon . . . almost everyday for my opinion . . . whether the legislature will pass a tax bill. . . . The legislature must promptly carry out . . . [the tax plan] or, be assured the credit of Maryland will so suffer that her stock in European markets will have but a nominal value." He was "most anxious that the legislature should adopt such measures as will permanently provide for payment of the interest on the debt . . . there is no other mode to adopt but immediate taxation." In 1841 the legislature responded to the exigency by enacting an increased general property

tax. When this measure proved insufficient during the succeeding years, lawmakers resorted to taxes on stocks and bonds, a stamp act, increased license fees, an income tax, and various other taxes on commercial groups. By 1848, following a basic reconstruction of the state's tax system, Maryland was able to resume interest payments.[50]

Yet throughout the state's resumption struggle the legislature remained sensitive to social-class pressures. Consistent with the predominance of modest, unincorporated producers among voters, the property tax exempted the produce of land in the hands of the producer and provisions consumed by him. Also exempt were the working tools of mechanics and hand manufacturers and the produce thereof while in the possession of the producer. Other exemptions included household manufacturers and the property of all persons whose possessions were assessed at less than $200. As was the case with the pre-1842 system, large, urban mercantile interests, capitalist investors, and corporations paid the highest proportion of the new levies. The Stamp Act of 1845 was indicative of public officials' preferences. It was "bitterly denounced," noted one keen student of the subject, but "as such a tax was exceedingly productive, easy to collect, and as, moreover, its chief burden fell upon the commercial interests of Baltimore City and not upon the rural districts, it was continued in force for several years."[51]

The strength of local control also shaped fiscal policy. The law of 1841 left tax collection to popularly elected local authorities who were sensitive to community opinion and wary of unpopular initiatives by the Maryland central government. Although the law received general support throughout the state, there was local resistance to it everywhere. Moreover, the local orientation of the collection process easily became entangled in grassroots political conflicts involving many public officials, including judges and juries. Throughout the redemption struggle the legislature confronted several counties that simply refused to collect the taxes. This outright opposition was overcome, but its persistence in less blatant forms influenced the government's role in development beyond the 1840s.[52]

Between the 1820s and 1840s no state did more to promote transportation development than Pennsylvania. Like the other mid-Atlantic states, Pennsylvania had significant experience with corporate enterprise, particularly canals and turnpikes, before 1815. During the 1820s, however, the heightened rivalry with New York and Maryland pushed

the Keystone state into a new era. In part lawmakers followed the developmental policies of New Jersey and Maryland. True to the constitutional values of legitimacy and accountability, they granted private corporations generous privileges in return for tax revenues and used public credit to underwrite particular projects on terms that seemed certain to augment the state's treasury. Yet Pennsylvania did more. It constructed a system of canals and railroads funded, owned, and operated by the state.

In Pennsylvania, as elsewhere, government promotion of transportation was subject to diverse local pressures. Philadelphia merchants, wanting better access to the Ohio Valley and the state's east-central coal region, initially were unconcerned about developing the northern counties, which therefore generally maintained stronger market relations with New York. Philadelphia also was engaged in intense competition with Pittsburgh, which due to mountain barriers in central Pennsylvania had closer commercial ties with Baltimore. Moreover, the southern counties divided their loyalties and trade between Philadelphia and Baltimore. Entwined in these struggles were the interests of numerous modest, unincorporated producers who desired development as long as it neither benefited others at their community's expense nor strengthened corporate promoters. And, of course, the entrepreneurial capitalists themselves were a potent force. Each of these groups justified its interests by appealing to the constitutional ideal.[53]

Meanwhile, the commitment to state-run enterprise further shaped fiscal policy. Consistent with the citizenry's desire to avoid increased taxation, Pennsylvania, like Maryland, financed its transportation program through deficit spending. Alert to the enormous patronage opportunities that state ownership provided, lawmakers understandably incurred this debt out of a desire to achieve the widest possible political gain. Yet the interplay of state control, the seemingly unlimited scope of expenditures that deficit spending invited, and political patronage influenced the particular course that Pennsylvania's transportation development took.[54] The policy nonetheless was consistent with the trade-off implicit in constitutionalism between corporate privilege and obligations. Lawmakers chose to spend most of their debt appropriations on canals rather than railroads. They made this choice in part because canal construction employed more workers than did railroad building, which increased the opportunities of local

contractors.[55] Moreover, the state imposed a toll structure which, while providing the state valuable revenues, nonetheless favored the canals and benefited among others the independent, unincorporated operators and shippers of the Schuylkill coal region. The canal tolls also served the interests of small producers in the state's more remote areas.[56]

Struggles in the coal region revealed how exchanging privileges for obligations shaped development. Following the Revolution the Pennsylvania legislature had incorporated the Lehigh Coal Mine Company to tap the rich black veins of the Lehigh coalfields. By the 1820s the company was so dominant that intense resistance arose from the just-emerging unincorporated Schuylkill producers nearby. Between 1825 and 1830 the number of Schuylkill shippers increased from 28 to 328. Although failure was a perpetual problem for them, these independent proprietors nonetheless acquired enough clout in the legislature to protect their competitive position. Railing against monopoly and demanding accountability, in 1833 they gained passage of a law which voided the charters of out-of-state corporate competitors doing business in Pennsylvania. They also won legislative approval for laws significantly limiting the right of in-state mining producers to charter transportation corporations used to transport the coal they mined. But perhaps the most impressive victory involved toll rates. Appealing to the constitutional ideal and using their support for the Delaware division of the state's canal system as leverage, Schuylkill independents bombarded the legislature with petitions demanding that lawmakers impose lower tolls upon the Lehigh Company (which had imposed a "monopoly rent"). Responding to the independents' antimonopoly rhetoric and the threat of legislative interference, the Lehigh Company reduced the tolls its transports charged by as much as 50 percent, which in turn served as a yardstick for those charged on the state-owned canals as they became operational, benefiting local communities along the state works and the independents which were also located there.[57]

In other ways localism and appeals to constitutional values significantly influenced fiscal policy making. New York and Ohio effectively managed the debt arising from transport construction by enacting general taxes.[58] Pennsylvania, responsive to the demands of producers and capitalists alike, however, pursued a plan of deficit spending which until quite late rejected such levies. To fund its transportation

system the state marketed long-term bonds issued at 5 percent; to pay the interest on this debt it relied upon indirect taxes and canal tolls. But as the legislature satisfied the ever-increasing demands of remote localities for canal service, costs increasingly outpaced the revenues collected from these sources. As the coal trade demonstrated, political factors, including antimonopoly rhetoric, also could result in lower toll rates, which further reduced the state's income. The waste and corruption associated with the locally oriented system of government-funded construction contracts exacerbated the problem. By the 1830s the legislature was compelled to resort to stopgap measures. Consistent with the trade-off sanctioned by the constitutional ideal, it negotiated large bank bonuses and loans in return for incorporation privileges or extensions of bank charters, thereby using new loans to pay off old ones. But as was the case in Maryland, the interest on the bonded indebtedness accumulated relentlessly. In 1835 the canal debt was nearly $22.5 million and the interest almost equaled the state's total revenues from indirect taxes and tolls.[59]

Even so, before the depression of 1839 political considerations encouraged lawmakers to reject general taxes. During the early thirties, in response to pleas from governors, there were occasional increases in indirect taxes and even in the property tax. The legislature repealed most of these, however, after the implementation of the bank-tax policy. At the same time, it failed to enact a levy on coal. The widespread popular opposition to all general taxation, particularly from producers, partially explained the legislature's unwillingness to face the deficit squarely. In addition, Pennsylvania instituted a system of centralized administrative control. Most states depended upon legislative committees and weak boards or commissioners to superintend transportation programs. Pennsylvania departed from the traditional approach by giving appointed officials unprecedent authority over the construction and operation of canals and railroads. Generally, the judiciary had only limited jurisdiction over the supervisors' decisions. Instead, the principal route of appeal was to the legislature, which strengthened the bond between particular private interests and legislative politics and the ideological advantages to be gained from appealing to constitutionalism.[60]

Nevertheless, by the 1840s pressure for increased taxes was irresistible. During the 1839 depression Pennsylvania's public credit in English and Continental markets disintegrated. *Hunt's Merchants' Magazine*

wrote that "every foreign poetaster, scribbler, and smatterer sneers at American slavery and Pennsylvania repudiation." The *London Chronicle* published another cutting observation: "I never meet a Pennsylvanian at a London dinner without feeling a disposition to seize and divide him. . . . How such a man can set himself down at an English table without feeling that he owes two or three pounds to every man in the company, I am at a loss to concede; he has no more right to eat with honest men than a leper to eat with clean men." This is when Wordsworth penned his rebuke in the sonnet "To the Pennsylvanians."[61]

Finally the legislature enacted new taxes. Yet the main source of revenues remained urban capitalist mercantile groups and corporations. Lawmakers in 1840 imposed a levy of one-half mill on every dollar of dividends made or declared by every incorporated company in the state. For years this tax was the Commonwealth's single largest source of revenue. Meanwhile, a law of 1844 established a tax on all personal income except (predictably) that of farmers. To collect these and other levies the legislature established a board of commissioners responsible for gathering triennial assessments. At last in 1849 legislators created a special fund for the liquidation of the state's debt.[62]

Through direct state involvement in transportation development, Maryland and Pennsylvania pushed the trade-off that constitutionalism sanctioned between capitalist privileges and obligations further than their smaller neighbors. Both states floated a hugh debt in order to satisfy as many community interests as possible. Responding to pressures for jobs and improved local services, lawmakers enacted elaborate transportation programs that failed to take into account the actual costs arising from local diversity, geographic barriers, and the insufficiency of tax revenues. Eventually, economic reality overcame political preference, forcing public officials to choose between repudiation and increased taxes. Yet even though new fiscal measures became law, corporations and other large entrepreneurial capitalists continued, as they had in the past, to pay the highest proportion of taxes. At least insofar as taxation was involved, producers were protected and faith in the constitutional ideal was affirmed. Thus, even though capitalists in New Jersey, Delaware, Maryland, and Pennsylvania undoubtedly gained enormously from the privileges received from the state, they nonetheless paid something in return. As a result, the interplay of governmental control, taxation, and diverse and fragmented social-class interests sustained the belief in capitalist account-

ability inherent in constitutionalism. Whether in the long run this would remain the case, however, was problematic.

### The Uneven Triumph of Corporate Capitalism

From the mid-forties to 1861 the managers of transport corporations and public officials increasingly struggled over fiscal policy. The conflict threatened to sever the link between corporate privileges and obligations that from the beginning had shaped the lawmakers' approach to incorporation and capitalism generally. During the 1840s corporate capitalists sought to weaken or eradicate altogether the legal rules that were consistent with traditional values of constitutionalism. The old order persisted in Delaware. A struggle fraught with ironies altered but nonetheless sustained limited corporate accountability in New Jersey. In the leading states of Pennsylvania and Maryland, however, two railroad managers succeeded in disrupting the market and social relations that had depended on appeals to the constitutional ideal, thereby facilitating the triumph of capitalist values.

A significant confrontation arose in Delaware. By the mid-1840s the Chesapeake and Delaware Canal had recovered from its struggle with Randel only to enter another with the Philadelphia, Wilmington, and Baltimore Railroad. The canal's charter granted it many privileges, but the provisions governing tolls did not permit a charge on passenger traffic. The charter of the PW&B, however, did allow passenger rates. Throughout northern Delaware the route of the railroad and the canal ran roughly parallel so that travelers could avoid paying the rail fare by going on the water. The canal wanted to develop a lucrative passenger business but could not without changing its charter. To alter the toll provisions the canal went to the legislature while the railroad fought to maintain the status quo. "The object of constructing the Canal was to carry freight," the railroad argued. It was "inequitable and unfair to defeat the just expectations held out to us by our Charter, by now transferring a portion of our business to others."[63]

This rivalry also involved the direct interests of the state and many of its citizens. Many residents of Sussex County who used the canal as passengers opposed giving up free transport. Furthermore, the railroad paid annually into the state treasury taxes and other revenues amounting to nearly $9,000. The passenger tolls provided much of the company's income that made the payment of these public levies possi-

ble. Moreover, in spite of significant indebtedness, the railroad spent over $100,000 annually within the state, primarily to pay the salaries of mechanics, laborers, and other employees. Thus the canal's attempt to change its charter challenged the benefits that taxpayers, independent proprietors, and other voters gained from the state's policy. Understandably, Whigs and Democrats found common ground against the canal in the appeal to constitutional values, exclaiming, "A chartered monopoly is against both Democratic and Whig principles" and "Down with monopoly!"[64]

The passenger toll struggle revealed the divisions among competing corporate capitalists. Prominent lawyers represented both the canal and the railroad as legislative lobbyists. John M. Clayton, one of those defending the railroad, was a leading railroad promoter who had been a United States senator, Delaware judge, and United States secretary of state. He had won Randel's damage judgment against the canal. On the canal's side was Caleb S. Layton, who was a noted local attorney despite criticism for "exceedingly bad taste . . . [and] common slang and vulgar anecdotes." The canal lost. The legislature not only refused to grant it the passenger toll privilege but also enacted a law "for the protection of the investment of this State in the loan" of the railroad.[65]

In 1847 a court case arose which further tested the canal's imposition of tolls on passenger traffic. The company levied the charge on an out-of-state shipper named John A. Perrine. The earlier struggle with the railroad had involved rights pertaining to corporations chartered and operating within the state of Delaware. Perrine claimed that the canal's charter also should be construed to prohibit tolls on those traveling from outside the state. As a nonresident of Delaware, the shipper filed suit in federal court. The federal tribunal decided against the canal, whereupon it appealed to the United States Supreme Court, but the canal fared no better there; Chief Justice Roger B. Taney delivered an opinion for Perrine. "A corporation created by statute is a mere creature of the law, and can exercise no powers except those which the law confers upon it," Taney held. It "has not, therefore, the same unlimited control over it which an individual has over his property. Nor has the company a right to refuse permission to pass through the canal. On the contrary, anyone has the right to navigate the canal for the transportation of passengers . . . without paying any toll on" them.[66]

The canal's defeat suggested the state's more general inhospitable-ness toward corporate promotion. During the late forties and fifties the chancellor of Delaware, Samuel Maxwell Harrington, led a campaign for the Delaware Railroad. He and his supporters conceived of the road as a "peninsular" facility connecting the northern and southern ends of the state with the markets of Virginia and greater Philadelphia. They attempted to mobilize public opinion through local meetings and legislative lobbying. Charles I. Du Pont expressed the developers' views: "In regard to the railroad I can only say that both Kent and Sussex *must wake up*, or be behind the age." It was necessary to "wake them up . . . with [the] *steamwhistle!*" The state's governor also attempted to arouse support by stressing that Delaware would receive "considerable sums . . . by way of . . . [a] tax" in return for the "privileges granted" under the charter.[67]

The arguments proved futile. There was too much resistance from "croakers" who opposed floating state bonds to provide the credit that the railroad desperately needed. In addition, downstate property holders feared that if the railroad brought increased property values, they would have to compete with outsiders for land purchases in Sussex and Kent. Appealing to local distrust of procorporate attorneys, opponents of the railroad emphasized further that they wanted "no other evidence of the weakness of the . . . [corporation's] cause than the fact that . . . [it had] bought up all the lawyers in Dover to advocate it." Moreover, the rivalry was so keen among the communities which were interested in the road that the legislative process became clogged. One lobbyist exclaimed "there are so many conflicting opinions and jarring interests . . . that it appears a matter of great perplexity on the part of the legislature to ascertain not only what course is expedient but what the people *really* want." Consequently, the steam whistle of the Delaware Railroad was not heard south of the canal until after the Civil War.[68]

Delaware was not opposed to development per se. But to the producers controlling local politics, corporate promotion was not an end in itself. Instead, it was regarded as the means to achieve social gains with the least threat to the established local order, including respect for the constitutional ideal. The tax revenues that the PW&B's charter provided, along with the employment its operation made possible, fostered an image of community accountability and public service. The D&C canal's attempt, however, to manipulate its charter solely to

increase its profits while providing no equivalent social contribution made it vulnerable to charges of monopoly, inviting defeat. Unless it appeared responsive to constitutional values, entrepreneurial capitalism was thus distrusted and resisted. And as the case of the Delaware Railroad showed, local opposition to non-resident developers was strong, promoters were often divided among themselves, and popular suspicion of corporate-serving lawyers was great.

Similarly, New Jersey's limited regulatory role and countenance of monopoly generated considerable controversy. Between the mid-1840s and the Civil War the united companies identified as the Camden and Amboy Railroad were central to political conflict in the state. Yet despite the antimonopoly rhetoric of Andrew Jackson's followers in national politics, the most stalwart defenders of the monopoly in New Jersey were Democrats. Whigs and later Republicans repeatedly used the Democrats' anticorporate shibboleths against them, warning New Jerseyans not to "yield to the dictation of managing cliques and mammoth incorporations" and other "wire-workers." Furthermore, they condemned the joint company as "that monstrous progeny of Democratic avarice, cunning and ambition! This vast machine, overshadowing the State . . . faithful to the men who gave it being." In response, the company and its party's supporters decried attacks from "socialists, speculators, or demagogues" who threatened "the rights of personal liberty and private property." Once in office, however, neither party tried to dismantle the monopoly: it was "deemed good policy . . . to tax those who . . . pass over her territory, or in other words the people of New Jersey, having power, make citizens of other states pay the expenses of their government by taxing travel instead of themselves."[69]

Indeed, the income flowing into the state treasury from the transit duties was substantial. In 1850 railroads contributed 93 percent of the funds necessary for the government's ordinary expenditures; up to that year they supported on average 69 percent of these public expenses. Between 1850 and 1860 the corporate revenue rose steadily from $66,298 to $152,307. The average amount due to the state from the taxes and dividends totaled about 11 percent of the Camden and Amboy Railroad's net operating receipts. Yet unlike the banks, virtually all of which paid the annual school fund tax, most transport corporations before 1851 paid no transit taxes and very few stock dividends. Thus the levies upon the few enterprises like the Camden

and Amboy Railway and the New Jersey Railroad that did provide public revenues were all the more vital. The failure to tax all transportation companies was a glaring inequity. But New Jerseyans no doubt found this unobjectionable in part because from 1848 to 1861 the state's fiscal policy significantly reduced the producers' tax burden.[70]

Lawmakers were under public scrutiny to keep taxpaying corporations accountable to local community interest and constitutional values. Perhaps the most conspicuous instance of this involved the campaign of noted political economist Henry C. Carey against the Camden and Amboy monopoly. Writing at first anonymously, then under his own name, Carey charged that the company's fares were too high. Moreover, he said, the rates discriminated against in-state and nonresident shippers as well as impeding transport development in other sections of the state. He challenged the constitutionality of the monopoly and urged the legislature to pass a general railroad law. The company defended the rates as necessary in order to pay the transit duties and stressed that the cost fell hardest on nonresidents, while New Jerseyans enjoyed freedom from direct taxation.[71]

After considerable political maneuvering the legislature thoroughly investigated Carey's charges. Although generally sympathetic to the company, the legislature found that it had not paid the full total of revenues due the state. The monopoly, as it had on other occasions during the 1830s and 1840s, escaped cheaply by reimbursing the state for the shortfall. The long-run consequences were more significant, however. The whole episode revealed that the state could not depend upon "anything so entirely imaginary as the liberality or generosity of a corporation." The legislature began requiring corporations to publish annual statements regarding the freight and passenger traffic upon which rates were based. Undoubtedly the new regulations influenced the doubling of tax revenues that the monopoly paid between 1850 and 1860. Beginning in 1850 the courts also circumscribed the company's control over rates. In the *Camden and Amboy Railroad Co.* v. *Briggs*, the New Jersey Supreme Court held that the railroad's charter required rate reductions, thus limiting its ability to pass on costs to the public.[72]

But perhaps the most remarkable consequence of these conflicts was that the monopoly felt threatened enough to pressure the Democratic party to seek political reforms. The party's platform called for increased public aid to education, the end to property qualifications

for jurors, tax exemptions for unincorporated enterprisers, a general incorporation law, and equal taxation.[73]

The transport corporation's concern about general tax liability was well founded. During the 1840s local assessors claimed the right to tax corporations, though the state courts usually decided in favor of the railroads. Increasingly after 1850, however, the judiciary's leniency gave way to a stricter policy. By then farmers who had benefited so long from the traditional, locally oriented taxation methods realized that many corporations were now exploiting the system. Of course, some railroads paid the transit duties and other levies that made direct taxation unnecessary. But most transportation companies made virtually no fiscal contribution to local communities. In 1851 the governor in his inaugural address called upon the legislature to reform the old system. "There is no subject which more urgently claims your faithful concern than the *equalization of taxes*," he urged. "That our present system of taxation is unequal in its operation, and imposes burdens upon landholders and others, from which the man of wealth and the capitalist are exempt, is indisputable." Lawmakers responded with legislation levying a tax on all personal and real property held by either individuals or corporations.[74]

The corporations fought the new rule but lost. The Camden and Amboy Railroad owned houses and lots that it rented to employees. In 1851 local authorities in Mansfield Township assessed this property; the railroad objected, claiming that the action violated its charter's tax exemption. The state supreme court embarked upon a new course of decision, however, supporting the community's right to tax the railroad. The court interpreted the charter to mean that the property absolutely essential to the company's operation was tax exempt, whereas that held merely to earn income was not. There "must be a limit somewhere," the court held, to the "power of the company to enlarge its operations and extend its property without taxation under this exemption clause, and that limitation . . . must be fixed *where the necessity ends and the mere convenience begins*." The "necessary appendages" of transport corporations were "one thing, and those appendages which might be convenient means of increasing the advantage and profits of the company are another thing." The company might find it "advantageous . . . to purchase land . . . to erect houses . . . for all their constant employees, to establish factories for making their own rails, engines and cars, even to purchase coal mines and supply

themselves with fuel," the court admitted, "but these are not among the *necessary* powers of such a company."[75] As in Delaware, then, New Jersey's otherwise minimal involvement in the economy ultimately did not impede the popular faith that corporate capitalists were accountable under the constitutional ideal.

Following the 1839 depression, corporate managers increasingly questioned the government's role in Maryland's economy. Between the mid-forties and early fifties the transport companies' need for government aid generally declined. Once direct government finance was no longer essential, the managers wanted to retain incorporation privileges while freeing themselves from the public obligations that charters imposed. Often state and local authorities held the majority of the corporate stock and therefore wielded considerable influence on the boards of directors. In the struggle to diminish public accountability directors claiming to represent the private stockholders were often at odds with the representatives of the community interest.[76]

Rates and the allocation of dividends were central to the controversy. Profits depended largely upon freight and passenger rates, but according to incorporation charters companies could not change these rates without legislative approval. Yet the construction of transportation facilities altered markets and heightened competition, which along with mounting operating costs put considerable upward pressure on rates. Managers representing the private stockholders sought greater discretion over rate setting to increase the dividends of their supporters. By contrast, the directors favoring the public wanted to strike a balance between protecting the government's income and promoting the interests of diverse local producers whose enterprise depended upon favorable rates.[77] The 1847 report of a legislative committee investigating the matter stated that the "most difficult problem to be solved in the management of public works is the adjustment of the rates . . . so as to produce the maximum revenue; and that the difficulty is increased by the present case by the fact, that the Pennsylvania State Railroad is a rival work . . . leading to [a] rival city." Uniform increases "might not be [the] best policy," the report admitted, but a selective "revision is necessary" in the items bearing upon the "interests of the State."[78]

Maryland's leading transportation enterprise was the Baltimore and Ohio Railroad. The state and the city of Baltimore held more than half of the B&O's stock. A significant benefit flowing from public control

was the tax that the railroad paid on passenger traffic between Baltimore and Washington, D.C. The legislature used the tax to "support . . . common schools . . . forever," one-half going to the city of Balitmore while the rest was appropriated equally among Maryland's counties. Reflecting the force of constitutional values, a legislative report stated, "If the credit of the whole state were used, its exercise . . . [ought] to procure, if possible, benefits for all citizens; and . . . [the B&O and other enterprises] must in some respects be regarded as local works."[79]

The company's ability to pay the tax depended significantly upon rates. In 1856 the railroad contributed $73,000 to the school fund, an amount equal to 20 percent of the company's passenger receipts and 30 percent of its net earnings. The B&O's directors preferred to have control over rate making, but as its annual report had stated in 1844, "it pleased the legislature . . . to withhold such discretion from the Board of Directors." The reason for the rejection, a legislative report explained, was that "this construction would make the corporation the master and the State the slave . . . reversing all our preconceived ideas of State sovereignty."[80]

The legislature usually acquiesced in part to the B&O's rate requests. But this support represented negotiations and compromises among competing interests rather than unquestioning deference to corporate power. During the forties the company asked the legislature for rate increases on various goods, particularly flour. But probably because the milling industry around Baltimore was a strong local interest, the legislature approved higher rates on every item except flour. Similarly, the B&O's rates on coal mined in Allegany County favored Baltimore. By 1856 the railroad acknowledged its policy of "price drawbacks" established "in favor of all coal delivered and consumed in Baltimore. The discrimination has been adopted as a measure of protection and encouragement of the manufacturing and other interests of the city."[81]

By the late 1850s the rates favored Baltimore over other areas. In 1858 western counties—which had previously supported public aid to the B&O—inundated the legislature with "several hundred" memorials "complaining of onerous charges made by said company on local freight."[82] The railroad responded that it maintained this "careful discrimination" partially to support "agricultural interests" elsewhere in the state and in order to "favor . . . the mercantile and general

interests of Baltimore [which] have been vigorously maintained and
. . . resulted in most beneficial effects upon the trade of the city." The
legislature then ignored the western counties' petitions because, a
report of 1860 stated, it accepted the opinion of "our most respectable
merchants—largely engaged in selling goods to the West . . . that . . .
the present policy . . . tend[s] largely to the increase of their business
transactions."[83]

The B&O had maintained such a policy for at least a decade and a
half. In 1844 it reported to the legislature that the "inequality in rates"
was necessary in order "to attract the largest amount of trade from the
greatest distance, so as not only to accommodate the largest extent of
country and increase the revenue of the road, but to foster and increase the trade of the State, and the City of Baltimore."[84] Public
influence over rates thus resulted in an unequal distribution of costs
and benefits.

But that which benefited Baltimore merchants, millers, and other
unincorporated, independent producers was not necessarily good for
the capitalists who held stock in and ran the railroad. Between the
mid-forties and 1860 private stockholders and the directors representing their interests on the B&O's board objected to the company's
dividend policy. Throughout the years following the depression private stockholders received dividends only erratically. Yet the state
received a steady revenue from taxes and other levies. "A Stockholder" complained in an open letter to the legislature that even
though the "state receives her dividends, she should not allow individual stock holders to suffer." The "only reason the directors pay the
dividends to the state" was, the letter writer argued, "that they are
afraid in default of this an investigation will take place." A no more
"rotten concern existed," it concluded, resulting in "a system of swin-
dling not exceeded by anything on record."[85]

The private stockholders did not accept this policy without resistance. In 1847 the railroad's board voted a larger dividend to the
private stockholders than it did to the state and Baltimore. The action
reduced the state's fiscal revenues and, coming as it did during the
struggle over debt repudiation, engendered controversy. Was the dividend lawful under the railroad's charter? The B&O's attorney said it
was; Maryland public officials disagreed. The governor noted the
danger inherent in diminishing the state's income from the corporation. The B&O's decision impaired the legislature's ability to "restore

the public credit," and it "could only be entertained and expressed . . . by one who has no interest or feeling in common with the people of our State." Moreover, it was *"humbuggery!"* Indeed, he exclaimed, appealing to the constitutional values of legitimacy and accountability, "Are the apprehensions originally expressed by the opponents of . . . internal improvements, that those overgrown corporations would become too powerful for the welfare of the State, already realized?" Faced with such criticism the company returned to the dividend policy favoring the public stockholders.[86]

Until the early fifties the B&O depended on legislative appropriations to complete its route to the Ohio River. After it lost a bid in the Pennsylvania legislature to procure a more favorable terminus at Pittsburgh, the railroad hammered out an agreement with Virginia to strike the Ohio at Wheeling. Yet political lobbying and lawsuits—particularly involving a disgruntled lawyer who had represented the corporation—so slowed the appropriations process that the B&O did not reach Wheeling until 1853.[87] The delay was particularly costly because the Pennsylvania Railroad reached the Ohio first, giving Philadelphia the initial trade advantage over Baltimore. Nevertheless, with the increased traffic the western throughway brought, the B&O's profits steadily increased. Meanwhile, the directors representing the private stockholders demanded greater control. By 1860, following the skillful maneuverings of B&O president John W. Garrett, the railroad acquired virtually full authority over its rates and profits. Garrett triumphed in part because he maintained the flow of tax and dividend revenues into the state treasury. Not until the railroad freely ignored the general interests of Baltimore and Maryland after the Civil War did the consequences of diminished public control become apparent. By then, public officials no longer had the power to guide corporate policy in ways favorable to diverse local groups.[88] More than ever before, the link between corporate privileges and obligations was disrupted, undercutting the constitutional ideal.

In Pennsylvania the decline of public control was even more pronounced. With the depression over and the new tax system in operation by the late 1840s, the threat of repudiation slowly diminished. At the same time, the state's rivalry with Maryland and New York generated demands for new railway projects. The most important enterprise to emerge from this struggle was the Pennsylvania Railroad. To prevent the B&O from reaching the Ohio at Pittsburgh, Philadelphia

and its allies won incorporation of that company during a tense legislative session in 1846. The city's merchants and other local promoters triumphed because in return for the charter they agreed that the railway would pay the state a lucrative tonnage tax. Construction of the Pennsylvania Railroad progressed rapidly, and the company not only beat the B&O to the Ohio but also paid the state good tax revenues. Yet by the mid-fifties the board of directors yearned to be free of taxation and the competition from Pennsylvania's public works system of canals and short spans of railroad.[89]

The Pennsylvania Railroad's resistance to public accountability merged with a controversy involving municipal subscription to corporate stock. In Philadelphia and other communities property holders who had supported state indebtedness to fund transportation development now opposed the creation of municipal debt for the same purpose. The tax program that the legislature implemented in the early forties to fend off repudiation placed the heaviest burden on entrepreneurial capitalists. But municipal stock subscription incurred local community indebtedness, which made virtually inevitable increased taxes upon real estate interests. Consequently, Horace Binney, one of Philadelphia's foremost attorneys, joined influential lawyers and property holders from other communities in a vigorous antisubscription campaign. Arrayed against Binney and his allies were the railroad promoters and their lawyers. In the heated debate that followed, each side developed legal and moral arguments consistent with constitutionalism to defend its position. Underlying the rhetoric, however, was an intense conflict among local interests.[90] "The people in one section of a county may derive valuable advantages from the construction of a public work," one observer exclaimed, "whilst those of another section, equally taxed for payment of interest and principal of debt, so contracted, may possibly not benefit at all."[91]

The antisubscription struggle reached a climax in 1853 in *Sharpless v. The Mayor of Philadelphia*. Philadelphia's mayor and town council, with legislative approval, had authorized the city's subscription to stock in two railroad companies. Although neither road reached the city, one of them was to be a feeder line for the Philadelphia-based Pennsylvania Railroad. Three property holders in the city sought an injunction to prevent the subscription. The case reached the Pennsylvania Supreme Court, where Chief Justice Jeremiah Black described it as "beyond all comparison, the most important cause that has ever been in this Court

since the formation of the government."[92] Counsel for the property holders argued that even with legislative authorization, municipal officials' investment in the railway stock was unconstitutional. This was a bold contention because since Independence the Pennsylvania legislature had repeatedly given legal sanction to such financial practices. Indeed, as the defendant's lawyer rebutted, "It is too late . . . upon any abstract ground, depending upon the mere theory of our form of government, to deny those powers to the Legislature of an independent sovereign State."[93]

The judges of the state supreme court were divided in their decision. Upholding the public interest strand of constitutionalism, the majority held in favor of the city's purchase and the legislature's authority to authorize it. Chief Justice Black admitted that only those governmental actions were constitutional which sought to achieve some public purpose. Yet clearly the construction of railroads was a "public duty". It was a "grave error," he declared, "to suppose that the duty of a state stops with . . . the administration of justice, the preservation of the peace, and the protection of the country from foreign enemies. . . . To aid, encourage, and stimulate commerce . . . is a duty of the sovereign, as plain and as universally recognized as any other."[94]

But drawing upon the values of accountability and legitimacy, two of the court's five judges dissented. The official report of the *Sharpless* case did not include the dissenting opinions, but Justice Walter H. Lowrie's was published in the *American Law Register*. In spite of numerous precedents favoring the majority's position, Lowrie urged, "Let us not be afraid of unduly reducing the province of government." History "proved," he contended, that "the corruption of government increases with its powers. . . . When its power is large, there are strong, and even ferocious, contests to get the use of its power." The granting of public purposes to private corporations had "subjected government to the worst temptations, and given rise to intrigue, fawning and favoritism, and has annually attracted to our capitals swarms of voracious and unprincipled speculators." But what was ultimately at stake ran deeper. "Our governmental stability depends much," Lowrie asserted, "upon . . . our reverence for the principle that natural rights of the individual [including the sanctity of property] are sacred against the touch of government." The court's decision was, he declared solemnly, "a long stride towards the very worst form of government . . . socialism."[95]

Only after the people amended Pennsylvania's constitution did the antisubscription cause triumph. Defeated in the majority opinion but encouraged by the dissent in *Sharpless* case, the opponents of public investment campaigned to revise the constitution. Other states had enacted amendments abolishing state and local investment in corporate enterprises; now Pennsylvania would do the same. In 1855 the legislature considered several measures that prohibited state and local governments from pledging or loaning their credit "to any individual, company, corporation, or association." Moreover, these proposals barred the state from assuming the debt of either municipalities or private corporations and denied the legislature the power to authorize any local government to invest in private enterprises. Other amendments imposed limits on the state's debt, established a sinking fund for the elimination of the current debt, and reduced Philadelphia's representation in the legislature. Voters and their representatives overwhelmingly approved these measures in 1857. The combined House and Senate vote approving the amendments was 102 to 19; the popular vote on the amendments was 122,663 for and 13,653 against. The same political pressures and constitutional values that originally had ameliorated the tension between producer and capitalist interests now exacerbated it.[96]

The constitutional amendments undermined the canal system and worked to the advantage of the Pennsylvania Railroad. The new limits on public debt threatened the financial lifeblood of the state-funded canals and short spans of railroad that consistently operated at a loss. Railway President J. Edgar Thomson offered to alleviate the state's debt burden by purchasing the public works for $9 million. In return, he wanted the tonnage tax repealed and exemption from all other taxes forever. The state's public officials consented to these terms in 1857, but before the deal was consummated, the courts intervened. Supported by the numerous localities that had benefited from the canals, the state-funded transportation system's commissioners challenged the sale in *Mott* v. *Pennsylvania Railroad Company* (1858). The commissioners argued that the perpetual exemption from taxation upon which the sale depended was unconstitutional. The railway's counsel rebutted that the legislature had granted similar exemptions in numerous corporate charters.[97]

The state supreme court was unanimous in its *Mott* decision. It held that the state could sell the public works, but not on terms granting a

perpetual tax exemption. The linking of the sale and the exemption was, exclaimed Chief Justice Black, "one of the most magnificent exhibitions of a 'mock auction' that the world has ever witnessed!" He perceived a threat to the future of governmental authority itself. "If the power to raise revenue may be sold today, the power to pass laws for the redress of civil rights, may be sold the next day," the chief justice declared. "If the legislative power may be sold, the executive and judicial powers may be put in the market with equal propriety."[98]

Thomson responded to the court's decision with defiance. The tonnage tax significantly cut into the railroad's profits: in 1857 alone the company paid $200,000. In addition, the panic that year reduced business, forcing the president to skip the November dividend. In 1858, claiming that it violated the United States Constitution, he refused to pay the tonnage tax; by 1861 the company owed the state $661,158. The legislature prepared to revoke the railroad's charter. After further legal battles Thomson and the state finally compromised: the legislature would repeal the tax in return for several financial commitments from the company. The railroad agreed to invest the sum of the back taxes in several railways serving various localities, particularly western counties that had been hurt by the Pennsylvania's discriminatory rates. Moreover, the company had to pay the state additional funds and also to placate western opposition by reducing local rates in an amount equal to the tax. While it diminished Thomson's victory in the short run, it gave him independence that led to market domination in the long run.[99]

As the nation moved toward civil war, entrepreneurial capitalists in the mid-Atlantic states began to triumph. During the initial stages of corporate development fiscal policy and appeals to constitutionalism had protected producers. Conflict among lawyers, politicians, and mercantile promoters, along with the associational bonds encouraged by local markets, community rivalry, and local control, had given producers leverage within the lawmaking process. To be sure, the policies emerging from this constitutional process perpetuated inequality and undercut social-class solidarity. But they also had made it possible for producer values and community interest to persist despite the rise of corporate capitalism. Undoubtedly influenced by the confined scope of struggle that heightened the clout of the two more isolated Kent and Sussex counties, the traditional order continued in Delaware. New Jersey was distinctive in that the interdependency

between producer and capitalist groups survived in altered form, owing in large part to the ironies that made the "monster monopoly" Camden and Amboy company sufficiently responsive to constitutional values that it became an agent of modest reform. In the two major states of Pennsylvania and Maryland, which had evolved the strongest connection been corporate privilege and obligation, however, the ultimate triumph of capitalist values was most apparent. Thomson's and Garrett's successes from 1861 on pointed toward a new era in which corporate capitalist power steadily weakened the constitutional ideal. Thus, the decline of the producers' influence was an early casualty of America's Civil War.

# 4

## Taking Property

Eminent domain, the right of government to take private property for public use, has been central to American economic development. The delegation of this right to private corporations was significant to the process of industrialization and the rise of capitalism. Yet at least during the initial stage of railroad and canal construction before 1860, diverse factors shaped the impact of the law. Under constitutional provisions neither the government nor private corporations could take property without paying "fair compensation." Accordingly, the exercise of eminent domain was contingent upon the mode of assessing property values. The tension between the privilege of condemning property and the requirement of paying a just price for it encouraged local confrontation.[1] Society's faith in the constitutional ideal and the producer economy, as well as the associational relationships they encouraged, was at stake in this conflict.

The assessment process indicated how constitutionalism fostered a divergence of interests between capitalist developers and property holders. The United States Constitution's Fifth Amendment and similar provisions in state constitutions making property taking contingent upon the requirement of paying just compensation reflected

the values of legitimacy and accountability embodied in the constitutional ideal. Constitutionalism legitimated the competing market interests of both property owners and property developers. Yet despite their increased dominance, corporate and mercantile capitalists benefited from this legitimacy only in conjunction with the accountability represented by the assessment process. The constitutionally imposed trade-off between corporate privilege and obligation sanctioned, moreover, property holders using this process to their advantage in the name of local control. While the law attempted to check the abuse of local control, the degree of social fragmentation often prevented capitalists from overcoming local resistance through appeals to developmental enthusiasm.

The Supreme Court sanctioned the states' protection of the more community-oriented market relations that local control embodied. Holding that the Constitution's Fifth Amendment applied only to the federal government's use of eminent domain, the Marshall Court affirmed the states' delegation of the assessment process to local authorities and the market interests they represented. The Taney Court elaborated upon this principle, declaring that corporate capitalists could not use the contract clause to prevent states from enforcing their police powers. Even so these and other decisions by the federal judiciary merely confirmed, at least in the four mid-Atlantic states, a tradition of responsiveness to and the protection of producer groups. A protectionist policy did not forestall the eventual triumph of capitalist values; it did, however, reinforce a popular faith that corporate capitalism could be held accountable, thereby deflecting social-class tensions.

### The Struggle for Local Control

A critical factor shaping the acquisition of right-of-way was local control. "I will here say," wrote Thomas S. Fernon, president of the Northern Pennsylvania Railroad, "that the utility and propriety, if not necessity, of conciliating neighborhood sentiment on the subject of street occupation by railroads—in our case a grave and serious local question," were a vital consideration. Since the right to take property depended upon "just compensation," which in turn was determined through a process of local assessment, Fernon's observation was not surprising. During the initial stage of transportation development,

when promoters relied heavily upon public finance, community influence was pronounced. To be sure, society wanted improved transportation, but it perceived this goal in local terms. Popular faith in community control, producer independence, and the accountability inherent in the constitutional ideal enmeshed transportation projects in grassroots political conflict. Although promoters usually acquired a right-of-way, they rarely were able to do so without first satisfying local demands.[2]

As Fernon admitted, his concern about the "local question" was rooted in experience. During the mid-fifties supporters of the Northern Pennsylvania Railroad lobbied Philadelphia public officials and private groups for financial backing. To succeed, the company required a coal depot located at a convenient point on the Delaware River.[3] Other companies also were seeking community subscriptions, and the Northern Pennsylvania road made little headway. If, as a municipal report stated, commerce was "a civil strife" which made "conquest of communities without the sword," Fernon and his fellow directors were losing.[4] As a result, although the charter of the company granted the power to condemn property, financial strictures interacting with the accountability imposed by the assessment process limited the practical usefulness of the right. To acquire the depot, Fernon eventually entered into private negotiations with a local merchant. But in order to complete the transaction it was necessary to gain the agreement of approximately thirty property holders along one street in the area. After some negotiations, in which the merchant requested and received the promise of a $10,000 fee for handling the matter, he wrote Fernon that he had obtained petitions granting the right-of-way from every resident except one.[5]

The man who refused to cooperate was R. M. Johnson. He argued that the railroad would harm his property and force him to pay future upkeep. The merchant went to the local court to condemn the site proposed for the depot and a portion of the street leading to it. Following the assessment process, the court appointed several viewers to ascertain the value of the condemned property, which delivered a judgment favorable to the railroad. But consistent with the constitutional value of accountability, Johnson appealed and got the decision overruled. The merchant then asked the local judge for a letter explaining the entire situation; he sent it and a bill he had prepared to the state legislature. The bill passed both houses and was signed by the

governor. The measure stipulated the damages due Johnson and directed the highway commissioner to open the road for the use of the railway while Johnson kept his property. The railroad company paid the merchant a fee for services rendered and Johnson for damages.[6]

Thus there were several dimensions to the local operation of property condemnation. The financial condition of a company influenced whether it exercised its charter rights at all. In some cases it was cheaper to resort to an intermediary. But of greater significance was the degree to which the condemnation process itself gave the property owner leverage to extract increased expenses from the railroad. Johnson's neighbors apparently went along with the railroad project without opposition. He, however, used the law to set in motion a process which resulted in winning a damage judgment while he retained his property. By forcing the merchant to resort to the legislature, Johnson encouraged faith in local control.[7]

Local confrontation could involve large stakes. The Baltimore and Ohio Railroad needed an appropriation from the legislature of one and a half to two million dollars in order to complete a branch to Washington. To construct the road the company also needed to build a bridge over the Patapsco River. Mrs. Rebecca Smith owned a bridge over the river which yielded from tolls about $4,000 per year. Initially, the railroad's president offered Mrs. Smith an indemnity for damages; complications arose, however, and the railroad failed to make good its promise. The woman's husband then demanded a "reasonable indemnity." He began lobbying through friends in Annapolis with the result that the Baltimore and Ohio was not able to get the money for the Washington branch until matters were settled with Mrs. Smith. With little delay the company paid the lady and got its appropriation.[8]

Yet more was involved than the mere clash of political and financial self-interest. On the face of it, a single property holder and her husband seem a poor match for Maryland's most powerful transportation corporation. Deserving emphasis also was the fact that the railroad considered the issue sufficiently important that from the start the company wanted to negotiate with Mrs. Smith rather than fight. Presumably this accommodationist urge sprang principally from the obligation imposed by the company's charter. In addition, the B&O's financial status was shaky enough, as indicated by its continuing need for the state appropriation, that the $4,000 indemnity was not an insignificant cost. The Smiths won the appropriation ultimately be-

cause the company's failure to fulfill its promise to them violated the values of legitimacy and accountability that the company's charter embodied. Because of these values the husband's lobbying touched the interests of property holders throughout Maryland. Indeed, the fact that the legislature held up a $2 million appropriation until the indemnity was forthcoming suggests the range of political and market factors that the B&O had aggravated.

Elected officials also defended local control for practical political reasons that nonetheless involved the constitutional ideal. A branch of what became the Philadelphia, Wilmington, and Baltimore Railroad encountered some of these realities in 1835 while attempting to construct a bridge over the Gunpowder and Bush rivers. "Awake and attend [to] your rights and privileges," a local newspaper urged the citizens of Hartford and Baltimore counties. The bridge threatened the shallop traffic that served farms whose wharves were located along the river. Closer investigation revealed, however, that a "Jackson Van Buren kitchen cabinet politician" who was losing constituents had seized upon the bridge issue to stir up flagging support, appealing to the constitutional values of accountability and legitimacy inherent in antimonopoly rhetoric. The company sent its land agent into the area to "operate quietly with some of the substantial men in the neighborhood." He began spending between fifty and a hundred dollars to fend off attacks. The opposition had hoped only to change the route of the road but petitions to the legislature from both sides heightened the controversy. Both groups sent lobbyists to Annapolis; after two months of agitation a committee report declared the bridge illegal. Eventually, the bridge was built, but the constitutional values represented by this sort of local resistance helped to impede establishing the company's right-of-way until the end of the 1850s.[9]

Communities also used the assessment process to influence corporate behavior in their favor. Sometimes such efforts failed. When "numerous" landowners attempted to "extract every possible penny," the Sunbury and Erie Railroad chose to build an expensive bridge elsewhere along the river in the "Muncey vicinity" rather than gave in to local pressure. The Delaware, Lackawanna and Western Railroad twice took a more costly route instead of paying the "extortions" of local property holders, causing "uncertainty as to just where and how the railroad would reach its Morristown terminus." But in Lancaster a line which eventually became part of the Pennsylvania Railroad was

unable to escape local pressures. When the road surveyed a route which circumvented the town, a petition of two-thirds of the county's taxpayers urged the legislature to have the route changed so that it would go through the center of Lancaster. A new survey was made, and the company bowed to the taxpayers' demands. The same road became entangled again with local interests when it attempted to locate its machine shops. Building the shops in a large town at one end of the line would have been reasonable, but a damage dispute involving John G. Parke led them to be constructed in an "agricultural" area. Parke was a member of a "large and influential" family, and after the dispute the railroad's chief engineer, "deeming it politic to heal their wounds," located the buildings in the place Parke preferred.[10]

In the mid-Atlantic states the assertion of local control and appeals to the constitutional ideal thus shaped railroad behavior. The Smiths and Johnson, as well as entire communities, linked political leverage and constitutional values to satisfy their demands. At other times the railroads incurred increased costs in order to avoid such pressures or suffered delays that significantly retarded their progress. But in either case, the right of condemnation in and of itself was insufficient to get the railroads what they wanted. Instead, the interplay of market, political, and social realities governed the establishment of a right of way, fostering the perception that corporations were accountable and that community and private interests were equally legitimate.

Confrontations with local authority also could strain the limits of social order and result in a defeat for a railroad. To achieve more economical operations, the New Jersey Railroad and the Morris and Essex Railroad decided to connect in Newark. The latter wanted to avoid a burdensome transshipment by wagon between its dock on the Passaic River and the proposed juncture of the two roads. Yet political pressures within the town led to an order by the common council that the company remove its tracks. When the railroad refused, the street commissioner and his laborers began to do the job. The company halted this action through a court order. With the injunction, however, a mob collected and a near riot ensued. The city then sued the Morris and Essex in court, charging trespass. Newark's "war of the tracks" ended when the chancellor ruled in the city's favor and the company dutifully pulled up its rails. Mob action was a powerful tool in controversies involving right-of-ways; one state report referred to "gates pulled down and houses set on fire." In another instance, from 1840 to

1842, sporadic rioting by the residents (including nonproperty-holding workers) of Front Street in Kensington, Pennsylvania, blocked construction of a railroad. Finally, the company gave up on the location. In yet another case, during a dispute with the New Jersey Railroad in 1849, the town council of New Brunswick warned that there was a "feeling growing in our community, which we will not be able to resist much longer, and if that *feeling* should urge our citizens to some ulterior measures, the members of the common council feel as if the Rail Road Co. will have provoked it."[11]

The part that mob action could play in determining a transportation route reflected a general social fragmentation. Rioting in this period (as in other eras) was an extension of political activity through extralegal means. Francis Grund, a defender of Andrew Jackson's Democratic party, stated the prevalence of this view in 1837 in his book *The Americans in Their Moral, Social, and Political Relations*. A riot was "not properly speaking an opposition to established laws of the country . . . but rather . . . a supplement to them—as a species of *common law*." Recent historians have noted the extent to which mob actions were a "regular social phenomenon" between the 1830s and the Civil War; more than 1,000 people were killed during riots.[12] The disorder in Kensington, Newark, and elsewhere was a manifestation of this phenomenon, directed against the location of transport routes.

Yet even without social unrest railroad promoters could lose. In Delaware railroads experienced innumerable delays due to conflicts associated with the condemnation process. Some of the opposition merely involved property owners who were seeking to gain better prices for their land. In other cases, particularly in the two underdeveloped southern counties, landholders and storekeepers resisted because they feared that improved transportation would increase property values and thereby attract outsiders as purchasers. "Foreign" competition and higher prices in turn could limit the opportunity of locals to enlarge their own holdings. At the same time, several intercommunity disputes involving right-of-way clogged the legal process, bringing development projects to a halt. Thus even though promoters enjoyed the right of condemnation in Delaware, local interests used the very same power to check transportation development.[13]

Struggles over right-of-way pitted landholders—the backbone of the producer economy—against capitalist promoters. Each group, of course, fought for their own vested interests; but more was at stake in

their confrontations than competing perceptions of individual possessiveness. Although the locals no less than promoters wanted to get the most for the least, their priorities of values often were at odds. The general yearning for development undercut neither the landowners' nor the community's commitment to local control and reliance upon constitutionalism. Johnson, the Smiths, and Parke did not hesitate to challenge the power of entrepreneurial capitalists through their own influence in the governmental process, employing appeals to constitutional legitimacy and accountability. In towns such as Newark and Kensington and rural areas like lower Delaware, there was enough residential and social-class cohesion that the community as a whole exercised political pressure upon lawmakers. At times the interaction between individual enterprise and community welfare even strained social order. Responsive to these conflicting values and interests, politicians searched for compromises that reconciled the corporations' privileges and obligations within constitutional limitations. As a result, the process of property condemnation sustained the belief that corporate capitalists were accountable, that community welfare and individual property rights were protected, and that the constitutional ideal was attainable.

### The Imperatives of Law

The law of eminent domain reflected tensions among communities, property holders, and promoters. In corporate charters lawmakers attempted to reconcile society's yearning for development and the producers' and communitys' desire for accountability, protection, and local control. The command of constitutional provisions that compensation was necessary in order for property to be taken for public use thus imposed upon lawmakers potentially conflicting legal imperatives having important social implications.[14] Developers demanded the privilege of condemnation while property and community interests claimed the right of just compensation, which in turn was tied to the method of assessment. The Supreme Court sanctioned this process. Under the law, then, the exercise of privilege and the mode of determining property values were manifestations of the constitutional ideal.

Between 1820 and 1860 most railroads and canals were chartered through special legislation. Pennsylvania passed a general law reg-

ulating railroads in 1849, but throughout the 1850s roads incorporated under it were generally treated as special franchises. The provisions of special charters (and the general regulatory law of Pennsylvania) were often the object of considerable lobbying in the legislature, especially the sections conferring the power of eminent domain. Yet despite certain variations in the provisions from state to state, the basic form of the grant of eminent domain was nearly uniform in Pennsylvania, Maryland, New Jersey, and Delaware. Railroads and canals incorporated in these states were given the power to condemn private property, not only for purposes of establishing a right-of-way but also for taking materials necessary for construction. In virtually all charters the use of the eminent domain privilege depended upon a process of determining the price of the property. Under the law, if the company and the landowner could not agree on a price, recourse to this process was essential in order for construction to proceed. In Pennsylvania this procedure applied even to private railroads and canals that connected with the state works.[15]

The assessment procedure involved several features. Either party made application to the county justice of the peace or sheriff (usually the latter), who issued a warrant to summon a panel of viewers. Each party had the right to challenge a certain number of the individuals selected. After removals by challenge, the total number of viewers that were to compose the jury or inquisition was set by statute. The number varied from state to state, sometimes from charter to charter. In Maryland there were always twelve viewers on a panel; in New Jersey there were between three and ten; in Delaware usually five; and in Pennsylvania the general regulation law set the figure at seven. The local official was to take care that none of the viewers was "related to, nor in any wise interested" in the property or its owners. The official then administered an oath that each juror would "justly and impartially value the damages which the owner or owners will sustain by the use or occupation . . . by the company." Usually, too, the provision contained a requirement that the jurors include in their estimate the "benefit resulting" to the owner from the construction of the road or canal. The decision of the inquisition (as the jury was also called) was written down, sealed, and filed in the local courthouse. Either party could appeal to the court to have the decision set aside or another inquisition called to view the property again.[16]

Intermittently, the Supreme Court upheld local control of the as-

sessment process. The first major test of the federal judicial role arose in 1833. Baltimore's expansion of public byways harmed a resident's wharf. Failing to get satisfaction in state court, the property holder appealed to the Supreme Court, arguing that the city had violated the Fifth Amendment's requirement for just compensation. The Court declined to consider the merits of this claim, deciding at the threshold the question of jurisdiction. Chief Justice John Marshall held that the provisions of the Bill of Rights, including those of the Fifth Amendment, applied only to the federal government. Marshall's decision closed the federal courts to such property-taking questions, thereby affirming local control.[17]

The Taney Court enlarged upon the states' authority over the local assessment process. During the depression of 1839 Vermont employed eminent domain to take over the private West River Bridge Company, whose 1795 charter granted power to collect tolls. Before the government determined appropriate compensation, a group of property holders sued in local court, arguing for a toll-free bridge. Complying with the state constitution's assessment process, local commissioners awarded the company $4,000 for its property and franchise. The judgment resulted in state court litigation that affirmed Vermont's authority. The company appealed to the United States Supreme Court where its counsel Daniel Webster charged that the state's action violated the contract clause, representing the "most levelling ultraisms of Anti-rentism or agrarianism or Abolitionism." The Court, however, upheld Vermont's enforcement of eminent domain as an exercise of the state's inalienable sovereign power.[18]

A similar case arose in Maryland. The legislature granted the Baltimore and Susquehanna Railroad Company the power of eminent domain, subject to the process whereby a local assessment jury determined the property's value in order to award compensation. A local circuit court, in turn, could review the assessment. Under these charter provisions the railroad condemned a property holder's land; the local jury settled the assessment, and the local court affirmed it. When the company attempted to pay the original assessment, the property holder balked, and the local authorities supported his refusal to accept the agreed-upon amount, whereupon the railroad appealed to the Supreme Court, charging that the state's action violated the contract clause. Representing the property holder, one of the nation's foremost attorneys, Reverdy Johnson of Baltimore, argued that the state's inter-

vention in the assessment process represented a legitimate exercise of its sovereignty and therefore was not contrary to the contract clause. Basically, the Court upheld the exercise of the state's power to protect the interest of the property holder against that of a corporation.[19]

These cases suggest how broad was the eminent domain power that the state delegated to local authorities. The Supreme Court limited the exercise of its jurisdiction to questions arising under the contract clause. In construing the clause the court upheld the states' authority, which depended on citizens of a local community serving as members of assessment commissions or juries. Appeals to local courts were permitted, but those courts were also agents of local authority. Either the property holder or the corporation could bring further appeals to higher state courts and even the legislature. Even so, property takings were such politicized issues that neutral treatment by either legislators or courts was difficult. Thus the assessment process was linked to political and social interests who could turn the constitutional values of legitimacy and accountability to their advantage. The Supreme Court strengthened this connection by favoring the value of local control inherent in federalism.

Due to this process the condemnation privilege could indirectly encourage cooperation. One road which eventually became part of the Philadelphia, Wilmington, and Baltimore Railroad initially procured a charter without the power to condemn property. But it soon became clear that because property owners refused to give up their land, construction was impossible without the right. The company urged the governor to give a speech calling for an amendment to the charter; he did so, and the legislature granted the privilege. The amended charter authorized the railroad to call upon commissioners appointed by the state to estimate the value of the property that the company condemned. The landowner was entitled to the price that the commissioners set as compensation. "We have done famously at Dover," wrote a company director. Yet the significance of the railroad's victory in this case was not just that it established a process of assessing property values which the landholder could not escape. The principal result was that now the company possessed the legal means to take the property but at a price determined by representatives of the local community. Without the right of condemnation the company was dependent upon the will of the property holder; but with the privilege, the way to compromise was open.[20]

The law's coercion brought about cooperation in part because of the influence of local control. As was evident in the federal cases, despite efforts to ensure impartiality, the mode of property assessment was open to the play of local self-interest. In Pennsylvania localism was such a problem that general legislative supplements were passed applying to all private incorporated companies allowing jurors to be selected from counties adjoining the one in which the land in question was located. In other cases, where local prejudice might influence a verdict, a trial involving an inquisition's decision could be moved to an adjoining county. The statues also allowed direct resort to a state judge who would then choose the sheriff who would summon the jury. Companies such as the Baltimore and Ohio Railroad that were incorporated in more than one state were required to accept the inquisition process of each state through which they passed. But whether a transportation corporation was chartered within or outside a given state, the method for determining the value of its right-of-way gave a great deal of influence to local authority.[21]

Events in Delaware suggest how local interest swayed the operation of the assessment process. Since corporate charters granted each party the right to influence the choice of commissioners, local pressures often influenced their decisions. The legislative vote on one such charter provision revealed how powerful local considerations could be. The measure passed 11 to 9; of the supporters the majority were from New Castle County where at the time the land-condemnation issue was most controversial. Under authority of this proviso the railroad attempted to condemn property in New Castle County, but the commissioners allowed "offensive compromises." The company director criticized the "rank injustice done by these proceedings to a company struggling." But underlying the conflict were the powerful local tensions evidenced by New Castle's role in the original passage of the law. A stockholder in Kent County reacted bitterly to the delay: "This great public improvement so hopefully begun has . . . met with obstacles in your county, which threaten to destroy it. We of the lower counties are slow to believe that a spirit of unjust speculation of the company exists exclusively in your county; and we will be still slower to yield to it." Even so, such problems prevented the railroad from reaching Kent until after the Civil War.[22]

Lawyers were central to property assessment disputes. Corporations employed attorneys to represent their interests during the initial

stage when the sheriff set in motion the inquisition process and later if the company decided to appeal the inquisition's decision. But the same pressures that shaped the operation of the law in other instances could work to the advantage of local lawyers. The Chesapeake and Ohio's encounter with J. J. Merrick was a case in point. Merrick was a prominent lawyer from Washington County. An early supporter of internal improvements for the development of his county, he had helped draft Maryland's first internal improvement legislation in the 1820s. Upon retirement from politics, Merrick became an active and highly sought-after lobbyist for western Maryland in favor of railroads and canals. But until his appointment as a state judge, he made his living as a lawyer known for his unusual ability to extract large damage judgments from western Maryland juries. The directors of the Chesapeake and Ohio Canal, who too often were on the losing end of such verdicts, finally decided that in order to stop Merrick they would have to hire him themselves. Merrick could, said one canal official, "obtain higher damages against . . . [us] than anybody else; this was a great motive with me in embracing the suggestion to employ him for the company." In this effort, however, the company failed. It refused to cover one of the lawyer's drafts; he appealed to his friends in the Maryland legislature, which ordered the company to pay $10,000 in personal damages.[23]

An argument in a damage suit suggests how lawyers like Merrick performed before their neighbors. A corporation's attorney complained that the landowners' council had used "unjust and improper means" to influence the jury to give "high and excessive damages against" his clients by claiming that their neighbors would "regard them [the jurors] as personal enemies." A jury of local people, opposing counsel rebutted, appealing to the values of legitimacy and accountability, should "take care of the people," especially when a "corporation of foreigners were taking their lands against their wishes and consent." This sort of appeal to the constitutional ideal was used by no less an establishment lawyer than Horace Binney, Jr., in an attempt to keep a railroad off some Philadelphia streets. In a public "appeal" to the legislature for "more than *twelve hundred* . . . fellow citizens, owners of property, or residents" along these streets, Binney charged that a corporation with "almost unlimited" powers and without the "consent of owners and occupants of property" threatened what were already "most *narrow* and *crowded thoroughfares* of this great city."[24]

Thus the relationship between lawyers and the privilege of condemnation was ambivalent. The same desire for local control and corporate accountability that encouraged attorneys like Merrick to serve as lobbyists in the legislature for corporations provided incentives to work against them under other circumstances. As an elected official, Merrick had responded to the demands of his western Maryland constituents in supporting railroads and canals. Yet the public wanted development in order to preserve community welfare and to protect producer independence. As a lawyer who in court served local landholders by winning higher assessment damages from corporations than "anyone else," Merrick no doubt appealed to these same values. Since the rules governing property condemnation were similar everywhere, Merrick's dual market for legal services probably was not exceptional. Indeed, when a property owner dissatisfied with an arbiter's decision wrote a friend in Philadelphia for advice, the reply he received was: "Let me urge you to call immediately on Mr. John Cadwalader. He is perhaps the safest counsellor you could consult in our city." Cadwalader was a prominent attorney and a future judge.[25]

Federal cases confirmed a dual market for legal services in the eminent domain field. Counsel for the parties coming before the Supreme Court in cases concerning the contract clause and other cases included nationally prominent lawyers Daniel Webster and Reverdy Johnson. Members of the Court's elite bar, these men argued the comparatively few but important suits that found their way to the nation's highest court. As was true of Merrick and Binney in the state legal arena, Webster and Johnson epitomized the fundamental fact of the American adversarial system of justice: that both sides deserved the best defense. In eminent domain litigation each side appealed to the competing values of corporate privilege and property rights. Inherent in the property holder's position, however, was the belief that private agents of power such as corporations must be held accountable in order to retain constitutional legitimacy. The institutional apparatus for maintaining this accountability was the assessment process and the local control it represented. Thus when Johnson's argument defeated the railroad, he, like his counterparts at the bar, gave normative force to the constitutional ideal.

The practical impact of eminent domain law depended significantly, then, upon the method of property assessment. Although lawmakers readily granted transportation corporations the vital privilege of tak-

ing property, they did not ignore local producer and smaller property-holding interests. The same process that enabled capitalist promoters to establish a right-of-way, provided the means to determine its cost through local assessment, the institutional means of enforcing constitutional legitimacy and accountability. The role of lawyers symbolized the ambiguities inherent in the operation of the imperatives of law. Sometimes the immediate result was interminable delay; in other cases it was cooperation and compromise. But the broader consequence was to facilitate the belief that community welfare, the protection of producers, and economic development were compatible with and dependent upon the corporate accountability and local control embodied in the constitutional ideal.

### Constitutionalism and the Stakes of Conflict

The interplay of eminent domain law, local control, and capitalist development reflected the American commitment to constitutional government. Tocqueville observed that "civic spirit is inseparable from the exercise of political rights." He asked, "How does it come about that each man is as interested in the affairs of his township . . . and of the whole state as he is in his own affairs? It is because each man in his sphere takes an active part in the government of society." The right of condemnation tested the link between democratic participation in governmental affairs and the constitutional parameters of the operation of individual self-interest. The exercise of the condemnation privilege revealed the degree to which in America, as Tocqueville said, it "is not disinterestedness which is great, it is interest which is well-understood."[26] This attention to interests was true of the full cross section of social-class groups including farmers, workers, other smaller property-holding producers, and capitalist promoters. A local elected official and his fellow citizens implemented the process of assessment upon which the power of condemnation depended. The sheriff and the inquisition were the means by which corporate privilege was held accountable to constitutionalism, which in turn helped to deflect social-class tensions.

The extent to which developers used their power suggested the influence of constitutional limitations. The company or its agent could negotiate directly with a landowner to arrive at a price for his property. When negotiation failed, the company could resort to condemnation

and the assessment proceedings, thereby turning the matter over to local authorities. If the inquisition's decision was unsatisfactory, either side could try the case in court and, if necessary, appeal the result to the state supreme court. But choosing condemnation, and the possibility of litigation it engendered, raised the issue of time. The grant of eminent domain no doubt gave transportation corporations the means to reduce costs as long as other factors did not intervene. But since, in keeping with the values of legitimacy and accountability, statutory provisions acknowledged the interests of local property owners, the assessment process could increase costs because of the time necessary to resolve disputes over what constituted fair compensation. Through the exercise of their own lawful rights, local people and communities possessed, then, leverage in their dealings with developers.[27]

The property holder's preference for inquisition judgments over uncoerced deed agreements suggested that this was so. Records of the Chesapeake and Ohio Canal show the amount of money paid for lands in Allegany and Washington counties in Maryland, the names of the owner with whom each transaction was made, and how the property was acquired (by deed or inquisition). For the period between 1835 and 1838 there were ninety-three real estate transactions listed. Of these, fifty-nine, more than 63 percent, were settled by inquisition, and the remainder by deed. Similarly, property records of Baltimore County showed that from 1835 to 1837 the Northern Central Railroad made twenty-one land acquisitions, of which fifteen, or 70 percent, were by condemnation. Other records revealed a similar pattern.[28]

Moreover, the price of the deeded property tended to be lower than that arrived at by inquisition. In one instance about forty acres were sold by deed for $1,000, whereas in another case roughly the same amount of land was appraised by a jury as worth $2,100. In two other transactions involving the same property holder about thirty acres went for $4,000 when assessed by a jury but another section went for $2,500 when transferred by deed. The deed books of Middlesex and Somerset counties in New Jersey show the cost of the roadbed of the Elizabethport and Somerville Railroad. For a right-of-way twenty-five miles long and about seventy feet across, the company paid nearly $52,000. There were great variations within even this short distance. Amounts ranged from $800 an acre to $800 for four-hundredths of an acre to as little as $100 per acre. Despite such diversity, inquisitions still tended to set higher prices than those arising out of private agree-

ment. The Pennsylvania Railroad estimated the total cost of damages for the right-of-way of one section at about $130,000; the inquisition awards for land of similar value totaled, however, over $167,000.[29]

The assessment process shaped the behavior of both property owners and corporations alike. In most cases transportation companies resorted to condemnation. But this was no doubt because property holders knew that they would receive higher prices from inquisition judgments than by relying upon one-on-one bargaining with the corporation. Hence property owners had good reason to wait to be coerced. Generally, citizens relied upon the assessment procedure not to thwart developers altogether but rather to hold them accountable to local control. Accordingly, ample opportunity existed for both sides either to exploit or to receive justice from the system. A newspaper editorial summed up the delicate balance that the law fostered: "The land-holders have mostly been willing to accept a fair compensation for their land. . . . [H]owever, there are a few individuals, who appear determined to make a large speculation in the shape of damages."[30] Thus the law offset the corporations' eminent domain privilege with a process by which individuals and communities received protection, generally remaining true to constitutional accountability and local control.

Recourse to litigation was exceptional. The annual report of the Pennsylvania Railroad stated that assessment of land damages had been "very satisfactory." Inquisitions assessed property on "just and fair grounds"; where judgments seemed too high, cases were taken to court. This situation was a great improvement over the "flagrant injustices' occurring in another county where it had been necessary to initiate litigation. The court had overruled the inquisitions' assessments and ordered new ones, and the report expressed confidence that the new inquisitions would arrive at fairer prices. Farther down the road, the company accepted without litigation assessments that were above their own estimates.[31] Moreover, the minutes book of one of the branches of the Philadelphia, Wilmington, and Baltimore Railroad acknowledged that the company's charter granted it the right to condemn land. However, because the use of the right required that the county sheriff appoint a panel of local men to determine the value of the damages, costly delays were likely. Yet resort to court action was even more time-consuming. Thus, but for exceptional cases, the company preferred to settle with the landowners privately or even to

accept the judgment of the sheriff's inquisition, rather than go to court. Such vicissitudes suggest why the minutes book of the same company praised its land agent when he was able to negotiate seventeen land cessions without trouble. Little wonder, too, that another railroad accepted delay and higher prices created by the "extravagant value put on their timber by farmers," rather than resort to trial.[32]

These considerations suggest that the connections between capitalist development and eminent domain were ambiguous. Rather than the one-sided exploitation of a defenseless class, the law encouraged a distribution of costs and benefits within constitutional limitations. It was not only the pecuniary interests of developers and property owners and the increased costs associated with delay that were at stake in this distributional process. Central also to confrontations over condemnation was local political participation represented by the role of elected officials and inquisitions in assessment proceedings. Property holders could accept the coercion of condemnation rather than merely rely upon negotiated settlements because the law preserved local control. Of course property holders might have been as susceptible as corporations to abusing the system, yet this did not obscure the degree to which each group "well-understood" its interests and looked to the law for its protection. The result was continued faith in local control and values of constitutional accountability.

The assessment process also weakened social-class solidarity. The pervasive influence of localism working through the legal process for establishing rights-of-way did not allow for the dominance of any single "entrepreneurial group." Instead, decisions determining a company's route were shaped by its interaction with different local interests. In 1835 farmers living outside one Pennsylvania community "bitterly opposed" construction of a railroad, while many townspeople favored it. The vote in the town meeting on giving the corporation a right-of-way split along these lines. In New Holland, Pennsylvania, representatives from the whole community petitioned against allowing a railroad to enter their town. In other areas, construction companies, teamsters, and hotel interests supported or opposed railroads and canals depending on whether the improvement helped or hurt their standing, both within the local area and in comparison with other localities. Interestingly, managers of corporations could appreciate the value of the assessment process where their own property was involved. The deed books of Somerset County show that I. Southard

and Jacob DeGroot sold the Elizabethport and Somerville Railroad some property at a good market price. Southard was a director of the railroad, and DeGroot was the captain of an affiliated steamboat company. One of the presidents of the Sunbury and Erie Railroad handled the American investments of the queen of Spain. Several of these investments were in real estate along the right-of-way of the railroad. The queen no doubt got a good price for her land.[33]

A close relationship existed between the local sociopolitical leadership and the process of acquiring a right-of-way. Three distinctive stages of local market development—strictly agricultural counties, those undergoing a transition from marginal to greater commercial market activity, and large, urban mercantile centers—characterized the socioeconomic and political landscape of the mid-Atlantic region before the Civil War. Leading groups in localities at each stage favored the idea of internal improvements (at least in the abstract). Support for particular projects in a particular locality depended, however, on numerous considerations. The persistent, sometimes bitter, commercial rivalries that dominated community relationships below the state level determined decisions concerning the location of transportation routes. Thus, even though powerful groups might want an internal improvement project for a locality their support or opposition depended upon the potential impact of similar projects elsewhere. The same principle was at work within individual communities. Coalitions of groups—even single property holders—could encourage or impede the establishment of right-of-ways depending upon their view of their particular self-interest. Moreover, a mix of old-style agricultural, artisan-worker, and rising professional elites dominated the local process of property assessment. Thus decisions concerning land condemnation reflected a cross section of class interests and attitudes, which undercut social-class cohesion.[34]

Confrontations over the routes of what became the Philadelphia, Wilmington, and Baltimore Railroad suggest the divisions among local groups. During the 1830s Baltimore promoters went to the legislature and asked for and received a charter of legal privileges from Maryland which granted, according to one observer, "more than the Lord's Prayer!" Yet later, when members of an influential Quaker milling dynasty in Wilmington, Delaware, enthusiastically called for local support of another branch of the road, the rest of the Quaker millers declined, stalling construction for years. In Pennsylvania the legisla-

ture granted developers a charter to construct a road between Philadelphia and Delaware County. Philadelphia merchants, however, opposed the project because they believed their "interest have been not
merely neglected, but entirely sacrificed" to rival communities. As a
result, the road initially failed. Although clashes among prominent
local interests involving right-of-way were not the only factors producing conflict, considerations relating to condemnation were nonetheless significant. In the long run these controversies were important not
primarily because they delayed railroad building but because they
encouraged the eventual distribution of losses and gains among diverse communities. Only after the various local groups agreed to
compromise did the three state legislatures sanction a unified company serving Philadelphia, Wilmington, and Baltimore.[35]

Related to these struggles was the importance of contractors to
railroad construction. Government financial and credit resources underwrote the contractors who actually built the railroads and canals in
the mid-Atlantic states. The availability of state credit encouraged the
construction companies to negotiate high assessment awards from
inquisitions. This was a notorious problem on the Pennsylvania Public
Works, where, in response to an investigation concerning collabora-
tion between assessors and contractors, Peter Utz admitted that he
had "asked for [an excessive award] . . . but did not get it." After
several such disappointments, Utz said, "I seen it was time to quite."
But other builders were successful enough that the problem reflected
what Louis Hartz called the "chaotic history of the works administration." Moreover, where private corporations were involved, as in the
case of the Chesapeake and Ohio canal, there were similar practices.
During a dispute with the Baltimore and Ohio Railroad over right-of-
way, the canal company found that the railroad was in collusion with
locals to raise the price of property and materials.[36]

Despite the unsavory nature of such practices, they weakened class
solidarity within the context of local control. Large urban contractors
handled the general finance and construction of major roads. Yet these
companies parceled out jobs to small, local enterprisers on a sub-
contract basis. It was often these modest-sized, local subcontractors
who were among the most immediate beneficiaries of the determination of the condemnation proceedings. Since the land agent of the
transport company was primarily responsible for making right-of-way
purchases, a strong financial bond existed between the developer and

the local producer. Similarly, the competition among rival communities for transportation projects put pressure upon the state fiscal resources available for use by contractors. Condemnation awards were usually among the major expenses of the company and were directly related to employment opportunities of both large and small contractors. To make more effective use of limited state finance, it was thus in the interest of developers, their major contractors, and local community and producer interests to cooperate.[37]

Interclass cooperation weakened the bonds among producers themselves. As improved transportation opened up larger markets, merchants contracted with buyers in distant places and local producers in urban centers like Philadelphia or Baltimore. Many of the local producers were "small employers" whose productivity depended upon groups of specialized workers. Greater transportation facilities increased the incentive for these employers to slash piece rates as demand grew. Thus, as happened in the Kensington, Pennsylvania, riots of the early 1840s, producers had good reason to oppose the location of a railroad terminus in their neighborhood because it symbolized the threat to their independence.[38] However, it was the same desire for independence that motivated the local subcontractors to work for the developers. Most of the local contractors who built several roads in the mid-Atlantic states were Irish. According to one observer, "they were probably fairly recent immigrants who had been laborers and had risen through the ranks to become [local] construction company heads." In Maryland and Delaware free blacks were among those working for the local producers, first on a segregated basis and then not.[39]

Perhaps this opportunity to achieve at least modest self-sufficiency explained why a vocal defender of the producer economy, Stephen Simpson, urged producers to support improved transportation. "Hitherto the sons of industry have viewed with a jealous eye . . . [transportation development] under an erroneous impression that it would reduce their wages, and deprive them of employment," he said. It was of course necessary to prevent the "profits" of railroads and canals from being "exclusively engrossed by monopoly and capital." Nevertheless, he affirmed, "the ultimate and general effect cannot fail to benefit the productive classes, by an enlargement of their comforts, and increase of their intelligence, and an accession to their importance and knowledge in the scale of society." Because they constituted

an "American System" which was the basis of "independence, industry, virtue, diffusive comfort, and general happiness," he concluded,
internal improvements "ought to unite all classes in their prosecu-
tion."[40]

As a result, the law deflected interclass tensions, and local producers
and their communities received the benefits of state-supported, capitalist finance. Although the distribution was never equitable, it was
consistent with Tocqueville's faith in democratic government and
broad enough to sustain the belief that community and individual
enterprise were accountable to local control and other constitutional
values.

### The Triumph of Judicial Discretion

If either party to a condemnation proceeding was dissatisfied with the
outcome, corporate charters granted the right to sue in court. Yet
because the judicial process took time and therefore usually increased
costs, transport companies resorted to it only in exceptional cases.
Moreover, the pressures favoring local control that were evident in the
assessment process also influenced trials before local judges and
juries. Although state appellate courts were more removed, they, too,
were unable altogether to escape local tensions. In the mid-Atlantic
states the triumph of the elected judiciary roughly coincided with the
boom in transportation development occurring before the Civil War.
Hence, both trial and appeals judges were accountable to the democratic process at the same time that condemnation disputes arising
from transportation development were on the rise. The United States
Supreme Court further strengthened this judicial role by holding that
eminent domain litigation was primarily a matter for state rather than
federal jurisdiction. Also during this period, state appellate judges
rode circuit, expressly in order to keep in touch with local needs.
Furthermore, as the experience of J. J. Merrick in western Maryland
suggests, both trial and appeals judges often came from the ranks of
politically and socially prominent local lawyers. None of this means
that local circumstances necessarily determined the result in eminent
domain cases; but it at least suggests that courts were not insulated
from the local interests.[41]

The central purpose of the court was to reconsider the results of
condemnation and assessment proceedings. Isaac F. Redfield, chief

justice of Vermont and author of an influential treatise on railroad law, stated in 1858 that the "inquiry" involving "what compensation shall be made, for land taken for public works, would on the face of it, seem to be a very simple one. One would naturally suppose the value of the land taken or damage sustained, to be the fair measure of compensation and there could be no serious difficulty in ascertaining the amount." But, the chief justice observed, "in consequence of numerous ingenious speculations in regard to possible advantages, and disadvantages, arising from the public works for which lands are taken, the whole subject has become in this country especially, involved in more or less uncertainty." As a result, many decisions were "contradictory."[42]

There were several sources of this uncertainty. Jurists were divided over whether the basis of the principle of fair compensation was natural right or simple expediency. In fact, however, there was little question that private companies were bound to pay for the property they damaged in establishing their route. The real question involved what constituted fair compensation. In assessing real estate values, for example, the value of "plough-land" could be set lower than other, more developed land (such as urban lots). But beyond such concrete problems were more amorphous considerations that could be taken into account to determine market value. As Redfield pointed out, all sorts of "ingenious speculations" were behind any attempt to set property values. Location, comparison with other sales in the neighborhood, the influence of the property owner, his relationship with his neighbors, and the climate of opinion for or against internal improvement in a local area were a few of the factors that could influence whether an owner would sell his property to a company or how an inquisition would assess property damages when there was no private agreement.[43]

Factors within the judicial process itself compounded the problem. English courts maintained predictability in their decisions by adhering to stare decisis, the principle that precedent controlled the result in like cases. In the United States, by contrast, judges gave much less weight to precedent. Judge Hugh Henry Brackenridge of the Supreme Court of Pennsylvania expressed the general view in 1814. "Certain it is that . . . stare decisis, is a salutary maxim," he said, "but it has appeared to me, that it has been carried sufficiently far in this country."[44] James Kent was more explicit some years later in his classic

work, *Commentaries on American Law*. "I wish not to . . . press too strongly the doctrine of stare decisis, when I recollect there are more than one thousand cases to be pointed out in the English and American books of reports, which have been overruled, doubted, or limited in their application." Given these considerations, Kent urged the value of wise experimentalism in judicial decision making. "It is probable that the records of many courts in this country are replete with hasty and crude decisions," he said. "Such cases ought to be examined without fear, and revised without reluctance, rather than to have the character of our laws impaired, and the beauty and harmony of the system destroyed by perpetuity of error. Even a series of decisions are not always conclusive evidence of what is law," the judge concluded; "the revision of a decision very often resolves itself into a mere question of expediency." The exasperation of a Maryland legislative report in 1854 was not surprising, then, when it exclaimed that the "lawyer can only reason upon law and justice of a case . . . but every Judge can decide the case one way or the other without good reason."[45]

The democratization of the courts no doubt encouraged judicial discretion. Pennsylvania lawyer Edward D. Ingrahm conveyed something of the pressures that judicial choices posed in a letter addressing the problem arising when a state supreme court judge died. "Our judicial affairs are not, as regards . . . candidates, very harmonious here," he said. "I wish we were more united." The tensions associated with democratic accountability influenced the relationship between the judge and jury. Delegates to the Maryland constitutional convention in 1850 noted that "prejudices arising from local causes" might "fly in the face of the plainest principles of law." Yet this did not justify giving the judge increased control by weakening the role of the jury as the decider of both law and fact. The convention voted to accept the practice of a prominent local judge who "invariably said that he had no right to instruct the jury," although "if asked his opinion he would give it."[46]

The fact that judges often were personally involved in development probably also indirectly enhanced discretion. Throughout the mid-Atlantic states judges like Samuel Maxwell Harrington, chancellor of the state of Delaware, were prominent developers. Harrington was a prime supporter and president of the Delaware Railroad. Even though he held judicial office, he led petition drives in the southern counties favoring corporate charters that had been introduced in the legisla-

ture. In addition, he owned land in the southern part of the state. Eventually Harrington resigned as the company's president due to, he admitted, "considerations of propriety connected with the condemnation of lands for the right-of-way." He promised to return to the post, however, once construction was completed.[47]

These considerations suggested why American courts approached decisions with flexibility. In England the more rigid social-class system shaped the selection of judges by appointment. Social-class status did not necessarily weaken the judges' independence, but it did facilitate the sort of cultural consensus that was consistent with a strict regard for precedent.[48] By contrast, the greater pluralism of American institutions fostered a consensus in which values were more diverse, at least insofar as the respect for precedent was concerned. A judge like Harrington clearly had a direct personal stake in favoring development. But as a public official he was part of a democratized governmental order which was responsive to social-class, market, and political pressures. Government authorities from other areas in the state were influenced by the same mix of values and interests rooted in their own locality. The same pressures were significant enough throughout the mid-Atlantic states to promote the degree of judicial discretion that Kent and others advocated.[49]

In some cases courts exercised this flexibility on behalf of corporations. The Maryland legislative report complained that Maryland courts permitted transportation companies to take property after it had been condemned but before the compensation awarded by the inquisition was paid. Eventually the landowner received her due, the legislative report observed, if the company remained solvent. Even so, the property holder had to bear the expense of litigation to force the company to pay. "These corporations [thus] became pets of all the courts, and in their favor the most latitudinarian constructions extended the powers of their charter to an alarming degree."[50]

But what were the losses and gains of such "latitudinarian constructions"? The action of the court delayed but generally did not prevent the property owner's just compensation. It was true that insolvency might prevent payment, though, as was noted in the discussion of debtor-creditor relations, this was a risk facing virtually everyone in antebellum society. In addition, the court shifted the burden of litigation to the injured party. Nevertheless, the essence of the court's favoritism was the restriction rather than destruction of the

property holder's rights. And eventually the court would be called upon to reconsider the entire issue when the angry owner sued the company for failure to pay what it rightfully owed. A letter from John Gibson to a railroad suggested that in such cases litigation was likely. "I have already notified you that I would not permit my land . . . to be taken or used until . . . [I received] compensation," he wrote. "Contrary to this prohibition . . . persons in your employment have actually commenced digging on . . . my farm. For this I consider the Company . . . [and its employees] as trespassers," Gibson concluded, "and shall take measures to assert my rights accordingly, as well as for an indemnity for the injury done to me." As a result of such pressure the Maryland Constitution of 1851 prohibited the taking of property until the owner received compensation.[51]

But courts also defended the property holder's rights. The troubles of the Northern Pennsylvania Railroad concerning its right-of-way in a place called Green Lane suggest something of the risks involved. The company's engineer had estimated the cost of the route at about $50,000. But the "anxious desire" of Henry Ingersoll of Green Lane that the road should be "as far as possible from his house" led to a trial. The jury decided in Ingersoll's favor, with the result that the railroad ended up paying nearly $121,000 for its right-of-way. The company grudgingly accepted the verdict, but the president could not restrain himself in a private letter to the chief engineer. "In order . . . that the Chief Engineer may not be in doubt as to my intentions . . . I convey to him my warning and my defiance." There was, however, no appeal.[52]

The Green Lane case was not unique. The trial of *James Bartram v. Philadelphia, Wilmington, and Baltimore Railroad* before Judge John Cadwalader in Pennsylvania suggests something of the situation of corporations in damage cases before local tribunals. The railroad attempted to negotiate with Bartram for three acres necessary for its right-of-way. When they failed to agree, the company initiated condemnation proceedings. An inquisition was called; it awarded the landowner a "sizeable" judgment. The railroad challenged the decision in Cadwalader's court. During the trial three of Bartram's friends were called to give their opinion as to the fairness of the judgment. George Fuhr said that he would not have sold the three acres to the railroad for $4,000. The company had wrecked a fine meadow, including gravel deposits and mica, and had not even raised the value of the land it had ruined. A second witness was less specific but stated that he thought the whole

property worth between $1,500 and $2,000. John M. Justice agreed with Fuhr that the land was worth more than the railroad company offered to pay but estimated the worth of the land around $1,200 per acre. Cadwalader took a liberal view of the testimony and adjudged an award of $4,615. This broke down to $1,200 per acre, plus a thousand dollars for general damage to Bartram's farm. There was no appeal in the case.[53]

In addition the courts could promote cooperation indirectly. Because of diverse political pressures the Maryland legislature granted both the Baltimore and Ohio Railroad and the Chesapeake and Ohio Canal a claim to the same route going west. But it became clear that the state lacked the fiscal resources to pay the construction and damage-assessment costs of the two companies on a separate basis. The B&O then attempted to preempt the canal's claim by initiating the condemnation process along the disputed right-of-way. The canal, however, obtained an injunction to stop local authorities from proceeding with the condemnations and the contractors from building. Arguing that the B&O's charter gave it precedence, the railroad appealed, but the state high court decided in favor of the canal.[54] A deadlock ensued which the legislature broke only through a compromise whereby it provided funding for "conjoint construction," including both projects under the same contract. If "both the works were included in one contract," a report concluded, "the interest of the contractor to promote the economy here contemplated would be direct and unequivocal." A corporate director admitted that the court decision had forced all the interests involved to cooperate. No group would receive "acts of grace at the hands of the legislature without a generous support from the friends of the other," he said, "in fine . . . united they would be strong, divided they would fall."[55]

The pattern of judicial discretion evident in these cases was consistent with decisions of state appellate courts. Transportation companies had, at best, only a mixed record of success on appeal. There were cases in New Jersey, Maryland, and Pennsylvania where high courts refused to award any damages at all. A New Jersey court refused recovery where an owner had voluntarily given away his land, then sued to have it returned after it had been improved by a company, even though the owner agreed to pay any damages. In another case, a New Jersey court denied an injunction to the owner of an urban lot who feared that the construction of a canal might injure his property.[56]

In Pennsylvania a high court refused to give compensation to a property owner who had freely turned over his land to a company for the
construction of shops but after they were finished had sued for damages.[57] Pennsylvania in some cases did not recognize the right of
landholders along a stream to recover damages resulting from flood-
ing due to the construction of a canal.[58] The state also had a similar rule
with regard to consequential or indirect damages in some cases.[59]
There were other cases in which the awards of inquisitions were set
aside due to procedural irregularities.[60]

But the outright refusal to allow compensation was rare. In most
cases the courts either let a judgment stand or, after setting it aside,
would order a new trial which could lead to a new assessment. A New
Jersey lower court had awarded a landowner $6,800 in damages,
which was nearly double the amount determined by the inquisition.
Because of the disparity, the Supreme Court ordered a new trial.[61] In
other cases assessments were set aside and new ones ordered when it
was shown that inquisitions had included in their judgment factors
which were improper. One controversial Pennsylvania decision reduced an award of $1,687 by a thousand dollars because it had in-
cluded future or possible damages.[62] At least one decision set aside an
award of six cents because it was "incurably bad." A new trial was
ordered to ascertain fairer compensation.[63]

In a majority of cases state supreme courts upheld the decision of
inquisitions in setting property values. A Maryland court stated suc-
cinctly the general view toward fair compensation: failure to give it
was "an exercise of power such as to shock our very idea of justice."[64]
In each state there were cases in which courts granted injunctions
against companies until they submitted to the inquisition process.[65]
New Jersey established the principle that landowners along navigable
streams could recover for damages resulting from a corporation's construction of a public waterway. New Jersey also expressly provided for
the inclusion of consequential damages under certain circumstances.[66]
Despite decisions to the contrary, Pennsylvania sometimes followed
New Jersey's lead on similar questions.[67] In other cases state supreme
courts gave property owners the means to recover damages from
corporations through a variety of procedural remedies.[68] And in a
number of cases where damages depended on title of ownership or
the right to occupy a roadbed, Pennsylvania courts decided in favor of
the landowner.[69] This diluted the impact of the state's stricter opinions

against compensation. There were also several cases where land-owners challenged the judgment of inquisitions that had favored the interests of corporations. In these cases the courts upheld the decision of the inquisition.[70] Cases involving the conflicting rights of companies revealed a similar pattern of mixed decision in state tribunals.[71] Where eminent domain issues were taken to federal court, property owners also often won.[72]

In these cases a struggle for local control, legal imperatives protecting property-holding producers, and constitutionalism encouraged judicial discretion. Diverse values and local interests impeded the eventual dominance of entrepreneurial capitalists in the construction of the transportation system. It was no doubt true that the right of eminent domain gave a tremendous advantage to railroads and canals. Resort to the right could further the progress of developmental programs and perhaps reduce the initial incidence of what amounted to a sort of "blackmail" between property holders and promoters. But it was also true that both in lobbying pressures leading to its initial grant in the corporate charter and through its practical operation in the assessment procedure, the right became enmeshed in a mass of political and social pressures reflected in appeals to the constititutional values of legitimacy and accountability. Examining the operation of assessments from the grassroots level reveals that local interests could get what they wanted from transportation facilities or even obstruct their construction. Whatever benefit railroads and canals received from eminent domain law could be offset by localism; and working against such realities, the corporations either struck a bargain or looked elsewhere for a route. Either way, the operational impact of the assessment process was increased costs. Thus while the right of eminent domain could potentially facilitate capitalist development, it also encouraged the belief that individual and community interests were subject to local control.

At the same time, the condemnation and assessment process deflected potential class tension. The attitudes and interests behind the operation of eminent domain reflected pervasive social and political fragmentation. The Smiths in their confrontation with the Baltimore and Ohio Railroad, the "Jackson-Van Buren" politician in his attack on the Philadelphia, Wilmington, and Baltimore Railroad; the Green Lane, Bartram, and Johnson cases; the ambivalent interests associated with large and small contractors; and even the workers of Kensington,

Pennsylvania, who rioted against putting a railroad in their neighborhood and won were instances of locals turning the legal system and constitutional values to their advantage.[73] In part this was possible because during the years before the Civil War transportation promoters in the mid-Atlantic states were not united enough to deal effectively with a highly diversified and influential array of local interests.[74] In addition, as the multiple financial involvements of promoters like Southard and DeGroot of the Elizabethport and Somerville Railroad suggests, even the "corporate power" itself could have a stake in vigorous use of the assessment process. Moreover, these confrontations involved local groups whose social composition cut across class lines, rather than fights between a capitalist elite and the dispossessed masses. Such factors also point to the improbability that—at least during this period—corporate interests were sufficiently unified and organized to disguise their activities by appearing to oppose government policies that they in fact favored.

The interaction between local market forces and corporate promotion thus resulted from a legal order which maintained popular faith in constitutionalism. Even such leaders of the bar as Merrick, Binney, and Reverdy Johnson could have good reasons to work against transportation corporations. These and other prominent attorneys would seem to be natural allies of railroads and canals. But considering the diversity of attitudes and interests and the degree of social-class fragmentation reflected by transportation development, it is not surprising that in relying upon the constitutional ideal through appeals to judges and juries, these lawyers could be found defending local control. Appellate court decisions revealed a similar tension. Although there were certainly opinions favoring unrestrained capitalist exploitation, the triumph of judicial discretion also protected the producers' and smaller property holders' interests.

# 5

## Railroad Accidents and

## Capitalist Accountability

**W**hile the connection between railway accident law and constitutional values was perhaps attenuated, it was not insignificant. Railroad accidents raised moral issues requiring the assignment of culpability or fault under the tort principle of negligence. The substantive content of negligence—especially as the principle related to the economic consequences of the standard of liability and whether that standard originated in fault or strict liability—were problems central to the evolution of the common law.[1] At the core of the negligence system nonetheless were judgments regarding the legitimacy and accountability of conduct. At least on one level of popular perception, these were the same values inherent in the constitutional ideal. Railroads, moreover, owed their existence to a public franchise and served customers as a public utility. This "public" character encouraged officials and citizens to view the railroads' conduct in terms of moral and constitutional values that were mutually reinforcing and interdependent.

Judgments regarding the railroads' accident liability occurred within a federal system characterized by significant local control. Be-

fore the Civil War a few accident cases involving business's standard of tort liability arose in federal court on diversity jurisdiction. The standard that the federal courts applied in these cases was the same one the state courts employed in railway accident suits, at least in the four mid-Atlantic states. State judges charged local juries on the bases of enduring common-law principles of justice and morality to promote due care and reasonable behavior, to minimize the risk of injury, and to promote honesty and fairness in the economic relationships of railroads and the wider society. In certain kinds of cases these principles led judges and juries to hold defendants to a standard of absolute or strict liability. In other cases local courts decided the question of whether defendants acted carelessly under a standard of fault. Regardless which rule of decision judges and juries applied in any specific case, tort law constituted a system of principles, policies, and rules grounded in popular notions of morality and justice.[2]

Moral and legal presumptions blended with popular faith in constitutionalism. In the American popular imagination from the 1840s on, railroads symbolized both the nation's potential for growth and the evils associated with "soulless" corporations. Faced with the necessity of reconciling these perceptions industry spokesmen such as H. V. Poor's *Railroad Journal*, railroad executives themselves, and legal commentators agreed that railroads and society alike should be held liable for harm or death caused by human error or misconduct. Even so, as public officials and courts applied moral principles central to the negligence system, the legal status of the railroads as public utilities engendered popular concerns about the constitutional legitimacy and accountability of corporate conduct. Accordingly, middling-class groups and federal, state, and local authorities held railroads to a higher standard of care. Workers clearly suffered, but not without offsetting considerations. Reflecting diverse values, social fragmentation, and the managers' restricted ability to pass costs on to other groups, railroad executives disagreed on the appropriate response, leaving corporate capitalism responsible to the interdependency of moral and constitutional values.

The law controlling accidents reflected the values and interests of the wider antebellum society and culture. During much of the nineteenth century producers no less than capitalist entrepreneurs welcomed the productivity that new technology made possible.[3] But the

desire for growth erased neither a deep-seated suspicion of corporate capitalism nor the conviction that it should be held accountable to the interests of small-to-medium-size, unincorporated property holders.[4] Similarly, the urban middle-class culture and evangelical Protestant values that dominated the media also favored development; they assumed, nevertheless, that universal moral principles governing individual human conduct applied with equal force to corporate capitalists, regardless of possible adverse economic consequences.[5] Lawmakers translated these ambiguous perceptions into policies that granted railroads generous privileges but subjected their use to governmental regulation. Although the potential for lax regulatory enforcement always existed, democratic political pressures arising from local rivalries and social tensions often resulted in policies that benefited noncorporate interests.[6] Moreover, unlike England and Continental regimes that dealt with the problems of industrialization through centralized administrative institutions, Americans relied upon legislative and judicial discretion exercised within a tradition of constitutionalism. Consequently, American railroad managers possessed much less governmentally enforced authority over workers than did their European counterparts, which no doubt mitigated class conflict.[7]

During the antebellum era railroad accidents were a conspicuous test of how law and society accommodated industrialization. Lawmakers in Pennsylvania, Maryland, New Jersey, and Delaware decided whether railroads would pay for accidents and the maintenance of operational safety as a business expense or would be able to shift the burden of cost to workers and society in general.[8] This was a critical issue because corporate competition and the influence of local groups transmitted through government control of rates restricted the railroads' ability to pass increased costs on to shippers and the consumer.[9] The interests of producers, middle-class presumptions regarding moral responsibility, and constitutional values also shaped governmental policy toward accidents. Given these factors, both legislatures and courts in the four mid-Atlantic states were under pressure to strike some balance between demands for capitalist development and moral as well as constitutional accountability. Consequently, government sought to spread the costs of accidents throughout society, thereby protecting modest-sized property interests.[10]

### Negligence and the Social Milieu

During much of the nineteenth century the legal principles governing accidents were in a state of transition. Standards of liability were discernible as strict liability or fault but did not yet exist in the modern doctrinal categories or forms. Instead, a claim generally existed where it could be shown that it fit within various common-law pleading categories, such as the writ of trespass, the writ of case, and the doctrine that there was no recovery for nonfeasance. These technical provisions were tied in turn to that traditional immunities and privileges that the law defined as contract or property relationships. Gradually, however, a uniform principle did emerge known as negligence. The moral cause of injury or damage resulting from some fault was central to the negligence approach to liability. Under the negligence principle a "pure" accident might happen in which there could be no recovery because no one's fault had caused it. Conversely, if it was possible to locate an accident's cause in someone's reckless, imprudent, or careless conduct, a basis for recovery existed. Thus where negligence was the basis of liability, there was no liability without culpability. At least since the seventeenth century a strict liability standard was also distinguishable in certain common-law cases, according to which there was liability for pernicious conduct without fault.

There were various ways to approach the issue of liability standards in railway accidents. Some scholars have argued that in some form either strict liability or fault characterized tort law before the nineteenth century. The form that negligence took in the nineteenth century nonetheless represented a departure from the past in which judges used old doctrines in new ways to reduce the costs of capitalist enterprise.[11] Other scholars have contended, by contrast, that continuity existed between the early principles of tort law and those which during the nineteenth century became dominant as the system of negligence. Under that system, however, courts generally reflected populist sentiments favoring community interests over the costs accruing to developers, including railroads.[12]

Yet another approach embraced the theme of continuity and the populist orientation of decision making. In addition, it argued that nineteenth-century American judges "used tort law to make people [and corporations] behave in morally appropriate ways by holding

them to community standards of reasonable behavior in the circumstances in order to minimize injuries and losses, and to promote honesty and fairness in economic relationships." In certain litigation this meant judges decided issues according to a standard of strict liability; in other cases the rule applied was one of fault. Ultimately, however, attaining morally responsible and accountable conduct was of greater importance than shifting the costs of development from capitalists to weaker groups. This overriding concern for the enforcement of moral imperatives was especially apparent in cases involving railroads that had injured passengers or strangers, those who experienced most such accidents.[13]

Little wonder, then, the leading nineteenth-century treatise on the law of negligence could say that probably no area of law "has had greater or more interesting growth." During the first half of the nineteenth century the choices inherent in the law resulted in rules that generally favored the community. Reflecting constitutional values of legitimacy and accountability, a treatise on accident law stated that railroads were "public servants," subject to the "public policy of the State," which prohibited carelessness toward the "person or property of a citizen." Accompanying the "extraordinary privileges" that railroads had received from the states were "commensurate duties" imposed by law. The "key" to this law was not a private contractual relationship between the railway and the public; instead it was a "solemn obligation of her [the law's] dignity, *the contract between the common carrier and the State.*" "Nothing" could excuse "any degree of recklessness" on the part of railroad employees or managers. A "universal rule" for the "promotion of the right and suppression of the wrong" bound railroad authorities and workers through a "public policy" controlling every law and contractual obligation.[14]

Attachment to local control helped shape the balance struck in state courts between procapitalist privilege and "public policy." Antebellum Americans understood local control in terms of the commitment to a general community interest which coexisted alongside an equally firm belief in private rights. The constitutional institution of local control that significantly influenced accident liability was the jury. A lawbook's treatment of the doctrine of contributory negligence reveals how contemporary lawyers looked upon the jury's authority. Under the rule of contributory negligence, injured persons forfeited their entire right of recovery if their own fault in part caused harm. The

treatise noted that most courts did not apply the rule in this extreme form, however. Instead, most judges left application of the doctrine as a "mixed question of law and fact" to the jury, and it was "safer" for a railroad's attorney to accept this without objection.[15]

Another factor contributing to the primacy of the jury was the local bar. Virtually from the beginning railroads recognized the usefulness of lawyers, and managers often retained the leading attorneys of a state as their company's counsel. But several realities retarded the effectiveness of big-time lawyers, especially in rural areas where most railroad tracks lay. The system of jury selection, which in many states was not uniform, might give local firms certain advantages. Some counties selected jurymen from a list of property holders; others relied upon bystanders. Under either system local attorneys were generally more familiar with the method of selection and the individual citizens actually being chosen and were often less distrusted than outsiders. Moreover, in some counties, through close social or political contacts with sheriffs or judges, local lawyers could directly influence the choice of jurors. Of course railroads might hire local counsel themselves, but often this was difficult because the individual belonged to the community's social and political establishment. Representing outsiders under such circumstances could have long-term disadvantages that the local attorney might understandably not want to risk.[16]

The contingency fee also facilitated the success of the local lawyer. Under this practice an injured plaintiff's attorney got nothing if he lost; but if he won, his fee amounted to a large percentage of the settlement. Historians have identified the emergence of the contingency fee as a postbellum phenomenon. It was already being used at least by the 1850s, however, as a complaint of one railroad president indicated in 1853. He agreed to a large out-of-court settlement in part to avoid "the effect upon juries of ingenious advocates who are working for a contingent fee." The availability of the percentage provided incentive for local lawyers to challenge railroads in the local courts. If the attorney had an advantage over the corporation's counsel because of a more intimate familiarity with the jury, this incentive was even stronger.[17]

All this bore directly on an attorney's ability to predict jury behavior. Local lawyers kept lists that included names, residences, and occupations of citizens assigned jury duty for a court's seasonal terms. Doubtlessly this practice arose in part out of a desire to keep informed about those before whom the attorney would be arguing cases. More

specifically, it gave him a basis for weighing the attitudes, customs, and previous jury experience of the individuals who would in most cases ultimately determine his client's fate. In small towns successful lawyers likely knew personally everyone on a given jury, so they probably did not need to keep formal records. But social contacts and experiences constituted what amounted to a list of particulars maintained in the practitioner's head. Given the conspicuous impact of railroads on antebellum society, few if any areas of civil litigation were more subject to the whims of community values and pressures than railroad accident cases. By knowing what courtroom tactics would likely influence his neighbors in such cases, the local lawyer had an advantage over outside counsel.[18] Even if a verdict was overruled, accident cases were usually sent back to the local court for retrial. With another trial, the factors contributing to localism would remain as strong as in the original litigation.

The social composition of juries may also have influenced verdicts in railroad litigation. Lists from Philadelphia for three different local court terms in the 1840s revealed the sorts of people who served as jurors in cities. The class and occupational mix was quite democratic: individuals identified as gentlemen and merchants served alongside farmers, various small wholesalers, clerks, professionals, artisans, and laborers. Of the total of 144 individuals on the three lists, the overwhelming majority were artisan-mechanics, such as carpenters, bricklayers, and plumbers. Nearly 49 percent were artisans, while just under 10 percent were farmers, three were "gentlemen," seven were laborers, six were service people or professionals, nine were clerks, and 25 percent were merchants or small wholesalers. By contrast, in rural areas most jurors tended to be farmers or small-town artisans.[19] Thus in both urban centers and the countryside individuals serving on juries generally belonged to the "producing classes."

These factors shaped the decisions that railroad managers made regarding accident compensation. Thomas Fernon, a Northern Pennsylvania Railroad executive, suggested the degree to which the local environment influenced his judgment. Numerous claims arose from a collision occurring during the summer of 1857. At the same time, the railroad was lobbying the city of Philadelphia for aid in an effort to negotiate a first-mortgage loan. The "disaster" directly threatened the city council's willingness to support the loan. "That lamentable occurrence has rendered it impossible to sell the remaining mortgage

bonds, on which reliance was placed, without such a sacrifice as the Board do not feel themselves justified making, without first exhausting every means to avoid it," Fernon reported. The pressures arising from adverse public opinion thus made the railroad quite conciliatory. During the months following the accident there were no lawsuits because the company made "amicable arrangements . . . with all." "Sensible that no human aid can allay the distress which such a catastrophe has entailed, the Board have, nevertheless," Fernon noted, "exerted their utmost ability to show their sympathy for all who have suffered, by as much liberality as it was possible for them to manifest."[20]

This handling of the accident by the railroad was consistent with the faith in constitutional values when debtor-creditor rights, taxation, and eminent domain were at issue. Corporations certainly possessed privileges and power, but the environment in which they operated nonetheless encouraged political and economic pressures that helped to make them accountable to community opinion. Although communities may have wanted railroads, there was little desire to gain them at the price of local control. Moreover, labor struggles occurred that were often "community uprisings" in which day laborers, artisans, shopkeepers, and professionals supported striking railwaymen. Thus the local response to railroads ran the gamut from public acquiescence to the demand for accountability to outright resistance. Of course, community authorities could directly influence corporations only as long as they were subject to government regulation and dependent upon government for financial support which was the case before 1860.[21]

These considerations influenced the role of lawyers in accident cases. As the remarks of railroad managers suggest, accidents created a dual market for legal services. The railroads themselves, of course, hired counsel in accident suits; they also paid attorneys to negotiate settlements in order to avoid litigation. At the same time, the emergence of the contingency fee indicated that injuries and deaths associated with railroads created another market for lawyerly skills. What linked the need for legal services and the pressures fostering community accountability was the managers' concern about adverse public opinion, which included the consequences resulting from defying constitutional values. In such an environment there was as much need for lawyers representing the maimed and dead as there was for those

defending railroads. Perhaps it was understandable, then, that rail-road managers granted "liberal accommodations" to avoid litigation.[22]

Local courts and juries were also vital to the enforcement of corpo-rate accountability. Since the right of removal to federal tribunals was quite limited before the Civil War, the great majority of accident cases came before state courts. Particularly in eminent domain proceedings community justice was entwined with a tenacious attachment to local control. The success or failure of corporations in local courts depended more upon the perception that public accountability was being pre-served than on a routine, unbridled enthusiasm for development. Probably the same was true in accident litigation. The market for contingency-fee lawyers, the preference of railroad executives for out-of-court settlements, and the interrelationship between financial de-pendency and public opinion suggest this was so. Moreover, the majority of jurors belonged to the class sharing producer values; very likely when producers sat as jurors, they measured the risks associ-ated with railroads by their own standard.[23]

Favorably disposed toward economic growth as long as it was not dominated by corporate capitalism, producers did not reject out of hand the industrialization that railroads symbolized. But given the social and market pressures growing out of constitutionalism and the localistic orientation of the jury system, it was understandable that the values of small, unincorporated producers and their desire for protec-tion would influence the emergence of negligence in American law. Thus since the actual economic impact of the adoption of various liability rules was at the time unclear, other social interests and consti-tutional values were a mental starting point for the evolution of the negligence system.

### The Moral Imperative

A cultural force which also shaped negligence doctrines was protes-tant morality. Growing out of middle-class evangelical Protestantism, the new moralistic faith had gripped the minds of many Americans by the 1830s. Initially, an elite "American gentry" constituted its primary exponents; but eventually its assumptions penetrated small-town gen-teel and urban working-class culture and dominated the thinking of the urban middle class. This vision rested on a belief in objectively identifiable, universal moral principles that were believed to be as

inviolable as the laws of Newtonian physics. Moral absolutism inspired American evangelicals with an earnest purposefulness which combined a belief in self-reliance, self-discipline, and individual obligation. In sum, it instilled what evangelical Protestants called "character." Individuals possessing such character needed no reminders to do their duty; an internal sense of obligation made them reliable. Moreover, a society constituted of such citizens required only a limited government; and tying individual liberty to moral conviction in private life promoted a concern for the general welfare of the community and nation. Opinion leaders sharing these values dominated American publishing in law, religion, and science; and they hoped through persuasion rather than vigorous governmental action to infuse the rising industrial order with standards of individual moral accountability and social responsibility that were consistent with constitutional values.[24]

Moralistic cultural values pervaded contemporary discussion of accidents. "Clearly most" railroad "catastrophes," noted one writer confidently in 1856, occurred because of "moral rather than physical factors . . . [resulting from] ignorance, or recklessness of man . . . not material causes . . . beyond the control of ordinary human care and knowledge." A stockholders' report for the New Jersey Railroad observed in 1853 that the surest "safeguards against danger" and the "greatest safety" consisted in "multiplying individual responsibility and care" on the road.[25] Without question, those "in the wrong" causing injury were to be held accountable. Whenever "wanton carelessness" resulted in death, it would be "blamed and punished as the highest degree of manslaughter."[26]

Assumptions about individual responsibility rather than a narrow preoccupation with development alone shaped views regarding negligence. If an accident resulted from the railroad's error, the managers of the company should pay damages. Similarly, when the conduct of a company employee caused harm, he should be held accountable. Passengers, too, were not exempt from liability if injury or death occurred because they "trespassed" railroad regulations or the "dictates of ordinary prudence." Moreover, strangers—members of the general public who either by chance or their own fault were involved in an accident—might be found liable in certain instances.[27] But regardless of the limitless variations in accidental circumstance, the preoccupation with moral causation sustained the moral assumption

that objectively identifiable individual misconduct was the basis of liability. And, consistent with their belief in universal moral principles, evangelical protestants believed that the standard by which such behavior should be measured was "THE COMMON SENSE OF MANKIND."[28] Thus railroad accidents raised the specter of the "soulless" corporation representing a collective will which threatened the regime of personal moral standards that was consistent with values of legitimacy and accountability inherent in constitutionalism. Apologists argued that individuals acting in a collective capacity should not be held personally accountable. True believers in evangelical morality, however, rejected such claims.

According to these moral presumptions, neither retarded development nor lost profits should weaken the personal duty to maintain safe railroad operation. Henry Varnum Poor, editor of the *American Railroad Journal* and leading spokesman of the industry, admitted that a chief purpose of railroads was "*money-making*." However, capitalists and managers needed to distinguish "*legitimate* from illegitimate projects." Railroads built for purposes of speculation were not legitimate and therefore exposed both the public and the industry itself to "danger," in part because such enterprises lacked the economic means to ensure adequate safety standards. Poor's journal conceded that rules imposing liability standards of "undue severity" could render railroad property "unstable," reduce it in value, and thereby threaten development. But protection from accidents through enforced individual accountability was a higher value. Even though "companies may suffer in being compelled to pay for injuries resulting from their mismanagement," Poor concluded, "they should also be accountable to the law."[29]

Evangelical Protestant moralism provided a distinct perspective on profits in general. The bland pages of the stockholders' report of the New Jersey Railroad suggested in 1854 that the moral impact of railways on society was as important as profits. "Receipts and disbursements" were indeed vital "material interests," the report stated. But these were "not comparable" to the beneficial influence that railroads exercised by facilitating systematic business habits and free trade and by "advancing the general welfare . . . [and] enlarging the moral machinery of mankind in Church and State." Attention to moral considerations did not preclude candid notice, however, that despite hazards and "injurious opposition" the railroad would pay its stockholders a dividend of about 10 percent.[30] Regardless of emphasis upon

moral priority, then, profitability remained the central consideration. Nevertheless, in the minds of believers, moralism was potentially a countervailing value.

The belief that moral responsibility and profitability were compatible influenced perceptions of the costs of accidents. Passengers, strangers, and the railroads themselves shared a "concomitant interest" in avoiding accidents, noted one observer, because they impaired the public's confidence in railroad operation. The links joining safety, economic costs, and "public confidence" were critical. It was an age in which, noted the *American Railroad Journal*, "we want railroads extended, improved and made valuable to the *proprietors*." Why? Not solely out of concern for stockholders or a company's profit margins, but because the "public will be better served." Thus, to garner the public's confidence and business, railroads had to learn that "economy and safety" meant the "same thing." And railroad managers would understand this lesson if juries and legislatures raised operational costs by imposing stiff penalties in accident cases. "All corrective measures, in fact resolve themselves to this," the *Journal* asserted bluntly in 1842: "the Legislature should not only see that a proper penalty is annexed to every accident, but the public should take the matter into their own hands, by giving exemplary damages in all cases that come before a jury."[31]

There was, of course, disagreement over the limits of the moral and constitutional accountability. Accidents often generated opposing views of responsibility, with one side railing against the abuse of monopolistic corporate privileges and the other side claiming the railroad's infallibility. But even champions of railroad development held managers singularly responsible for avoiding accidents. *American Railroad Journal* editor Poor exclaimed that the "great peril" to public safety was railroad "*management*." The risk arose in part because "most" companies were "dumb." In addition, managers were too often careless, indifferent, or even dishonest in carrying out their duties; these deficiencies in turn meant that the subordinates they employed frequently possessed similar traits.[32] Thus, evangelical Protestants believed, forcing railroads to pay for accidents that resulted from operational mismanagement encouraged among all the company's personnel a sense of individual responsibility for the maintenance of safety standards.

Moral assumptions were particularly ambivalent regarding the connection between labor-management relations and safety. The fellow-

servant rule, of course, limited employer liability for accidents resulting from the negligence of employees. Simultaneously, however, the
jury system, producer values, and the emphasis on personal accountability and moral causation could mitigate the impact of the doctrine
by imposing liability upon corporate management. Reinforcing this
pattern was the institutional relationship between railroad supervisors
and workers. The hiring, firing, disciplining, and general personnel
management of workers on early nineteenth-century railroads was
highly decentralized, most authority resting with foremen and other
local officials. Arbitrariness, paternalism, family connections, favoritism—all the uncertainties associated with face-to-face supervisory
discretion—significantly influenced the average worker's status. In
such a system individual responsibility and expertise controlled the
enforcement of regulations governing the employee's conduct.[33] But
as the observations of Poor and others attested, in many cases the
likelihood that subordinates might cause accidents did not free managers from liability when the safety of the public was endangered.
Thus conflicting values and social realities shaped the personal accountability of workers and managers alike.

Railroad executives responded to these tensions in several ways.
Consistent with evangelical Protestant values, a stockholders' report
of the Philadelphia, Wilmington, and Baltimore Railroad offered one
widely accepted solution in 1855. "Could every operative be placed in
a position to share in the savings made by his extra care and exertion,
instead of being paid a stipulated salary," the report declared, "corporations would not only be large gainers, but the work would be better
and more promptly done." The company hoped, despite its "extended
operations" and large numbers of employees, "to attain the same
degree of personal supervision and care, as in the private business of
individuals. Could all corporations adopt a system that would secure
such supervision and care, many a railroad that is now scarcely earn-
ing its expenses, would become dividend paying." Such was the "infir-
mity of human nature," stated a report of the New Jersey Railroad in
1853, that no single individual was incapable of occasional erring
behavior. To correct for these lapses, railroads should follow the lead
of "mercantile operations" by establishing "checks and safeguards . . .
[and] requiring others promptly to correct any delinquency."[34]

Railroads also used informal welfare measures and various rewards
to encourage employee attention to safety. Some managers contrib-

uted funds to hospitals where their employees were treated for injuries. A few companies even provided worker accident insurance programs. Employees maintaining good safety records received bonuses, gratuities, and medals. On a less structured level, as official state accident reports noted, railroads often kept injured employees on their rosters during convalescence. In other cases when workers recovered but remained lame for the rest of their lives, companies would continue to employ them.[35] Frank Steward was a fireman for the New Jersey Railroad; one day he lost a toe and part of a heel attempting to jump from an engine. Although the wound slowed him down, the company kept him on. Another example involved a young brakeman named John Ryan who worked for the same company. "While unnecessarily reaching out and looking back" during a turn, the report read, the youth hit his head on the car, whereupon he fell from the train. Ryan's leg was amputated, but the company continued to employ him.[36] According to Walter Licht's pioneering study *Working for the Railroad*, such practices were not uncommon. The chief problem was that company generosity toward a worker usually depended upon the discretion of local supervisors, which permitted too much arbitrariness.

Another factor ensuring safety was comparatively good wages. Railroad workers were reasonably well paid by the standards of the time, and managers' desire to prevent the public dissatisfaction that resulted from accidents was one reason for this. Contemporaries stressed the interconnectedness of wages, public relations, and safety. It was a gross error, a writer observed, to lower wages because this would impair employee effectiveness and loyalty and thereby increase the risk of accidents, which in turn would foster public criticism of managers and result in diminished business. At the same time, managers should take care that every employee gave "a full equivalent for wages paid." The *American Railroad Journal* and certain railroad executives also shared the view that a "safe, sober, properly disciplined . . . [and] properly paid" worker would avoid accidents.[37]

Finally one range of opinion, probably held by only a few publicists, wanted to avoid accidents out of a concern for the welfare of workers themselves. Generally, the *American Railroad Journal* noted, the public cared only about passengers' safety. But the sad record of injuries and deaths involving "humbler parties" called for "wider sympathies" that included railroad workers who "hourly . . . [confronted the risk of]

disasters, which in a moment may reduce their families to want." The *Journal* regarded the "conductors, and enginemen, and firemen of trains as . . . the adventurous sailor, who exposes himself in all weathers and risks his life upon the farthest spar or the slenderest rope to preserve the comfort and safety of the inmates of the ship."[38] It seems unlikely that such attitudes had any direct impact on the behavior of courts, juries, or legislatures. But, insofar as Poor's ideas reflected a more general awareness of the connection between public safety and worker conditions, they were not insignificant. Although the public may have been generally unconcerned about workers, its interest in its own safety could have influenced governmental policies that nonetheless benefited those working for the railroad.

The issue of railroad safety thus created a tension between developmental cost factors and the cultural imperatives of evangelical Protestant morality and constitutionalism. The link between these polar extremes was the interest of passengers and other representatives of the general public in protecting their own lives and bodies. Publicists asserted that commitment to the economic growth that railroads symbolized should not subvert the duties emanating from moral accountability and individual responsibility. In order to balance competing and often conflicting demands arising from the concern for public relations, profitability, and accident prevention, Poor and others held managers, workers, passengers, and the general public firmly responsible for conduct that resulted in harm. These individuals apparently believed that greater care grounded in stronger personal character would significantly diminish a grave public evil. But because they were closest to and most experienced with railroad operations and possessed a public franchise, managers and their employees were deemed most responsible for accident avoidance and accountable to moral as well as constitutional values. Even though decentralized labor-management relations placed a heavy burden on rank-and-file workers in this connection, managers were not exempt from a comparable standard of care. To heighten managerial concern about safety, publicists like Poor urged legislators to impose upon railroads effective safety regulations and juries to hand down high damage awards in accident cases. In this way, the publicists argued, individuals acting in consort as a "soulless" corporation would be held morally accountable. Ultimately, antebellum American courts and legislatures translated these tensions into a protective policy which constituted the

working realities of the negligence rule and was consistent with re-spect for the constitutional ideal.

### Policy Impact: The Legislature and Social Fragmentation

Confidence in the influence of public opinion shaped accident preven-tion policy. By the 1850s, as railroad safety became a significant public issue, state laws began requiring companies to publicize statistics and other information describing injuries, deaths, and the status and con-duct of employees involved in particular incidents.[39] Publication of these data theoretically gave evangelical Protestants the means to determine whether individual culpability had caused or contributed to an accident. It reflected, too, the assumption that where government rested on popular will, resolution of social evils required holding public franchises accountable to the constitutional ideal. Moreover, given the hazards inherent in the producer economy, reports made unincorporated, small enterprisers aware of the risks that passengers, strangers, railroad employees, and managers confronted. This con-junction of constitutional, producer, and moral values encouraged the conviction that aroused public opinion could foster safer railroads. It reflected, too, diversity rather than unity of social-class interests. "Men of doubtful character are often kept straight by the force of public opinion," declared Poor's *Journal*. Reports of railroad opera-tions, including those concerning accidents, would "provoke commu-nity criticism" and thereby bring about improved railroad safety.[40]

New Jersey railroads began reporting accident information in 1852. Throughout the decade about a dozen companies annually supplied detailed accident-related data. The notorious Camden and Amboy Railroad and the New Jersey Railroad were among those that did con-siderable interstate business and possessed significant political clout. Other small concerns, such as the Warren Railroad, were involved pri-marily in local enterprise and had less political influence.[41] On the small roads years went by in which there were no reported injuries or deaths. The bigger railroads, however, were never so lucky. Three annual reports from the New Jersey Railroad suggested accident patterns: during the three years six passengers died and fourteen were injured, eighteen strangers were killed and the same number wounded, and five employees were killed and seven were injured.[42] During 1854 on

the Camden and Amboy Railroad four passengers were killed and five injured, four strangers died and six were wounded, and one employee was killed and one injured.[43] Totals from five annual reports of three different roads for the years 1852 to 1858 showed that twelve passengers were killed and nineteen were wounded, twenty-four strangers were killed and twenty-six injured, and nine employees were killed and eleven injured.[44]

These figures suggest significant implications for railroad managers' views of accidents. Taken together, injuries and death occurring to passengers and strangers outnumbered those suffered by employees more than four to one. Of course, because there were far fewer railroad workers than there were passengers and strangers, the employees' risk was much greater. But in terms of sheer political and social influence, the group suffering the most from accidents was that which also potentially possessed the most clout over lawmakers—the general public. In addition, the railroad's business itself depended upon these same people. Particularly during the competitive antebellum period, managers were concerned that an unfavorable public image fostered by an indifference to safety might result in loss of business. Since, as Charles Francis Adams observed, accidents were bad for public relations, railroads often settled with "their adversaries quickly." Hence, Adams pointed out the damages paid in three major accidents averaged $700,000. The cost may have been great, but as Fernon and other railroad executives noted, an inflamed public opinion would have exacted a higher price.[45]

When it came to prescribing governmental policy, however, managers disagreed. Few questioned the principle that some sort of governmental action to facilitate railroad safety was necessary, but beyond that general point consensus dissolved. One group urged that the law should focus upon and punish members of the general public whose involvement with railroads could or did in fact result in hazard and harm. Accordingly, the Board of Directors of the Camden and Amboy Railroad proposed to deal with one perennial cause of accidents with a law which made "all persons, trespassers, who without authority from the Company go on the road or suffer their cattle to go on it." Why should the law emphasize the conduct of the ordinary citizen? Because everyone should "have perfect protection in himself; why diminish it by placing the responsibility elsewhere and upon persons much less interested?" Consequently, the directors concluded, the "best means"

to achieve safety was for the legislature to avoid any laws that were "hostile" to railroads. After all, a railroad was a "useful public convenience entitled to the liberal support and just consideration of the people, and to that protection from the courts and juries which every American freeman has a right to claim." It was wrong to consider railroads "nuisances to be reviled . . . libelled . . . and persecuted."[46]

Other managers were more compromising. They rejected the one-sided policy espoused by the Camden and Amboy directors because it was "against the public." Noting the importance of public relations to business, the stockholders' reports of the New Jersey Railroad observed that "true economy" and safety demanded that the government should establish rules governing the actions of both railroads and the general public. "A more considerable public sentiment should . . . be cultivated . . . until there be a more complete comprehension of the causes of casualties . . . and corresponding remedies for their prevention," the report urged. Other managers bowed to the pressure of public sentiment but did so grudgingly. "I am satisfied that in these cases, certainly we paid more than it was honest for the parties to receive," wrote a former president of the Philadelphia, Wilmington, and Baltimore Railroad, William Henry Swift, in 1853; "still it appeared to be a lesser evil and one to be submitted to rather than force doctor's certificates of injured spines . . . bruises, blood spitting, and women three to six months gone in pregnancy."[47]

Of course, even conciliatory railroad executives wanted citizens and government to share with them a responsibility for accident prevention. One directors' report noted with satisfaction that there were fewer casualties from "persons walking on, or crossing the tracks" than in the past. But cattle on the rails continued to threaten passenger safety. The directors "admonished" owners to comply with laws requiring the fencing of stock along railroad tracks, which would avoid both a "pecuniary loss" and a "fearful responsibility" for the "destruction of human life" resulting from such "delinquency." Concerning other behavior that frequently caused "melancholy casualties," the directors hoped that the "public authorities" would "enact and enforce penal restraints for the prevention of such conduct."[48]

Divergent manager perceptions influenced legislative policy. Virtually all managers probably assumed that individual moral responsibility should determine liability. And no doubt both groups of managerial opinion understood clearly the connection between public

relations and competition. But some directors counted on the railroad's sheer economic importance to offset the threat of critical public opinion, while others sought to turn this concern to their own advantage by presenting themselves as friends of the public, acknowledging that railroads should share responsibility for improved safety conditions. Furthermore, despite conciliatory talk and emphasis upon moral uplift, a compelling motive behind the compromisers' position was likely little different from that of the Camden and Amboy's directors: an overriding preoccupation with potential pecuniary issues. Nevertheless, the difference in attitudes is important. It showed that the political influence of railroad executives upon lawmakers was divided, which in turn created tensions in the fashioning of policy. It also suggests that at least some managers, in keeping with moral and constitutional values of accountability, accepted a partial liability for accidents in order to assuage public opinion. Among railroad leaders themselves, then, the political constituency existed for an accommodating approach to policy making.[49]

Moreover, railroad employees had reason to look upon the law's treatment of accident liability with mixed emotions. As state reports demonstrated, railroad operation placed employees in constant danger, frequently causing maiming or death. Of course a worker's ability to recover damages was further limited by the fellow-servant rule. The availability of local attorneys relying upon contingency fees opened up for workers the possibility of legal action in accident cases; several considerations, however, could discourage an employee from going this route. Since producer values (which embodied a conception of risk rooted in the experience of the small shop or farm) and evangelical Protestant morality recognized a high degree of individual accountability, it was not surprising that trial courts scrutinizing particular cases at times would find employees at fault. And apparently employees who declined litigation and depended upon the potentially arbitrary local railroad supervisors got more money than those who won in the courts. Furthermore, a suit could disrupt any favoritism or sympathy inherent in the supervisory system and thus would threaten the workers' chances of receiving voluntary gratuities from employers.[50] The fact that only irregularly and infrequently would railroads remove workers who had been involved in accidents likely reinforced these considerations.[51]

But a potent political concern also may have encouraged workers to

be wary of lawmakers' involvement with the accident problem. In striking contrast to railroads in England, American managers were generally unable to impose upon railroad employees a fining system. Fines were fundamental to the system of discipline on English roads; a certain percentage of wages was withheld from an employee's pay for such rule infractions as recklessness or intoxication. Moreover, Parliament enacted laws that made violation of the railroad's private rules a criminally enforceable offense. American managers lamented that state and federal governments denied them such power. And even though laws did make carelessness or drunkenness resulting in accidents criminal offenses, the measures did not create a managerially sponsored, state-sanctioned discipline program. Railroad workers voted, possessed acknowledged political power, and even organized effectively in antebellum America. Yet when it came to mobilizing political support to improve safety conditions on railroads, railroadmen apparently acquiesced to narrowly focused legislation that punished only negligent, accident-causing conduct.[52] Perhaps this was because railroad employees feared that greater politization of the safety issue might eventually result in a comprehensive, state-enforced discipline system on the scale of England's.

In response to these pressures legislatures sought to distribute the costs of and responsibility for improved safety. In a few instances a state such as Maryland imposed sanctions that made railroads absolutely liable for negligently caused accidents.[53] Generally, however, legislators implemented standards intended to limit accidents by reducing the human error that was believed to be their primary cause. If moral culpability was the chief source of the problem, contemporaries believed, heightened individual attention could eradicate it. Thus states enacted laws that demanded of both railroads and the general public a higher standard of care in their relations with each other. Railroads were bound to use lights and whistles, to slow down, and to install gates and watchmen at crossings; they were required to publish regular reports, safety regulations, and accounts of accidents, to adopt the telegraph, construct double tracks, regularize schedules, build footpaths along rails, and punish employees who consumed alcoholic beverages on the job. At the same time, farmers were expected to fence in livestock near railroad tracks. Under certain circumstances strangers were designated as trespassers if they suffered injuries or

death while standing near, around, or upon the rails, though this often did not remove liability for a railroad's culpable conduct in such cases. Laws also required companies to maintain a safe, comfortable environment for passengers, recognizing that conditions appropriate for an "able-bodied man, might be altogether insufficient . . . [for] a lady, a child, or an infirm person." Conversely, passengers were expected to "use all reasonable prudence" while on board trains or otherwise present upon railroad property.[54]

Evangelical Protestant, constitutional, and producer values reflected in statutory standards provided, then, a protective orientation to railroad safety policy which facilitated public and capitalist accountability. Lawmakers rejected the claim that because they contributed significantly to economic development railroads should be virtually exempt from accident liability. Neither were American legislatures willing to follow the English example by establishing comprehensive safety systems under the control of centralized governmental administration. Instead, American law placed the responsibility for avoiding accidents upon the individual citizen, employee, or corporate manager. Through disciplined moral character and enlightened public opinion, railroad managers, workers, passengers, and the general public could together protect life and property from human error.

Theoretically everyone was accountable for failing to achieve this goal: ultimately, however, the law held railroad managers and workers to a higher standard of care than the general public. Fencing in livestock, making strangers trespassers, and requiring prudent conduct of passengers did not diminish the "higher duty" imposed upon railroad managers to implement and maintain new safety procedures and thereby to protect the public from harm. Compliance with legislative policy increased the railroads' fixed costs, which in the competitive antebellum environment was a significant economic factor.[55] One group of managerial opinion, hoping to limit these costs by creating a safer, more predictable business environment, advocated moderate government action. The fellow-servant rule also imposed a disproportionate liability upon workers, though informal welfare measures, comparatively high wages, local supervisory control, and above all the lack of a state-enforced discipline system may have mitigated this burden. Thus, statutory law was one component of an accommodationist policy underlying negligence doctrines; the common law was another.

### Policy Impact: The Courts

The case of *The Pennsylvania Railroad* vs. *Catharine G. Ogier* in the Chester County court of common pleas indicated how antebellum trial judges and juries meted out justice. At a dangerous intersection of a public road and railroad tracks, a locomotive smashed into Dr. Septimus A. Ogier and his wagon as he attempted to cross. Ogier was killed, whereupon his widow sued the railroad charging the company with negligence. The company's attorneys argued that Ogier's own conduct had contributed to the accident, freeing the railroad from responsibility. Numerous witnesses gave conflicting testimony concerning whether Ogier or the railroad was negligent. Under these circumstances the judge's charge was crucial in influencing the verdict of the jury. "Where," asked the judge, "was the negligence which occasioned this fatal collision?" The standard for negligence was "such care *as men of common sense and common prudence ordinarily exercised, in like employments*." In applying this standard, the judge said, the jury must strike a balance: "The Railroad Company, notwithstanding their right to travel along and over their road, were bound to exercise due care and diligence, in the use thereof, and Dr. Ogier, although on a road whereupon he had a right to travel, was also under the obligation of duty so to exercise his right as not to interfere with the rights of others." Following the judge's charge, the jury gave a verdict for the widow of $10,250. The Supreme Court of Pennsylvania sustained the verdict on appeal.[56]

The *Ogier* case suggested how lower courts interpreted and applied the negligence principle. The judge's instructions left to the jury the determination of responsibility for the accident. The standards governing the jury judgment depended upon its perception of the meaning of "due care and diligence" and "common sense and common prudence," which in turn was rooted in Protestant moral assumptions and the experience of living in a producer-oriented economy. The social composition of the jury and local institutional factors involving the role of the bar also no doubt influenced the verdict. In terms of policy, these factors resulted in a judgment which shifted from Mrs. Ogier to the railroad the economic costs of the accident. The outcome in *Ogier* was not atypical, but the interplay of interests and values shaping such results was nonetheless complex.[57]

Coroner jury verdicts suggested that popular attitudes did not uni-

formly favor unqualified railroad liability. Throughout the nineteenth century investigation of accidents was crude; only occasionally were inquiries made that went beyond those conducted by the coroner's inquests, panels of local citizens called by the sheriff or justice of the peace. The jurors were charged with determining what happened, why, and who, if anyone, was responsible. A typical coroner's verdict resulted from an accident occurring in 1855 involving the Camden and Amboy Railroad. There were twenty-four deaths and eighty wounded after the train backed into a horse and wagon crossing the tracks. The inquest concluded that the driver of the wagon had failed to exercise "due diligence," while the train's engineer and other employees had failed to observe the company's and the state of New Jersey's safety regulations. The jury urged that the state establish more effective safety measures governing the public's access over the tracks and the railroad's operation along its road.[58] In another case John Caffray was crossing Green Street in Jersey City one evening. A railroad's employees were switching cars in the area "by means of a switch rope attached to the engine." When Caffray attempted to cross behind the engine, he fell over the rope, "wheels passed over his arms, crushing and breaking the collar in several places," and he died of his injuries. The jury censured the railroad for not lighting the street better where the accident occurred and for not having a watchman stationed there to warn of the danger. In another incident Eugene McCarthy, a passenger attempting to get on a moving train, caught his foot, was thrown down, and the train rolled over him. McCarthy died shortly thereafter, but the coroner's inquiry exonerated the company from all blame. A passenger leaning out of the window of a train leaving the station hit one of the posts supporting the roof of the depot, resulting in the passenger's death. The coroner's jury exonerated the company from all blame but condemned the depot as a nuisance.[59]

Other factors complicated the assessments of coroner juries. A jury did not hold the railroad liable when, coming around a curve, one of its engines struck and killed instantly a man walking on the tracks who was later found to have been "deaf and dumb."[60] The New Jersey state accident reports show that injury or death involving someone who was intoxicated virtually always, absolved the company of blame.[61] James O'Brian, stated one such report, in attempting to jump upon a rapidly moving car "had his arm taken off" and died, "repeatedly lamenting, that his own carelessness and intoxication" had caused the

tragedy.[62] In another case John Smith "while intoxicated" left from a rear door of a train waiting on a bridge rather than from the passenger exit and fell many feet to his death. Both the coroner and Smith's friends "deemed an inquest unnecessary."[63] The difficulties of assigning responsibility became further involved when acts of heroism by railroad employees intervened, as when an unknown man walking on a track saw a train coming and tried to avoid danger by jumping to a parallel track but was struck by an engine coming from the opposite direction. A fireman on the forward section of one of the trains saved the injured man's life by pulling him onto the engine.[64]

Common-law juries, too, apparently sought to balance the interests of railroads and injured citizens. A report of the Philadelphia, Wilmington, and Baltimore Railroad declared in 1858: "Railroads perform a service to the community, valuable beyond all price, and yet, the watchful care which has transported millions in safety, by night and day, is forgotten when one out of these millions is injured by his own carelessness. Many of the Courts of justice countenance the most unreasonable demands upon Railroads, and allow juries to render the most unjust verdicts." Tempering the company's exasperation, however, was a discernible trend favoring a more balanced treatment. "A better day . . . seems to be dawning," the report continued; "some of the Courts have had the independence to give proper instructions to juries, and the justice to set aside unreasonable verdicts." "A few more such examples," the report concluded, "will do much toward preventing accidents, by teaching the community that they too are bound to exercise a reasonable care, and that they cannot recover damages from Railroads where accidents are the result of their own carelessness."[65]

The railroads' defeat in local courts was not, therefore, inevitable. The interplay of institutional factors, cultural values, and the particular facts of a case could result in a verdict favoring capitalist enterprise. This suggested that trial judges and juries took seriously their duty to do justice in a given case. But what was the essence of such justice? Did the judge's instructions governing the law and the jury's application of these to the facts represent only a quest for fundamental fairness? Or were courts, like the legislature, responding to conflicting social and cultural pressures, the resolution of which ultimately spread the human and economic costs of accidents among different interests? Appellate court litigation provides some answers to these questions.

Appellate cases were exceptional, comprising only a small proportion of the total railroad accident litigation before 1860. Furthermore, antebellum law often did not, according to James Kent's *Commentaries*, "press too strongly the doctrine of *stare decisis*." Consequently, trial courts could distinguish a suit from those governed by the precedents of higher tribunals, and appellate judges might do the same in cases coming before them.[66] "So long as the struggle between precedent and reason shall continue," wrote the *North American Review*, "legal opinions . . . will depend more on the character and turn of mind of the judge, who is to decide it, than any general principle."[67] This prevailing discretionary approach to decision making encouraged the diverse results noted by the Philadelphia, Wilmington, and Baltimore Railroad report.

Considerations of litigation strategy also diminished the significance of appellate litigation. Railroad lawyers did not take appeals except in very carefully selected cases. The railroad not only declined to appeal suits it had a strong chance of losing; it also would not appeal even a strong case if there was a likelihood that an unfavorable precedent might be established. If there was no precedent, the railroad's position was stronger than the plaintiff's because the pressure was on the individual's lawyer to settle. Nevertheless, as railroad executives and Pool's *Journal* noted, despite important instances to the contrary, juries tended to give verdicts against the railroad.

Still, an appellate decision determined the ultimate outcome in that particular case, so an examination of a number of appellate opinions can reveal whether any general patterns emerge from accident litigation as a whole. In Delaware, Maryland, New Jersey, and Pennsylvania between 1845 and 1860 appellate courts decided approximately forty railroad negligence cases. There were six discernible categories of accidents: those involving railroad employees, passengers, livestock on tracks, strangers crossing tracks, property (other than livestock on tracks), and the railroad as a nuisance. Of these 40 percent concerned property,[68] 22.5 percent concerned passengers,[69] 15 percent concerned crossings,[70] 12.5 percent concerned livestock,[71] 0.05 percent concerned employees,[72] and 0.05 percent concerned nuisances.[73] When it came to winning or losing, the railroad lost as often as it won—with twenty decisions for and twenty against. But the comparison of win/lose by category was perhaps more useful in determining whether there were noticeable patterns. Passengers won 70 percent[74] of the time, and

courts upheld property rights over the railroad's interests in 56 per-cent[75] of the cases; but the railroad won whenever a collision occurred between a train and livestock wandering on the rails.[76] The crossing cases split evenly[77] furthermore, when the railroad was a nuisance it did not win;[78] conversely, in the employee litigation the worker lost both times.[79]

In railroad accident cases mid-Atlantic appellate judges thus were not single-mindedly preoccupied with capitalist welfare and develop-ment. The courts sought instead to strike some balance between de-velopmental concerns and the public's desire for safety. Anyone aware of recent Pennsylvania decisions "on questions between railroad com-panies and those whom they have injured in person or property," as an opinion of that state's high court in 1859 read, knew that the judges accepted "no excuse" from those who "obstructed tracks" or otherwise interfered with a company's operation. But at the same time the court held railroads bound to "transport safely."[80]

Priorities were implicit in this balancing. Judges held railroads firmly accountable for passenger safety; only where harm clearly re-sulted from their own fault did passengers lose. Similarly, appellate tribunals had virtually no sympathy for railroads that created a public nuisance. In the crossing cases the courts favored neither railroads nor a particular social group, suggesting that their overriding goal was the attainment of impartial justice. Courts held livestock raisers rather than railroads liable in the livestock collision litigation, yet precisely whose interests the judges were most concerned about here was am-biguous; they may have wanted to protect passengers from collisions as much as they sought to reduce the railroads' liability.[81] The em-ployee cases seemed unequivocal enough: in the mid-Atlantic states, if a railroad worker's actions resulted in an accident, he almost certainly lost. Since so few cases involved workers, however, the policy implica-tion of these decisions was unclear. Without doubt mid-Atlantic judges, reflecting both producer and evangelical Protestant values, believed employees should be accountable for negligent conduct. But the appellate courts so rarely had the opportunity to enforce this judgment that the cost benefits gained by railroads from such anti-worker doctrines as the fellow-servant rule were minimal. Jury ver-dicts were generally sympathetic to railroad workers, but perhaps more importantly, railroads often treated their employees better than did the courts. Ultimately, then, beyond an apparent willingness to

enforce the cultural values of the time, the broader ramifications of the courts' antilabor decisions are problematic.[82]

Thus in the adjudication of accident cases appellate judges wanted both to do justice and to enforce managerial responsibility for safety. Unquestionably the courts were also concerned about the railroads' economic welfare, but not to the point of repudiating these other values and interests. The property damage litigation further suggests what goals the judges wanted to achieve from their balancing policy. Of sixteen cases the largest proportion, five, involved the question whether railroads should pay for nonfire damage to property. In four suits, the next highest proportion, liability for property damaged by fire arising from locomotive sparks was at issue. In addition, two cases concerned liability for loss of slaves, two involved harm to livestock being carried by railroads, two dealt with the railroad's culpability for damage to mills on streams, and one concerned a father's right to recover for the loss of his son's labor services. The railroad lost three of the five nonfire cases,[83] both of the livestock freight suits,[84] split even in both the mill[85] and slave litigation,[86] won three of the four fire cases,[87] and had to pay the father for the lost labor of his son.[88] Support for capitalist developmental enterprise nullified, therefore, neither the judges' commitment to justice nor their desire to maintain managerial accountability.

The few accident cases arising in federal court usually involved stagecoaches. But the liability standard was like that which state courts applied in railroad litigation. In two Ohio federal circuit court suits[89] and another case appealed to the Supreme Court from the circuit court sitting in Baltimore, jury charges held stagecoach company managers liable to injured passengers for the "least negligence, or want of skill, or prudence."[90] The company was liable if passenger injuries were "in any degree attributable to a want of skill or care" on the part of the firm or its employees. As the agent of the company the coach driver was bound to act "with the utmost prudence and caution."[91] Nevertheless, the company was obligated to pay the damages. In all three suits the jury followed the court's instructions, delivering a verdict against the company and requiring the payment of damages. In the Supreme Court case, the Court affirmed the same standard and jury verdict.[92]

One Supreme Court decision did hold a railroad's conduct to the same high standard of care. The management of a Philadelphia-based railroad invited stockholders to ride the train as guests. When one of

these nonpaying stockholders was injured, the company argued that it was liable only for the "grossest" negligence, which did not include individuals who had failed to purchase a ticket. Essentially, the railroad's argument was that any liability would have to be based on a contract represented by the purchase of a ticket. Since the stockholder had not entered into such a contract by tendering payment, the railroad owed him only the barest minimum of care. Justice Robert C. Grier of Pennsylvania rejected the contract claim in favor of the higher common-law tort standard. "When carriers undertake to convey persons by the powerful but dangerous agency of steam, public policy and safety require that they be held to the greatest possible care and diligence," Grier said. "And whether the consideration for such transportation be pecuniary or otherwise, the personal safety of the passengers should not be left to the sport of chance or the negligence of careless agents. Any negligence, in such cases, may well deserve the epithet of 'gross.' "[93]

Grier's decision upheld the railroad's liability, despite the claim that an employee's disobedience had caused the injury. The passengers' safety was of paramount importance. "Nothing but the most stringent enforcement of discipline, and the most exact and perfect obedience to every rule and order emanating from a superior, can insure safety to life and property." Accordingly, it was the company's duty to employ qualified workers; failure to do so was negligence itself. "The intrusting [of] such a powerful and dangerous engine as a locomotive, to one who will not submit to control, and render implicit obedience to orders," was, Grier asserted, "itself an act of negligence." Indeed, shifting the liability from the company to workers would undercut the need for discipline that was the passengers' protection from harm. "If such disobedience could be set up by a railroad company as a defence, when charged with negligence, the remedy of the injured party would in most cases be illusive, discipline would be relaxed, and the danger to life and limb of the traveller greatly enhanced." Thus Grier concluded, "Any relaxation of the stringent policy and principles of the law affecting such cases, would be highly detrimental to the public safety."[94]

In deciding accident suits antebellum appellate and trial judges exercised wide discretion. Juries' commitment to local control, combined with the likelihood that railroads could as easily lose as win on appeal, meant that the courts' balancing policy often did not favor

corporate capitalism. Judges, responding to diverse political pressures and cultural imperatives, often favored protectionist policies, placing passenger safety, property rights, and equity above the developmental interests that railroads represented. The judiciary placed a heavy burden on workers, though such inequalities were consistent with discretionary judicial action that defended producer and evangelical moral values.

In the mid-Atlantic states before the Civil War, moral and constitutional accountability and protectionism rather than a zeal for capitalist promotion alone were the guiding principles of railroad accident law. Lawmakers, leading spokesmen for the industry such as Poor's *Journal*, and railroad executives expressed the conviction that everyone was liable for damage, injury, or death resulting from human error and misconduct. As the law of negligence evolved, it imposed upon the general public a duty to avoid reckless behavior. But consistent with the constitutional values of legitimacy and accountability inherent in the grant of a public franchise, railroad managers and workers were held to a higher standard. Public safety regulations raised operational expenses just when competition and state control of rates limited the railroads' ability to pass these costs along to consumers and shippers. Divisions among railroad executives undercut the united front that was necessary in order to bring about changes in the law. In addition, the law encouraged a dual market for the services of lawyers, which further undercut group solidarity. Unquestionably workers suffered unfairly; but the railroads' own personnel practices, combined with their failure to establish a legally enforceable discipline system, partially offset this burden. Thus cultural values and producer interests checked corporate capitalism and preserved the apparent interdependency of moral and constitutional values.

# Epilogue

On the last day of May, 1860, Justice Peter V. Daniel, Virginian and Supreme Court justice, died. Born just three years before the drafting of the Constitution, Daniel spent a public career off and on the Court defending the agrarian way of life associated with Thomas Jefferson. He resisted unswervingly the commercial and corporate values and interests identified with the emergent capitalism of his day. For him, state sovereignty was the foundation of the Constitution and federal "consolidation" was an unmitigated evil. Daniel opposed national authority in large part because too often it was turned to the advantage of the capitalist classes he abhorred. During his middle age the agents of the Bank of the United States drove him nearly to ruin. Characteristically, he told fellow Democrat and friend President Martin Van Buren, "Damn the contemptible slaves of the Bank, I put them all at defiance." Daniel's intense conviction that the Bank represented not just one institution but a morally wrong style of life endured beyond the grave. Concerned for the welfare of his two small children, Daniel in his will recognized the need to convert his largest asset, real estate, into state bonds. The will categorically excluded such conver-

sion, however, into the "stocks or bonds of banks, railroads, or corporations or joint stock companies of any kind."[1]

Daniel's faith in a producer's way of life as distinguishable from one following capitalist values is suggestive. Unquestionably, as a justice the force of his views resulted in a frequency of dissents which made him the Court's most antibusiness, pro–states' rights advocate. Yet the ideological complexities inherent in that position were indicated by the fact that he joined the majority of his fellow Jacksonian Democrats in unanimously supporting the Whiggish Joseph Story's decision of *Swift* v. *Tyson* (1842). Future commentators have concluded that Story's extension of federal judicial authority over the negotiable contracts of commercial credit epitomized the Supreme Court's defense and promotion of mercantile capitalism. What this characterization ignores, however, is the degree to which the producer economy's use of credit differed from that of the corporate and mercantile capitalists'. The slaveholding planter Daniel viewed credit in terms of more personal market relations that, according to Eugene D. Genovese, were not capitalistic.[2] Thus, he went along with Story not because the two shared an underlying liberal capitalist consensus, but because producers needed to counter the capitalists' advantage.

Daniel's complex contribution to the Court has still wider implications. The popular scholarly presumption that the operation of the antebellum constitutional system, especially the Supreme Court, reflected the dominant liberal capitalist consensus leads to the conclusion that ultimately Daniel and the agents of the "monster" Bank he so hated agreed on basic market values. Put another way, the consensus argument assumes that in the core values of such private institutions as the church or the family, Daniel and his antagonists shared essentially the same cultural beliefs toward economic opportunity and obligation. One may have been an agrarian capitalist and the other a corporate or mercantile capitalist. But because they both accepted the primacy of private property and contract rights, the distinction represented merely a matter of degree. Thus individuals like Daniel fulminated against evils—privilege, monopoly, aristocracy, federal intervention—but within their souls they did not differentiate themselves from corporate executives and mercantile speculators. This was true, the logic of the consensus argument goes, of one justice's personal career struggle, it was true of the Court of which he was a member, and it was true of the entire constitutional order that he took an oath to defend.

This work offers another way of thinking about antebellum constitutionalism and capitalism. Relying as it does upon a case study format which considers in depth only a four-state region and just four broad areas of policy making, its conclusions must be regarded as preliminary at best. Despite these limitations, it may be useful to state more boldly my purpose, interpretation, and findings. A central goal has been to develop an analytical framework which takes seriously the point of view of people like Daniel and his opponents. Accordingly, I have placed the mid-Atlantic materials and the more well known elements of constitutional history, such as political party struggles involving federalism or the Marshall and Taney Courts, in the context of recent studies of social and cultural history. A focus of these studies has been the formal and informal institutions by which the small producers' attachment to independence eventually was amalgamated with liberal capitalist values of a more individualistic independence to form free-labor ideals. I have suggested that antebellum constitutionalism furthered this process of cultural accommodation.

In order to gain a clearer impression of constitutionalism's accommodationist role, reference to Daniel again may be helpful. Central to capitalism's emerging dominance was its disruption of the personal independence tied to locally oriented associational market relationships identified with the family household economy that Daniel's plantation, Crow's Nest, represented. In addition, his views of acceptable and unacceptable business conduct were consistent with the social and market reciprocity prevailing in his home community of Stafford County, Virginia. "Soulless" corporations and "foreign" big merchants thus threatened the private institutions and personal relations closest to Daniel. As a result, it was not difficult for him to believe that he and they were irreconcilably opposed.

Daniel nonetheless struggled to protect his way of life through law and constitutional interpretation. He and his opponents thus relied upon the same institutional process. But the willingness of both sides to confront each other in formal constitutional and legal channels did not mean that the economic values driving the conflict shared a fundamental consensus. Surely the producer class to which Daniel belonged felt too much threatened to believe that it was merely the consequences of the tendencies of capitalism which put them at risk. At the same time, the corporate and mercantile capitalists' ever-growing dominance rested upon legally and constitutionally sanctioned priv-

ileges and advantages. If the capitalists used the constitutional order to diminish the producers' independence, it was reasonable for members of the producer class to seek protective policies from that same constitutional order. Jackson's veto of the second Bank of the United States indicated symbolically and in practical terms that by working through the system, producers like Daniel could win. The Supreme Court's sustaining of the states' police power under the commerce and contract clauses gave producers further cause for faith in the ideals of constitutionalism.

As Michael Kammen has observed, the Constitution's symbolic and working meaning emerged gradually before the Civil War. The Federalists and Anti-Federalists eventually agreed (though for different reasons) that the nation's prosperity depended on ratifying the Constitution. Prosperity for whom and of what sort nonetheless engendered repeated conflict within the federal judiciary and the political parties that controlled the state and federal governments. The public discourse of party leaders was consistent with the ideas of political economists who accepted the fact that producers were the most important electoral constituency in a tripartite social structure including capitalists, producers, and dispossessed paupers. The social fragmentation dividing the interests supporting capitalist and producer values contributed to the politicians' search for policy compromises on both the federal and state levels. American federalism was so new, however, that social and ideological struggles heightened the significance of constitutional controversies. Over the long run the outcome was that the states rather than the federal government were principally responsible for promoting or protecting the values and interests of both producers and mercantile and corporate capitalists.

The Supreme Court and the federal judiciary it led also facilitated social and ideological accommodation. The Court under Marshall and Taney interpreted the contract, commerce, and judicial clauses to sustain property and contract rights. Throughout the antebellum period, however, political resistance from Congress and the states forced the Court to employ an extratextualist technique, code words, an evolving principle of original intent, and institutional secrecy in support of the theory that the judiciary merely found and declared law. While these devices deflected criticism, the process circumscribed the federal judiciary's independence. Within these limitations the Court's decision making sustained a broad police power and the state's pri-

mary role in the economic order. In order to preserve judicial independence, the federal judiciary thus formally sanctioned the process of accommodation occurring on the state level. As a result, the Court took a leading role in the cultural amalgamation of liberal and republican ideologies and the capitalist and producer values they embodied.

Daniel's public career suggests how constitutionalism contributed to the process of cultural accommodation. Daniel was a member of first the Old Republican Richmond Junto and then the new Jacksonian Democrat regime that controlled antebellum Virginia's politics. As a Jeffersonian and Jacksonian party activist, he espoused John Taylor's defense of producers against the threat of capitalist values. Like Taylor, for example, Daniel as a matter of principle opposed banks. He nonetheless once supported state-controlled banks, especially in opposition to the Bank of the United States. Although political opportunism was undoubtedly involved, his position drew upon the larger principle of state sovereignty. Accordingly, Daniel accommodated producer and capitalist values within an institutional framework of state authority. Accommodation of what he regarded as contrary values and interests was possible only through the instrumentality of local government, including juries, which could be counted on to protect producers.

On the Supreme Court, Daniel compromised his principles rarely if at all. Yet his rigid states' rights stance in cases involving the contract and commerce clauses and federal jurisdiction drove Taney and other Jacksonian members of the Court toward a more moderate conception of the states' police powers which emphasized the regulation of corporate and mercantile capitalism. State governments could satisfy the demands of both producers and capitalists and at the same time protect the weaker from the stronger. The reliance upon regulation thus permitted a degree of policy flexibility which encouraged the process of cultural accommodation.

Central to the accommodationist function of these constituent constitutional institutions was a fundamental constitutional ideal. The familiar principle of checks and balances incorporated a number of core values including local control, legitimacy, and accountability. More abstractly, the principle could be translated into the ideal that no center of private or public power was legitimate unless it was accountable to some external authority. On the level of working federalism, the values inherent in the constitutional ideal conditioned the conflicts

channeled through political parties; federal, state, and local popular governments; and the federal judiciary. Politically this meant that the legitimacy of a given economic policy depended upon the extent to which it seemed to be accountable to public authority and even other private groups. As producers and corporate or mercantile capitalists appealed to the constitutional ideal, economic policies resulted favoring both sides, thus furthering the accommodation of opposing values and interests.

Ironically, the producers' appeals to the constitutional ideal ultimately encouraged the triumph of capitalism. The political parties' and the Supreme Court's general deference to local control resulted in state legislative and judicial policies that protected the producers' values and interests through laws favoring debtors, the taxation of merchants and corporations, a process of taking property which largely depended on local implementation, and doctrines of accident liability that gave much weight to moralistic concerns. These and other policies effectively held big merchants and corporations accountable to local governmental institutions such as juries and to community standards of individual responsibility. The effect of successfully enforcing the constitutional value of accountability, however, was that corporate and mercantile privileges received constitutional legitimation. While this sanction of power was constitutionally limited, it reinforced national market advantages that in the long run were too strong for more locally oriented market relations to resist. By the 1850s the process was sufficiently advanced that the values of personal independence rooted in the traditional producer economy increasingly were amalgamated with capitalist values in a new order premised on free labor.

Daniel's response to the rise of free-labor ideals was characteristically defiant. Increasingly dominated by capitalist values, the North by 1850 was, he believed, incapable of producing "any thing" that was "good and decent." As for a society based on the free-labor ideology, he could "scarcely imagine a greater slavery, or any condition more absolutely vulgar, unrefined and unrefining than the scuffle and the selfish contention" it engendered in even the most mundane affairs of life.[3] Ultimately, such views reflected, as Genovese has argued, a noncapitalist worldview which was consistent with traditional producer values. Throughout his public career Daniel fought for constitutional interpretations intended to protect that world and those values. Finally, of course, the conflict between free and slave labor could not

be contained within the constitutional order, and Daniel, like most southerners, supported secession. In light of Daniel's commitment to core constitutional values of local control, legitimacy, and accountability, the failure to protect the producers' world contributed to the tragic conflict.

The mid-Atlantic region occupied the borderland between the world Daniel loved and the one he came to hate. Possessing a traditional producer economy which did not depend upon the evil of slavery, the states that have been the focus of this study were more ready to accommodate free-labor ideals. Even so, in Henry C. Carey's "harmony of interests" the need for government intervention to defend small-scale, locally oriented, unincorporated enterprise looked backward to a protectionist policy making role based on appeals to the constitutional ideal, which benefited producers. Thus, the traditional American faith in constitutionalism influenced the accommodation of producer values to the triumph of capitalism.

NOTES

INDEX

# NOTES

## Prologue

1. Forrest McDonald, *Novus Ordo Seclorum: The Intellectual Origins of the Constitution* (Lawrence, Kan., 1985); Michael Kammen, *A Machine That Would Go of Itself: The Constitution in American Culture* (New York, 1987), esp. 6, 23, 43–127, 228; Charles Grove Haines, *The Role of the Supreme Court in American Government and Politics, 1789–1835* (Berkeley, Cal., 1944).

2. R. Kent Newmyer, *The Supreme Court under Marshall and Taney* (New York, N.Y., 1968).

3. James M. McPherson, *Battle Cry of Freedom: The Civil War Era* (New York, 1988), 14; Allan Kulikoff, *The Agrarian Origins of American Capitalism* (Charlottesville, Va., 1992), 109.

4. Kulikoff, *Agrarian Origins*, 109.

5. Kammen, *Machine*, 43–127; G. Edward White, *The Marshall Court and Cultural Change, 1815–1835* (New York, 1991).

6. John Ashworth, *"Agrarians" and "Aristocrats": Party Political Ideology in the United States, 1837–1846* (London, 1983); John Ashworth, "The Jeffersonians: Classical Republicans or Liberal Capitalists?" *Journal of American Studies* 18 (1984): 430; Drew R. McCoy, *The Elusive Republic: Political Economy in Jeffersonian America* (Chapel Hill, N.C., 1980); Sean Wilentz, *Chants Democratic: New York City and the Rise of the American Working Class, 1788–1850* (New York, 1984); Eric Foner, *Free Soil, Free Labor, Free Men: The Ideology of the Republican Party before the Civil War* (New York, 1975), 19–20, 36–39. But see Jonathan A. Glickstein, *Concepts of Free Labor in Antebellum America* (New Haven, Conn., 1991).

7. McPherson, *Battle Cry*, 26; for the problems defining producer see Stuart M. Blumin, *The Emergence of the Middle Class: Social Experience in the American City, 1760–1900* (Cambridge, Eng., 1989), 1–17.

8. Paul Conkin, *Prophets of Prosperity: America's First Political Economists* (Bloomington, Ind., 1980), 6.

9. Ibid., 7. See also Millard Schumaker, *Sharing without Reckoning* (Waterloo, Ontario, 1992).

10. Conkin, *Prophets*, 12, and definitions of *capitalist* and *capitalism*, 23–24, 44, 58, 59, 60–61, 118–19, 156–58, 192–94, 252–53.

11. See ibid. for the following discussion of antebellum political economists.

12. As quoted, White, *Marshall Court and Cultural Change*, 66.

13. Conkin, *Prophets*, 281.

14. Ibid., and compare Glickstein, *Concepts of Free Labor*.

15. References for this and following paragraphs are notes 6, 7, 9, 10 above.

16. McPherson, *Battle Cry*, 15; and note 9.

17. Notes 1, 2, 5 above.

18. James Willard Hurst, *Law and Markets in United States History: Different Modes of Bargaining among Interests* (Madison, Wis., 1982), 97–98; see also White, *Marshall Court and Cultural Change*.

19. Daniel Walker Howe, "Victorian Culture in America," in Howe, ed., *Victorian America* (Philadelphia, 1976), 3–28, is an introduction to a large literature.

20. See especially chap. 2 below. My idea of associational market relations draws upon Schumaker, *Sharing without Reckoning*, and Carey's economic theory.

## 1. Constitutionalism, Capitalism, Antebellum Society

1. McDonald, *Novus Ordo Seclorum*, is an excellent introduction to a large literature.

2. See generally James Willard Hurst, *Law and the Conditions of Freedom in the Nineteenth-Century United States* (Madison, Wis., 1967); Kermit L. Hall, *The Magic Mirror: Law in American History* (New York, 1989), 9–128; Lawrence M. Friedman, *A History of American Law* (New York, 1985), 105–202, 230–570; Tony Allan Freyer, *Forums of Order: The Federal Courts and Business in American History* (Greenwich, Conn., 1979), 1–98.

3. The distinction between local and national market relations as it relates to emergent capitalism is implicit in the references cited in note 2 above. Its analytical significance is suggested more directly in Herbert Hovenkamp, *Enterprise and American Law, 1836–1937* (Cambridge, Mass., 1991), 79–92; McPherson, *Battle Cry*, 9–37. For the significance of federalism, see Harry N. Scheiber, "Federalism and the American Economic Order, 1789–1910," *Law and Society Review* 10 (1975): 57–118.

4. The relation of the Supreme Court to capitalism and its relation to slavery issues and antebellum constitutionalism generally are discussed in a rich and diverse literature to a certain extent summarized in the works cited in note 2 above. A good introduction to the Court under Marshall and Taney remains Newmyer, *Marshall and Taney*. See also Hovenkamp, *Enterprise and American Law*; Carl B. Swisher, *The Taney Period, 1836–1864* (New York, 1974); White, *Marshall Court and Cultural Change*; Haines, *Role of Supreme Court, 1789–1835*; Charles Grove Haines and Foster H. Sherwood, *The Role of the Supreme Court in American Government and Politics, 1835–1864* (Berkeley, Cal., 1957); Harold H. Hyman and William M. Wiecek, *Equal Justice under Law: Constitutional Development, 1835–1875* (New York, 1982), 1–202.

5. McPherson, *Battle Cry*, 33–42; Friedman, *History of American Law*, 202–29; Hall, *Magic Mirror*, 129–67; Joan Hoff, *Law, Gender, and Justice: A Legal History of U.S. Women* (New York, 1991).

6. Kammen, *Machine*, 3–126, esp. 20, 158.

7. Hurst, *Law and Markets*, 96–98. Hurst has restated the principle in similar terms as applicable in various contexts; see Hurst, *Law and the Conditions of Freedom* 5, 6, 8, 9, 10; Hurst, *Law and Social Order in the United States* (Ithaca, N.Y., 1977), 28, 45, 49, 57–58, 67–81, 220, 242–43, 270. But see Morton J. Horwitz, *The Transformation of American Law, 1780–1860* (Cambridge, Mass., 1977).

8. Note 5 above.

9. Notes 2–4 above.

10. Note 7 above.

11. McPherson, *Battle Cry*, 26; Rush Welter, *The Mind of America, 1820–1860* (New York, 1975), 85–86; Kulikoff, *Agrarian Origins*, 43, 95; Glickstein, *Concepts of Free Labor*, 4–5, 314–16; Blumin, *Emergence of the Middle Class*, esp. 1–17; Wilentz, *Chants Democratic*; Foner, *Free Soil*.

12. On the significance of credit, see Freyer, *Forums of Order*, 1–52.

13. Notes 2, 4; Tony Freyer, *Harmony and Dissonance: The Swift and Erie Cases in American Federalism* (1981), 1–43; Tony Freyer, *Discretion and Dependence: A History of Alabama's Federal Courts* (Brooklyn, N.Y., forthcoming).

14. White, *Marshall Court and Cultural Change*, 11–156; note 4 above.

15. Notes 1, 4, 6, 7, 11 above.

16. As quoted, Kammen, *Machine*, 13, 55.

17. Ibid., 3–125; McDonald, *Novus Ordo Seclorum*.

18. Kammen, *Machine*, 67; notes 4, 6, 7 above.

19. Hurst, *Law and Markets*, 97, though Hurst's formulation of the constitutional ideal includes but extends beyond, in terms of American history, the antebellum period.

20. Ibid., as quoted, 115.

21. Note 4 above; see also Andrew C. McLaughlin, *The Courts, the Constitution, and Parties*, 111–88.

22. Notes 2, 3, 4 above; chaps. 2 and 3 below; James Willard Hurst, *The Legitimacy of the Business Corporation in the Law of the United States, 1780–1970* (Charlottesville, Va., 1970); Hurst, *Law and Markets*.

23. Freyer, *Forums of Order*, 1–52.

24. Ibid., esp., 11, 28–29; notes 4, 5 above; Kammen, *Machine*, 95–124.

25. Alexis de Tocqueville, *Democracy in America* (New York, 1969), 99, 143, 148, 149, 276; notes 4, 23 above.

26. Alexis de Tocqueville, *Democracy in America*, (New York, 1945, 2 vols.), 282–83; legal file 51, "In the District Court for the city and county of Philadelphia," "List of Jurors for December Term 1844" and ibid. for Sept. term, 1847 and *Grant* v. *Farnum* file, legal file 52, Judge John Cadwalader Papers, Historical Society of Pennsylvania; "Laws Relative to Debtors and Creditors," *Hunt's Merchants' Magazine* 2 (1840): 491–92; Friedman, *History of American Law*, 155–56, 399, 470–71, 484–85.

27. Ibid.; Freyer, *Harmony and Dissonance*, 109–10; Hugh Henry Brackenridge,

*Law Miscellanies: Containing an Introduction to the Study of the Law* (Philadelphia, 1814), 458, 558.

28. William H. DeForest, "Trial by Jury in Commercial Cases," *Hunt's* 35 (1856): 303.

29. R. Kent Newmyer, "Daniel Webster as Tocqueville's Lawyer: The *Dartmouth College* Case Again," *American Journal of Legal History* 11 (1967): 127–47; Friedman, *History of American Law*, 94–102, 303–22, 606–54.

30. Blumin, *Emergence of the Middle Class*, 5, 10, 12 and see esp. his discussion of producers at 8–9. But see Glickstein, *Concepts of Free Labor*, 4.

31. The linkages between constitutionalism and class-based political party involvement and the corresponding ideology are suggested in Wilentz, *Chants Democratic*, in relation to the Democratic party's antimonopoly crusade, and in Foner, *Free Soil*, concerning the anticapitalist strain in Republican party free labor ideology. But, again, see Glickstein, *Concepts of Free Labor*, 314–15 and, in the legal context, Horwitz, *Transformation*.

32. Chap. 2 below. See also Freyer, *Forums of Order*, 1–98.

33. Compare discussions in works cited in note 4 above to Scheiber, "Federalism," *Law and Society Review* 10 (1975): 57–118. See also Freyer, *Forums of Order*, 1–98, and Freyer, *Harmony and Dissonance*, 1–43.

34. Maurice G. Baxter, *The Steamboat Monopoly: Gibbons v. Ogden, 1824* (New York, 1972), 58–60, 76–118.

35. Newmyer, *Marshall and Taney*; Haines, *Role of Supreme Court, 1789–1835*; Haines and Sherwood, *Role of Supreme Court, 1835–1864*; Dwight Wiley Jessup, *Reaction and Accommodation: The United States Supreme Court and Political Conflict, 1809–1835* (New York, 1987); White, *Marshall Court and Cultural Change*. For the methodology employed to define "code words," see ibid., esp. 4–8.

36. See White, *Marshall Court and Cultural Change*, esp. 4–8, and compare Swisher, *Taney Period*.

37. Ibid. See also Freyer, *Harmony and Dissonance*, 1–43.

38. Ibid.

39. White, *Marshall Court and Cultural Change*, 1–156; note 11 above.

40. Ibid.

41. Notes 35, 36 and 37 above.

42. The following discussion draws extensively from H. Jefferson Powell, "The Original Understanding of Original Intent," *Harvard Law Review* 98 (1985): 885–948. Powell's thesis in the main is consistent with Kammen, *Machine*, 68–94 and McDonald, *Novus Ordo Seclorum*.

43. Powell, "Original Understanding," 888.

44. Ibid., 944–47; Kammen, *Machine*, 68–116.

45. As quoted, Kammen, *Machine*, 87–88.

46. Newmyer, *Marshall and Taney*, 27, 28, 64; Freyer, *Harmony and Dissonance*, 1–43; note 4 above.

47. 9 Wheaton 1 (1824); Baxter, *Steamboat Monopoly*.

48. 4 Wheaton 518 (1819); Francis N. Stites, *Private Interest and Public Gain* (Amherst, Mass., 1972). See generally works cited, note 4 above.

49. 4 Wheaton 316 (1819); note 4 above.

50. Note 4 above; Hovenkamp, *Enterprise and American Law*, 17–29.

51. 11 Peters 420 (1837); 16 Peters 1 (1842); Stanley I. Kutler, *Privilege and Creative Destruction: The Charles River Bridge Case* (New York, 1971); Freyer, *Harmony and Dissonance*, 4–43; Freyer, *Forums of Order*, 53–98.

52. "The Law of Debtor and Creditor in Louisiana," *Hunt's* 15 (1846): 71; "Bankrupt Law," ibid., 10 (1841): 27.

53. Kammen, *Machine*, 43–94; White, *Marshall Court and Cultural Change*, 11–156; Freyer, *Forums of Order*, 1–52; Freyer, *Harmony and Dissonance*, 4–43; R. Kent Newmyer, *Supreme Court Justice Joseph Story, Statesman of the Old Republic* (Chapel Hill, N.C., 1985).

54. Note 5 above; see also Hyman and Wiecek, *Equal Justice under Law*, 1–19, 86–202; Kermit Hall, W. W. Wiecck, and Paul Finkleman, *American Legal History: Cases and Materials* (New York, 1991), 32–33.

55. Note 11 above.

56. Tocqueville, *Democracy in America* (1945 ed.), 2:156–57; notes 2, 3 above; John E. Sawyer, "The Entrepreneur and the Social Order: France and the United States," in William Miller, ed., *Men in Business: Essays on the Historical Role of the Entrepreneur* (New York, 1962), 16–17.

57. Diane Lindstrom, *Economic Development in the Philadelphia Region, 1810–1850* (New York, 1978); Thomas C. Cochran, *Frontiers of Change: Early Industrialization in America* (New York, 1981); Burton W. Folsom III, *Urban Networks: The Economic and Social Order of the Lackawanna and Lehigh Valleys during Early Industrialization, 1850–1880* (Baltimore, 1981); Glenn Porter, ed., *Regional Economic History: The Mid-Atlantic Area since 1700* (Greenville, Wilmington, Del., 1975).

58. Allan Pred, *Urban Growth and City Systems in the United States, 1840–1860* (Cambridge, Mass., 1980), 7–9; Lindstrom, *Philadelphia Region*, 41–57; Clarence H. Danhof, "The Farm Enterprise: The Northern United States, 1820–1860s," *Research in Economics* 4 (1979): 127–91; Glenn Porter and Harold C. Livesay, *Merchants and Manufacturers: Studies in the Changing Structure of Nineteenth Century Marketing* (Baltimore, 1971), 1–13, 228–32; Cochran, *Frontiers*, 134; J. W. Lozier, "Rural Textile Mill Communities and the Transition to Industrialization in America, 1800–1840," *Regional Economic History Research Center Working Papers* 4, no. 4 (1980): 78–95; Bruce Laurie, *Working People of Philadelphia, 1800–1850* (Philadelphia, 1980); Walter Licht, "Labor and Capital and the American Community," *Journal of Urban History* 7 (1981): 223; Eugene D. Genovese, *The Political Economy of Slavery: Studies in the Economy and Society of the Slave South* (New York, 1967); Fred Bateman and Thomas Weiss, *A Deplorable Scarcity: The Failure of Industrialization in the Slave Economy* (Chapel Hill, N.C., 1981); McPherson, *Battle Cry*, 26; Welter, *Mind of America*, 85–86;

Kulikoff, *Agrarian Origins*, 43, 95; Glickstein, *Concepts of Free Labor*, 4–5, 315–16; Blumin, *Emergence of the Middle Class*, 1–17; Foner, *Free Soil*, 18–23, 36–37.

59. Peter J. Coleman, *Debtors and Creditors in America: Insolvency, Imprisonment for Debt, and Bankruptcy, 1607–1900* (Madison, Wis., 1974), 287.

60. Chaps. 2–5 below; see also note 11 above.

61. Stephen Simpson, *The Working Man's Manual* (Philadelphia, 1831), 147, 149, 155, 196–97.

62. James Rogers Sharp, *The Jacksonians versus the Banks: Politics in the States after the Panic of 1837* (New York, 1970), 1–49, 285–309; chap. 2 below; note 58 above. But see generally Welter, *Mind of America*.

63. Chap. 2 below; Freyer, *Forums of Order*, 1–98.

64. Ibid.

65. Simpson, *Working Man's Manual*, 96, 102; note 11 above.

66. Simpson, *Working Man's Manual*, 128–29, 130; chap. 2 below.

67. Note 11 above.

68. As quoted, McPherson, *Battle Cry*, 27; notes 65, 66 above; Foner, *Free Soil*, 21–23.

69. Glickstein, *Concepts of Free Labor*, 314–15; compare Foner, *Free Soil*, 21–23.

70. Wilentz, *Chants Democratic*; John Ashworth, *"Agrarians" and "Aristocrats,"* 1–2, 24–29; Ashworth, "The Jeffersonians," 430; see also McCoy, *Elusive Republic*.

71. Chaps. 2–5 below; and notes 6, 7 above.

72. Merritt Roe Smith, *Harpers Ferry Armory and the New Technology: The Challenge of Change* (Ithaca, N.Y., 1977), 23; Herbert G. Gutman, *Work Culture and Society in Industrializing America: Essays in American Working-Class and Social History* (New York, 1976), 258; Eugene S. Ferguson, "History and Historiography," in Otto Mayr and Robert C. Post, eds., *Yankee Enterprise: The Rise of the American System of Manufacturers* (Washington, D.C., 1981), 6–7; Tony A. Freyer, "Reassessing the Impact of Eminent Domain in Early American Economic Development," *Wisconsin Law Review* (1981): 1263–86.

73. Sharp, *Jacksonians versus the Banks*, 1–49, 285–305; notes 56, 61, 65, 69, 70 above.

74. Note 5 above; Kammen, *Machine*, 98–99.

75. Thomas L. Haskell, "Capitalism and the Origins of the Humanitarian Sensibility, Part 2," *American Historical Review* 90 (1985): 547–66; chaps. 2–5 below; Freyer, *Forums of Order*, 8–9; Tony A. Freyer, "Antebellum Commercial Law: Common Law Approaches to Secured Transactions," *Kentucky Law Journal* 70 (1982): 593–608.

76. Howe, "Victorian Culture in America," 2–28.

77. Ibid.; chap. 2 below.

78. Notes 26–29 above; Freyer, "Localism and Eminent Domain."

79. Daniel Walker Howe, *The Political Culture of American Whigs* (Chicago, 1979); Welter, *Mind of America*, 184–85, 242–43; note 11 above.

80. George M. Stephenson, *The Political History of the Public Lands from 1840 to 1862: From Pre-emption to Homestead* (New York, 1917), 44–65; Daniel Feller, *The Public Lands in Jacksonian Politics* (Madison, Wis., 1984), 185–88, 194–98; Hall, *Magic Mirror*, 89–93.

81. Freyer, *Forums of Order*, 1–98; Freyer, *Harmony and Dissonance*, 1–43; note 4 above.

82. Notes 5, 7 above; chaps. 2–5 below. See also the following representatives of a large literature: Tony A. Freyer, "Government and Early American Capitalism: An Interpretation," *Essays in Economic and Business History* 3 (1984): 184–205; Hall, *Magic Mirror*, 87–128; Friedman, *History of American Law*, 177–201, 230–79, 258–301, 412–86, 511–71; Robert A. Lively, "The American System: A Review Article," *Business History Review* 29 (1955): 81; Harry N. Scheiber, "Government and the Economy: Studies of the 'Commonwealth' Policy in Nineteenth-Century America," *Journal of Interdisciplinary History* 3 (1972): 135–51; Carter Goodrich, *Government Promotion of American Canals and Railroads, 1800–1890* (New York, 1960); Oscar Handlin and Mary Flug Handlin, *Commonwealth: A Study of the Role of Government in the American Economy: Massachusetts, 1774–1861* (Cambridge, Mass., 1969); Milton Heath, *Constructive Liberalism: The Role of the State in the Economic Development of Georgia to 1860* (Cambridge, Mass., 1954); Bray Hammond, *Banks and Politics in America from the Revolution to the Civil War* (Princeton, N.J., 1957); G. Herberton Evans, Jr., *Business Incorporation in the United States, 1800–1943* (New York, 1948); John William Cadman, Jr., *The Corporation in New Jersey: Business and Politics, 1791–1875* (Cambridge, Mass., 1949); Edward Chase Kirkland, *Men, Cities, and Transportation: A Study in New England History, 1820–1900*, 2 vols. (Cambridge, Mass., 1948); Harry N. Scheiber, *Ohio Canal Era: A Case Study of Government and the Economy, 1820–1861* (Athens, Ga., 1969); Louis Hartz, *Economic Policy and Democratic Thought: Pennsylvania, 1776–1860* (Cambridge, Mass., 1948); Hurst, *Law and Social Process in United States History* (Ann Arbor, Mich., 1960); Hurst, *Law and Economic Growth: The Legal History of the Wisconsin Lumber Industry* (Cambridge, Mass., 1964); Harry N. Scheiber, "The Road to *Munn*: Eminent Domain and the Concept of Public Purpose in the State Courts," *Perspectives in American History* 5 (1971): 329–404; Scheiber, "Property Law, Expropriation, and Resource Allocation by Government, 1789–1910," *Journal of Economic History* 33 (1973): 232–51; Horwitz, *Transformation*; Harry N. Scheiber, "Back to 'The Legal Mind'? Doctrinal Analysis and the History of Law," *Reviews in American History* 5 (1977): 463; Scheiber, "Regulation, Property Rights, and Definition of 'The Market': Law and the American Economy," *Journal of Economic History* 61 (1981): 173–81; Freyer, "Localism and Eminent Domain."

83. Hartz, *Economic Policy and Democratic Thought*; Philip Scranton, *Proprietary Capitalism: The Textile Manufacture at Philadelphia, 1800–1885* (New York, 1983); Cochran, *Frontiers*; Lindstrom, *Philadelphia Region*; Folsom, *Urban Networks*; Porter, *Regional Economic History: The Mid-Atlantic Area since 1700*; Whitman H. Ridgway, *Community Leadership in Maryland, 1790–1840* (Chapel Hill, N.C., 1979); Lee Ben-

son, "Philadelphia Elites and Economic Development: Quasi-Public Innovation during the First American Organizational Revolution, 1825–1861," *Regional Economic History Research Center Working Papers* 2 (1978): 25–54; C. K. Yearly, Jr., *Enterprise and Anthracite: Economics and Democracy in Schuykill County, 1820–1875* (Baltimore, 1961); Gary Lawson Browne, *Baltimore in the Nation, 1789–1861* (Chapel Hill, N.C., 1980); Genovese, *Political Economy of Slavery,* 153; Barbara Jeanne Fields, *Slavery and Freedom on the Middle Ground: Maryland during the Nineteenth Century* (New Haven, 1985).

84. Pred, *Urban Growth,* 7–9; Lindstrom, *Philadelphia Region,* 41–57; Susan E. Hirsch, *Roots of the American Working Class: The Industrialization of Crafts in Newark, 1800–1860* (Philadelphia, 1978), xix; Scranton, *Proprietary Capitalism;* Harold Hancock, "The Industrial Worker along the Brandywine, 1800–1830," Hagley Museum Research Report (Greenville, Del. Eleutherian Mills Historical Library, 1956); Anthony F. C. Wallace, *Rockdale: The Growth of an American Village in the Early Industrial Revolution* (New York, 1978); Milton Cantor, "Introduction," 3–30, Charles Stephenson, "A Gathering of Strangers? Mobility, Social Structure, and Political Participation in the Formation of Nineteenth-Century American Working Class Culture," 38–46, 49–51, Alan Dawley and Paul Faler, "Workingclass Culture and Politics in the Industrial Revolution. Sources of Loyalism and Rebellion," 70 73, Michael Feldberg, "The Crowd in Philadelphia History: A Comparative Perspective," 79–85, 88–90, Bruce Laurie, "'Nothing on Compulsion': Life Styles of Philadelphia Artisans, 1820–1850," 94–95, 97–99, 103–5, 108, 113–16, 118–20, in Cantor, ed., *American Working Class Culture: Explorations in American Labor and Social History* (Westport, Conn., 1979); Hirsch, *Roots,* 12–13, 85–86, 89–90; Licht, "Labor and Capital and the American Community," 223.

85. Alfred D. Chandler, Jr., *The Visible Hand: The Managerial Revolution in American Business* (Cambridge, Mass., 1977), 244–45; Yearly, *Enterprise and Anthracite,* 15–16; Cochran, *Frontiers,* 134; Lozier, "Rural Textile Mill Communities" Wallace, *Rockdale;* Hancock, "Industrial Worker along the Brandywine."

86. Danhof, "Farm Enterprise," 127–91; Porter and Livesay, *Merchants and Manufacturers,* 1–13, 228–32.

87. Wallace, *Rockdale,* 62–65, 91, 95, 97, 98; Hirsch, *Roots,* 90–94; Stuart Blumin, "Mobility and Change in Ante-Bellum Philadelphia," 165–208 and Herbert Gutman, "The Reality of the Rags–to–Riches Myth," 98–124, in Stephen Thernstrom and Richard Sennett, eds., *Nineteenth–Century Cities* (New Haven, 1969); Folsom, *Urban Networks;* Ridgway, *Community Leadership,* 181–84; Carter Goodrich and Sol Davision, "The Wage Earner in the Western Movement," *Political Science Quarterly* 50 (1935): 161–85; Helene Zahler, *Eastern Workingmen and National Land Policy, 1829–1862* (New York, 1941); Cochran, *Frontier,* 135; Jeffrey G. Williamson, "American Prices and Urban Inequality since 1820," *Journal of Economic History* 36 (1976): 313 and n.; Donald R. Adams, Jr., "Workers on the Brandywine: The Response to Early

Industrialization," *Regional Economic History Research Center Working Papers* 3, no. 4 (1980): 1–29; Adams, "Wage Rates in the Early National Period," *Journal of Economic History* 28 (1968): 404–26; Adams "Some Evidence on English and American Wage Rates," *Journal of Economic History* 30 (1970): 499–511; Adams, "The Mid-Atlantic Labor Market in the Early Nineteenth Century," in Paul Uselding, ed., *Business and Economic History: Papers Presented at the Twenty-Fourth Annual Meeting of the Business History Conference*, 2d ser., 7 (Urbana, Ill.: Bureau of Economic and Business Research, 1979); Yearly, *Enterprise and Anthracite*, 59; Samuel Walker, "Workingmen of Scranton," in Cantor, *Workingclass Culture* 364; Charles Stephenson, "Gathering of Strangers?" 44–45; Cochran, *Frontiers*, 26–28; Coleman, *Debtors and Creditors*, 287–88.

88. As quoted, Foner, *Free Soil*, 17–18, 22.

89. Ibid., as quoted, 22.

90. Notes 83, 84, 87 above.

91. Hovenkamp, *Enterprise and American Law*, 74, 77, 186–87.

92. As quoted, Foner, *Free Soil*, 36–37.

93. Notes 84, 87 above.

94. Notes 11, 91 above.

95. Chap. 3 below; see also notes 7, 91, 92 above.

96. Hovenkamp, *Enterprise and American Law*, 67–78, 183–86.

97. Ibid.; notes 39, 70 above.

98. White, *Marshall Court and Cultural Change*, 201–91; Kammen, *Machine*, 77–78; Gary B. Nash, "The Philadelphia Bench and Bar, 1800–1861," *Comparative Studies in Society and History* 7 (1965): 209, 218–20; Glickstein, *Concepts of Free Labor*, 4–5.

99. White, *Marshall Court and Cultural Change*, 76–156, see also Kammen, *Machine*, 77–78.

100. As quoted, Freyer, *Forums of Order*, 26–27; Swisher, *Taney Period*, 147–54; *Bronson v. Kinzie*, 1 How. 311 (1843).

101. As quoted, Swisher, *Taney Period*, 151.

102. Note 100 above; see chap. 2 below.

103. *Sturges v. Crowninshield*, 4 Wheaton 122 (1819); *Ogden v. Saunders*, 12 Wheaton 213 (1827); *Dartmouth College v. Woodward*, 4 Wheaton 518 (1819); *New Jersey v. Wilson*, 7 Cranch 164 (1812); Hovenkamp, *Enterprise and American Law*, 19–27; Newmyer, *Marshall and Taney*, 68, 88.

104. Baxter, *Steamboat Monopoly*, 69–118.

105. Elizabeth Brand Monroe, *The Wheeling Bridge Case: Its Significance in American Law and Technology* (Boston, 1992); for social-class implications, see chap. 3 below.

106. *Martin v. Waddell's Lessee*, 16 Peters 397 (1840); Haines and Sherwood, *Role of Supreme Court, 1835–1864*, 218–19.

## 2. Constitutionalism and the Associational Economy

1. Freyer, *Forums of Order*, 1–98; Friedman, *History of American Law*, 269–75; Coleman, *Debtors and Creditors*.

2. White, *Marshall Court and Cultural Change*, 4, 114, 181–83, 595–675, 741–78; Swisher, *Taney Period*, 71–154; Hovenkamp, *Enterprise and American Law*, 17–35; Haines, *Role of Supreme Court, 1789–1835*; Haines and Sherwood, *Role of Supreme Court, 1835–1864*; Newmyer, *Marshall and Taney*; Freyer, *Forums of Order*, 1–98.

3. For more on the dual market for legal services, see Freyer, *Discretion and Dependence*.

4. Freyer, *Forums of Order*, 1–98; Newmyer, *Marshall and Taney*, 7–8, 40–48, 74, 79, 93; Maurice G. Baxter, *One and Inseparable: Daniel Webster and the Union* (Cambridge, Mass., 1984), 200–203, 207, 226–39, 258–59.

5. For details on negotiability, Freyer, *Forums of Order*, 36–48; Hovenkamp, *Enterprise and American Law*, 87–89; Friedman, *History of American Law*, 266–69.

6. "Legal Protection of Good Faith," *Hunt's Merchants' Magazine* 1 (1839): 230; Hurst, *Law and Markets*, 105–6; Freyer, *Forums of Order*, 1–18, 36–99; Freyer, "Antebellum Commercial Law"; Harold R. Weinberg, "Commercial Paper in Economic Theory and Legal History," *Kentucky Law Journal* 70 (1982): 567–92; Horwitz, *Transformation*, 211–52.

7. Notes 2 and 5 above. The most important cases are *Sturges* v. *Crowninsheild*, 4 Wheaton 122 (1819); *Ogden* v. *Saunders*, 11 Wheaton 213 (1827); *Bronson* v. *Kinzie*, 1 Howard 311 (1843).

8. Notes 1, 2, 3, 5 above.

9. Freyer, *Forums of Order*, 8–10; 56–60; Cochran, *Frontiers*, 24–27; Friedman, *History of American Law*, 238–43; Coleman, *Debtors and Creditors*, 287.

10. Lindstrom, *Philadelphia Region*; Porter and Livesay, *Merchants and Manufacturers*, 1–13, 228–32; Tocqueville, *Democracy in America* (1945 ed.), 2:156–57; Yearly, *Enterprise and Anthracite*, 15–16; Louis C. Hunter, *A History of Industrial Power in the United States, 1780–1930*, vol. 1, *Water Power in the Century of the Stream Engine* (Charlottesville, Va., 1979), 67; Cochran, *Frontiers*, 134.

11. Pred, *Urban Growth*, 13. The text here and below follows closely Freyer, *Forums of Order*, 8.

12. Lewis E. Atherton, "The Problem of Credit Rating in the Ante-Bellum South," *Journal of Southern History* 12 (1946): 354–56; James H. Madison, "The Evolution of Commercial Credit Reporting Agencies in Nineteenth-Century America," *Business History Review* 67 (1974): 164–86; Porter and Livesay, *Merchants and Manufacturers*, 29–34.

13. Madison, "Credit Reporting Agencies," 167.

14. Atherton, "Problem of Credit Rating," 355.

15. Wallace, *Rockdale*, 91, 95, 97; Yearly, *Enterprise and Anthracite*, 59; Herbert Gutman, "The Workers Search for Power," in H. Wayne Morgan, ed., *The Gilded*

*Age: A Reappraisal* (Syracuse, N.Y., 1963), 38; Stephenson, "Gathering of Strangers?" 44–45; Walker, "Workingmen of Scranton," 364; Cochran, *Frontiers*, 26–28; Coleman, *Debtors and Creditors*, 287–88; Hirsch, *Roots*, 92; Freyer, "Antebellum Commercial Law," 605–8; Weinberg, "Commercial Paper," 588–92.

16. For other factors contributing to weakened class solidarity, see Blumin, "Mobility and Change"; Gutman, "Reality of the Rags-to-Riches Myth"; Wallace, *Rockdale*, 62–65; Hirsch, *Roots*, 90–94; Zahler, *Eastern Workingmen*; Goodrich and Davision, "Wage Earner"; Cochran, *Frontiers*, 135; Williamson, "American Prices and Urban Inequality," 313, and n.; Adams, "Workers on the Brandywine;" Adams, "Wage Rates"; Adams, "Some Evidence on English and American Wage Rates"; Adams, "Mid-Atlantic Labor Market."

17. Tocqueville, *Democracy in America* (1945 ed.), 1:69–97, 417–21.

18. See, for example, Freyer, "Reassessing the Impact of Eminent Domain"; Freyer, *Forums of Order*, 1–79; Freyer, *Harmony and Dissonance*, 1–43; and Samuel Troth to Grinnell Minturn & Co., April 21, 1843, quoted in Porter and Livesay, *Merchants and Manufacturers*, 32.

19. Richard Kilbourne, "Securing Commercial Transactions in the Antebellum Legal System of Louisiana," *Kentucky Law Journal* 70 (1982): 609–41; *Fletcher* v. *Morey*, 9 F. Cas. 266 (C.D.D. Mass. 1843) (No. 4,864).

20. Freyer, *Forums of Order*, 1–52; Weinberg, "Commercial Paper," 570–71, 580–83. The credit report material is drawn from the R. G. Dun & Co. collection located in Baker Library, the Graduate School of Business Administration, Harvard University (used with permission of Baker Library and R. G. Dun & Co.). For the background and origins of R. G. Dun & Co., see, Freyer, *Forums of Order*, 8. See also Freyer, "Antebellum Commercial Law." Following each state the order of citation is: firm name, county-town, volume, page. Maryland: Levi Perry, Baltimore county & city, 7:7; Moses Lake, Anne Arundel, Annapolis, 2:9; Thomas Beck, Baltimore county & city, 7:6; David Hissonger, Frederick county & city, 2:151; George F. Webster, Frederick county & city, 2:7; Vernon Hebb, Allegany, Cumberland, 2:6; George L. Richardson, Worcester, Snow Hill, 8:89; Thomas W. Ellison, Kent, Chestertown, 2:90; Jesse T. Higgins, Montgomery, Poolsville, 2:126; O. Swingly, Washington, Hagerstown, 2:12; Albaugh & Delander, Carroll, Woodbine, 2:11; R. G. Reese, Cecil, Elkton, 2:11; Thomas G. Robertson, Washington, Hagerstown, 2:11; George W. Delander, Allegany, Oakland, 2:10; David F. Smith, Frederick county & city, 2:8; Edward I. K. Scott, Prince Georges, Marlboro, 2:9; S. H. Steel, Chesapeake county & city, 2:159; Spencer & Wright, Cecil, Perrysville, 2:151; Joseph Payne, Frederick county & city, 2:147; David Engel, Carroll, Sams Creek, 2:145; Comegys Semans, Cecil, Cecilton, 2:143; (Mrs.) R. A. Stansburg, Anne Arundel, Annapolis, 2:139; Henry Blackstone, Allegany, Cumberland, 2:135; Edward Mansfield, Kent, Chestertown, 2:130; Jesse Duval, Prince Georges, Laurel, 2:126. New Jersey: Rochus Heinisch, Newark county & city, 20:62; W. S. Hooper, Cape May, Cope Island, 8:22; Richard Casey, Cape May county & city, 8:25; John

Dougherty, Cape May county & city, 8:23; Joseph Perkin, Burlington, Beverly, 6:99; T. N. Emley, Burlington, Cook's Mills, 6:99; Henry E. Emley, Burlington, Cook's Mills, 6:97; George C. Davis, Burlington, Juliustown, 6:97; Thomas Knighton, Morris, Morristown, 60:210; Clark & Hughson, Morris, Walnut Grove, 60:159; Joseph B. Berry, Morris, Shipping port, 60:158; Jonathan C. Brunnel, Morris, Brunneltown, 60:155; Bragshaw & Keep, Morris, Madison, 60:155; John Emmons, Sr., Morris, Madison, 60:155; Charles Edwards, Morris, Madison, 60:154; Mahlon Minton, Morris, Madison, 60:154. Pennsylvania: C. M. McCauley, Fulton, McConnelsburg, 69:613; Michael Barndoller, Fulton, Fort Littleton, 69:612; Jesse Akers, Fulton, Emmasville, 69:612B; David Shoemaker, Fulton, McConnelsburg, 69:612a; Walter H. Knowlton, Erie county & city, 60:439; George Finch, Perry, Landesburg, 126:33. These are regional totals; there were variations within and among the states.

21. RG 21, U.S. District Court for District of Maryland Bankruptcy Records, Act 1841, case files 1842–43, nos. 1–30, Feb. 1 - Feb. 15, 1842, Federal Records Center, Philadelphia, Petitions of William H. Hayward, John W. Richardson, George Massope, Mathiew Keirle, James Power, Andrew Riley.

22. See note 20 above; and also Coleman, *Debtors and Creditor*, 287.

23. Henry Alexander to Archibald McCall, Dec. 3, 1819, file no. 77, Letters of James Partridge, Eleuthera Bradford Du Pont Collection, files 77–97, Acc. 146, box 7; Hagley Museum and Library.

24. The following paragraphs are taken from RG 21, Maryland Circuit Court Equity Cases, 1809–19, *Phillip Kierschner* v. *Jacob Kierschner* (1819), box 2.

25. The following paragraphs are taken from RG 21, U.S. District Court for District of Maryland Bankruptcy Records, Act 1841, case files 1842–43, nos. 1–30, Feb. 1 - Feb. 15, 1842, Petition of Bernard Schlesinger.

26. For the correspondence upon which the following is based, see Briscoe & Partridge to E. I. Du Pont de Nemours & Co., Baltimore, 1813–1818, in Records of E. I. Du Pont de Nemours & Co., ser. 1, pt. 1 ser, B, acc. 500, box 45, Hagley Museum and Library.

27. Samuel Briscoe to E. I. Du Pont, Jan. 21, 1819, ibid.; and Elias Glenn to E. I. Du Pont, Nov. 28, 1823, file no. 77, Letters of James Partridge; Eleuthera Bradford Du Pont Collection, files 77–97, acc. 146, box 7, Hagley Museum and Library.

28. Samuel Briscoe to E. I. Du Pont, May 21, 1818 (f. 3), Dec. 29, 1818 (f. 3); Records of E. I. Du Pont de Nemours & Co., ser. 1, pt. 1, ser. B, acc. 500, box 45, Hagley Museum and Library.

29. Maryland: William Torbet, Cecil, Elkton, 2:8.

30. Pennsylvania: C. M. McCauley, Fulton, McConnelsburg, 69:613; New Jersey: John Emmons, Sr., Morris, Madison, 60:155.

31. The claim of typicality is based on reading through the reports of the firms listed in note 20 above.

32. Pennsylvania: Joseph H. Hunter, Fulton, Burnt Cabins, 69:612c; Pennsylvania: Robert S. Hunter, Fulton, Speersville, 69:612.

33. New Jersey: John Dougherty, Cape May county & city, 8:22.

34. New Jersey: Rochus Heinisch, Newark county & city, 20:62.

35. The claim of typicality is based on reading through the reports of the firms listed in note 20.

36. Maryland: Thomas Beck, Baltimore county & city, 76.

37. Maryland: Mrs. R. A. Stransburg, Anne Arundel, Annapolis, 2:139; Mrs. O. C. Gephart, Allegany, Cumberland, 2:124; Edward Mansfield, Kent, Chestertown, 2:130; Edward I. K. Scott, Prince Georges, Marlboro, 2:9; New Jersey: Richard Casey, Cape May, 8:25; Hurst, *Law and Social Order*, 66. See also other secondary sources cited and analyzed in James W. Ely, Jr., review of Norma Basch, *In the Eyes of the Law: Women, Marriage and Property in Nineteenth Century New York* (Ithaca, N.Y., 1982), in *University of California Law Review* 31 (1983): 294–304.

38. Maryland: Moses Lake, Anne Arundel, Annapolis, 2:9.

39. Maryland: M. Soloman, Baltimore county & city, 7:6; K. H. Butler & McClaney, Allegany, Cumberland, 2:14; David Hissonger, Frederick county & city, 2:14; Pennsylvania: William S. Deil, Lehigh, Allentown, 86:265a.

40. Maryland: Levi Perry, Baltimore county & city, 7:7. See also Pennsylvania: William Gross, Catasauqua, Lehigh 86:285; John Gross, Catasauqua, Lehigh 86:285; Maryland: Mount Savage Iron Works, Allegany, Frostburg, 2:6.

41. Peter DuPonceau to Albert Gallatin, May 19, 1826, quoted in Richard Holcombe Kilbourne, Jr., *Louisiana Commercial Law: The Antebellum Period* (Baton Rouge, La., 1980), 2.

42. *Debates and Proceedings of the Maryland Reform Convention to Revise the Constitution*, 2 vols. (Annapolis, 1851), 2:408.

43. "The Connexion of Commerce and Agriculture," *Hunt's* 2 (1840): 480; "On the Moral End of Business," ibid., 1 (1839): 385; "Mercantile Law," ibid.

44. "On the Moral End of Business," ibid., 1 (1839): 388; "The Principles of Credit," ibid., 2 (1840): 195–96.

45. "The Principles of Credit," ibid., 2 (1840): 203.

46. "Beware of Over-trading," ibid., 1 (1839): 428.

47. "Morals of Trade," ibid., 7 (1842): 350, 352; "Evils of Commerce," ibid., 2 (1840): 76; "Theory of Profits," ibid., 2 (1840): 219; "Mercantile Law," ibid., 1 (1839): 422.

48. Anonymous, *Debtor and Creditor* (Philadelphia, 1810), 4–5, 11–13, 15.

49. Anonymous, *A Letter to the Senate and House of Representatives of the United States upon the Expediency of an Uniform System of Bankruptcy* (Boston, 1821), 4, 6, 14, 18, 31.

50. Robert Hare, *Proofs That Credit as Money in a Truly Free Country Is . . . Preferable to Coin* (Philadelphia, 1834), 5–12.

51. Anonymous, *Remarks upon the Necessity and Effect of General Bankrupt Laws Including Corporations* (New York, 1858), 8, 10, 12.

52. Virgil Maxcy, *Address to the Agricultural Society of Maryland* (Annapolis, 1820), 14; William Rawle, *An Address Delivered before the Philadelphia Society for Promoting Agriculture* (Philadelphia, 1819), 21; H. A. Boardman, *Suggestions to Young Men Engaged in Business* (Philadelphia, 1851), 11, 14–15.

53. George N. Eckert, *Letter to Governor James Pollack . . . on the Industrial, Commercial and Financial Troubles Now Existing in the United States* (Philadelphia, 1855), 5, 6, 13, 14.

54. Civis, *Remarks on the Bankrupt Law* (New York, 1819), 80.

55. Simpson, *Working Man's Manual*, 143. See also A Citizen of Maryland, Strictures on the Letter of Charles J. Ingersoll, Esq., Touching the Right of a Legislature to Repeal a Charter (Baltimore, 1836), 52–53; Sharp, *Jacksonians versus the Banks*, 44–45, 275–76, 280–96, 307–8, 349.

56. As quoted, Sharp, *Jacksonians versus the Banks*, 282.

57. Porter and Livesay, *Merchants and Manufacturers*, 29, 31–33, 44, 72–77, 101; Cadman, *Corporation in New Jersey*, app. 1, 443–44; John A. Munroe, "Party Battles, 1784–1850," in Henry Clay Reed, ed., *Delaware: A History of the First State*, 3 vols. (New York, 1947) 1:125–62, Thomas Law, *An Address to the Columbian Institute on the Question "What Ought to Be the Circulating Medium of the Nation?"* (Washington, D.C., 1830), 22.

58. See chap. 2 below; Freyer, "Reassessing the Impact of Eminent Domain"; Simpson, *Working Man's Manual*, 132.

59. *A Digest of the Laws of Pennsylvania . . . Relative to Banks* (Harrisburg, 1854), 129; Law, *What Ought to Be the Circulating Medium of the Nation?*, 4.

60. Andrew Jackson, "Farewell Address," in James D. Richardson, ed., *A Compilation of the Messages and Papers of the Presidents*, 12 vols. (New York, 1897), 2:1522, 1523.

61. "Ought Certain Creditors to Be Preferred in Making Assignments?" *Hunt's* 7 (1842): 274. See also Freyer, *Forums of Order*, 9–10, 37–41, 58–60; Weinberg, "Commercial Paper," 580–87.

62. As quoted, Freyer, *Forums of Order*, 10; "Preferences by Insolvents," *Hunt's* 7 (1842): 352–54; "Ought Certain Creditors to Be Preferred in Making Assignments?" ibid., 7 (1842): 273–75; "Preferring Creditors in Assignments: Its Morality," ibid., 7 (1842): 527–29. The problems with accommodation loans were discussed repeatedly in the contemporary commercial literature, examples of which are cited in notes 42–54 above. See also Freyer, *Forums of Order*, 9–10, 37–41.

63. William Holdsworth, *A History of English Law*, 16 vols. (London, 1972), 8:169; Freyer, *Harmony and Dissonance*, 1–45. See also Freyer, *Forums of Order*, 53–98.

64. Freyer, *Harmony and Dissonance*. For case law on negotiability of accommodation paper and related matters, see Weinberg, "Commercial Paper," 580–87; and *Cline & Francis v. Miller*, 8 Md. 274 (1855); *Muirhead v. Kirkpatrick*, 21 Pa. 237 (1853); *Hedges v. The Farmer's Bank*, 2 Del. Cas. 651 (1821); *Commercial Bank v. Ross*, 1

Del. Cas. 586 (1819); *The Farmers' Bank* v. *Robesan's Admn's*, 2 Del. Cas. 652 (1821); *Overton* v. *Tyler*, 3 Pa. 346 (1846); *Appleton* v. *Donaldson*, 3 Pa. 381 (1846); *West Branch Bank* v. *Fulmer*, 3 Pa. 399 (1846); *Dundass* v. *Sterling*, 4 Pa. 73 (1846); *Dundass* v. *Gallagher*, 4 Pa. 205 (1846); *Hughes* v. *Large*, 2 Pa. 103 (1845); *Esling* v. *Zantzunger*, 13 Pa. 50 (1850).

65. "Commercial Lawyers," *Hunt's* 14 (1846): 64–66; Freyer, *Harmony and Dissonance*, 21–25; "Laws Relative to Debtor and Creditor," *Hunt's* 2 (1840): 491–92.

66. See pamphlets and/or commerical periodical literature cited in notes 43–55 above.

67. P. S. Atiyah, *The Rise and Fall of Freedom of Contract* (Oxford, Eng., 1979), 229, 519–20.

68. The pamphlet and commercial literature cited above and discussed below is a valuable source for the study of the subject of comparative debtor-creditor relations in general and such vital particulars as the issue of preferring creditors.

69. Freyer, *Forums of Order*, 56–59; Coleman, *Debtors and Creditors*, 151, 173, 282, 291. See also notes 61–64 above and the following pamphlets: Anonymous, *A Letter to the Senate*, 25; Civis, *Remarks*, 14, 35–36; Charles M. Ellis, *Hints for Relief . . . betwixt Debtor and Creditor* (Boston, 1857), 8, 21–22, 24, 31, 35–37, 45, 47, 52–54; Anonymous, *Debtor and Creditor*, 26; Robert Young Hayne, *Speech of Mr. Hayne . . . on the Bill to Establish a Uniform System of Bankruptcy* (Washington, D.C., 1826), 4.

70. Ibid.; 21, Records of U.S. Circuit Court District of Columbia, Insolvents Case Papers, 1814–42, *Abijah Adams* v. *John D. Russell*, 1820 (box 4), General Archives Division, National Archives, Suitland.

71. "Preferences by Insolvents," *Hunt's* 7 (1842): 352; note 62 above.

72. *Memorial of the Citizens of Charleston praying for . . . an Uniform System of Bankruptcy* (Washington, D.C., 1822); *Memorial of the Chamber of Commerce of the City of New York Praying for a General System of Bankruptcy* (Washington, D.C., 1823); *Memorial of the Chamber of Commerce of the City of Philadelphia* (Washington, D.C., 1824); *Memorial of Sundry Citizens of . . . Troy . . . New York (Against a System of Bankruptcy)* (Washington, D.C., 1822); and see note 68 above.

73. Hayne, *Speech*, 4, 6, 9; Charles Warren, *Bankruptcy in American History* (Cambridge, Mass., 1935).

74. Civis, *Remarks*, 21–30, 35–36; Ellis, *Hints*, 25–26, 33, 37–41, 45; Hayne, *Speech*, 9, 10; Anonymous, *Debtor and Creditor*, 26; John Sergeant, *Speech of Mr. Sergeant in the House of Representatives . . . on the Bill to Establish an Uniform System of Bankruptcy* (Washington, D.C., 1823), 2, 10, 15, 35; Anonymous, *A Commentary on the Bankrupt Law of 1841* (Washington, D.C., 1841), 17, 47.

75. *Memorial of the Chamber of Commerce of Philadelphia*, 4.

76. Sergeant, *Speech*, 2, 14, 24.

77. Coleman, *Debtors and Creditors*, 131, 134–36, 140, 146, 149, 154, 158–59, 174–75, 208, 214, 244, 275. For case citations, see note 7.

78. Hayne, *Speech*, 10–11.

79. Debtor wins: *Immel* v. *Stoever*, 1 Penrose & Watts 262 (1830); *Power* v. *Hollman*, 2 Watts 218 (1834); *Mitchell's Estate*, 2 Watts 87 (1833); *State* v. *Goldsmith*, 1 Harris & Johnson 101 (1800); *Landsdale* v. *Ghequiere*, 4 Harris & Johnson 257 (1815); *State* v. *Krebs*, 6 Harris & Johnson 31 (1823); *Cole* v. *Albers*, 1 Gill 412 (1843); *Malcolm* v. *Hall*, 1 Mary. 172 (1847); *Williamson* v. *Wilson*, 1 Bland 418 (1826); *Baylies* v. *Ellicott*, 9 Gill 452 (1851); *Evans* v. *Sprigg*, 2 Mary. 457 (1852); *Bailey* v. *Seal*, 1 Del. Rep. 367 (1834); *Lewis* v. *Norwood*, 4 Del. Rep. 460 (1847); *Samuel Fortner's Case*, 2 Del. Rep. 461 (1838); *Tunnel* v. *Jefferson*, 5 Del. Rep. 206 (1849); *Hale* v. *Ross*, 3 New Jersey 373 (1811); *Vreeland* v. *Bruen*, 21 New Jersey 214 (1847); *Stokes* v. *Middleton*, 28 New Jersey (1859). Creditor wins: *Seal* v. *Duffy*, 4 Pa. State Rep. 274 (1846); *Englebert* v. *Blanjot*, 2 Wharton 240 (1837); *Betz's Appeal*, 1 Penrose & Watts 271 (1830); *In Re Wilson*, 4 Pa. State Rep. 430 (1846); *Manro* v. *Gittings & Smith* 1 Harris & Johnson 492 (1804); *Michael* v. *Schroeder* 4 Harris & Johnson 227 (1815); *Farrow* v. *Teakle*, 4 Harris & Johnson (1815); *Larrabee* v. *Talbot*, 5 Gill. 426 (1847); *Smith* v. *Donnell*, 9 Gill 84 (1850); *Poe* v. *Duck*, 5 Mary. 1 (1853); *Wire* v. *Browning & Hull*, 20 New Jersey 364 (1845).

80. James Barbour, *Remarks . . . on the Bill for Abolishing Imprisonment for Debt* (Washington, D.C., 1824); *The Petitions of Rufus Davenport to the Twenty-four States for the Adoption of the Free Debt Rules . . . [and] the . . . Abolition of Imprisonment for Debt* (Boston, 1828); Coleman, *Debtors and Creditors*

81. Creditors win: *Voorhees* v. *Thorn*, 21 New Jersey 77 (1847); *Rogers* v. *Brundred*, 16 New Jersey 159 (1837); *Lillburne Harwood's Case*, 4 Del. Rep. 541 (1847); *William Hooper's Case*, 3 Del. Rep. 320 (1841); *Egbert* v. *Darr*, 3 Watt's & Sergeant 517 (1842); *Heilner* v. *Bast*, 1 Penrose & Watts 267 (1830); *Dean* v. *Patton*, 1 Penrose & Watts 271 (1830). Debtor wins: *Clark* v. *Ray*, 1 Harris & Johnson 318 (1802); *Lewis* v. *Norwood*, 4 Del. Rep. 460 (1847); *Fisher* v. *Stayton*, 3 Del. Rep. 271 (1840); *Samuel Fortner's Case*, 2 Del. Rep. 461 (1838); *The State* v. *Ward*, 8 New Jersey 120 (1825); *Hillet* v. *Hunt*, 20 New Jersey 476 (1845).

82. *Debates and Proceedings of the Maryland Reform Convention*, 2:407–9; and citations in note 79 above.

83. Gaol Calendar, Sheriff, West Chester County, 1813–1816 (West Chester County Historical Society, no page number).

84. Freyer, *Forums of Order*, 13, 29. But see note 85 below.

85. *Power* v. *Hollman*, 2 Watts 218 (1834); *Mitchell's Estate*, 2 Watts 87 (1833); *In Re Wilson*, 4 Pa. State Rep. 430 (1846); *Stoever's Appeal*, 3 Watts & Sergeant 154 (1842); *Wire* v. *Browning & Hull*, 20 New Jersey 364 (1845); *State* v. *Krebs*, 6 Harris & Johnson 31 (1823); *Powles* v. *Dilley* 9 Gill 222 (1850); *Beaty* v. *Davis*, 9 Gill 211 (1850); *Manro* v. *Gittings & Smith*, 1 Harris & Johnson 492 (1804); *Farrow* v. *Teorkle*, 4 Harris & Johnson 271 (1815); *King, Boyd & King* v. *Johnson*, 5 Del. Rep. 31 (1848). For negotiability of accommodation paper, see note 62.

86. *Maberry & Pollard* v. *Shisler*, 1 Del. Rep. 349 (1834); *Larrabee* v. *Talbott*, 5 Gill 426 (1847); *Evans* v. *Sprigg*, 2 Mary. 457 (1852); *Union Bank* v. *Kerr*, 7 Mary. 88 (1854); *Hale* v. *Ross*, 3 New Jersey 373 (1811); *In Re Wilson*, 4 Pa. State Rep. 430 (1846).

### 3. Taxation and Capitalist Accountability

1. Foner, *Free Soil*, 18–23, 19–20, 36–39. See also the works cited in chap. 1 above.

2. Ibid.

3. See particularly Freyer, *Forums of Order*, 1–98; Haines, *Role of Supreme Court, 1789–1835*; Haines and Sherwood, *Role of Supreme Court, 1835–1864*; Newmyer, *Marshall and Taney*. For fuller citation, see note 4, chap. 1 above. Cases are cited below.

4. Edwin R. A. Seligman, *Essays in Taxation* (New York, 1895), 10–22; Bernhard Grossfeld and James D. Bryce, "A Brief Comparative History of the Origins of the Income Tax in Great Britain, Germany, and the United States," *American Journal of Tax Policy* 2 (1983): 211–51; Hurst, *Law and Markets*.

5. Hartz, *Economic Policy and Democratic Thought*; Cadman, *Corporation in New Jersey*; Joseph G. Blandi, "Maryland Business Corporations, 1783–1852," *Johns Hopkins University Studies in Historical and Political Science* 52, no. 3 (1934); Hugh Sission Hannah, "A Financial History of Maryland, 1789–1848," ibid., 25 (Aug.-Oct. 1907). Compare Scheiber, *Ohio Canal Era*.

6. See note 3 above; and discussion below.

7. As quoted, J. Alton Burdine, "Government Regulation of Industry in Pennsylvania, 1776–1860" (Ph.D. diss., Harvard University, 1939), 45–46.

8. Ibid., 46.

9. *Dartmouth College* v. *Woodward*, 4 Wheaton 518 (1819); Newmyer, *Marshall and Taney*, 64–68, 75–79; Haines, *1789–1835*, 309–39, 379–419; Stites, *Private Interest and Public Gain*; Hovenkamp, *Enterprise and American Law*, 32–34.

10. *Charles River Bridge* v. *Warren Bridge*, 11 Peters 420 (1837); Newmyer, *Marshall and Taney*, 95–98; Haines and Sherwood, *Role of Supreme Court, 1835–1864*, 28–43, 347–48; Swisher, *Taney Period*, 71–99; Kutler, *Privilege and Creative Destruction*; Hovenkamp, *Enterprise and American Law*, 110–14.

11. 12 Wheaton 419 (1827); Newmyer, *Marshall and Taney*, 52, 54, 63, 85, 102, 103, 107, 115; Haines, *Role of Supreme Court, 1789–1835*, 533–35; Haines and Sherwood, *Role of Supreme Court, 1835–1864*, 143–50; Swisher, *Taney Period*, 357–422.

12. *Bank of Augusta* v. *Earle*, 13 Peters 519 (1839); Freyer, *Forums of Order*, 19–30, esp. 28–30; Swisher, *Taney Period*, 115–21, 464–65; Haines and Sherwood, *Role of Supreme Court, 1835–1864*, 60–76.

13. 16 Peters 1 (1842); *Louisville Ry. Co.* v. *Letson*, 2 Howard 497 (1844); Freyer, *Forums of Order*, 73–98, esp. 92; Haines and Sherwood, *Role of Supreme Court, 1835–1864*, 76–82; Swisher, *Taney Period*, 461–64; Freyer, *Harmony and Dissonance*, 55, 56, 75–76, 78. See above, notes 9–12.

14. Hartz, *Economic Policy and Democratic Thought*, 39–81; Cadman, *Corporation in New Jersey*, 327–416; Blandi, "Maryland Business Corporations," 39–89; Robert

M. Blackson, "Thirteenth Annual Research Conference at Harrisburg," *Pennsylvania History*, 65 (1978): 333–35; Hurst, *Law and Markets*, 66–67; notes 12–13 above. See Hagley Museum and Library: *An Act to Recharter Certain Banks, Passed the Twenty-fifth Day of March, 1824* (Pottsville, Pa., 1831), 8; *Report of the Committee on the Petition of the Directors of the Farmers and Mechanics Bank* (Lancaster, Pa., 1808), 6; *Charters, Laws, By-Laws of the Bank of Pennsylvania* (Philadelphia, 1830), 17, 20.

15. Cadman, *Corporation in New Jersey*, 389–416; Blandi, "Maryland Business Corporations," 72–88; Hartz, *Economic Policy and Democratic Thought*, 138, 141, 187, 292; John Anthony Muscalus, *The Use of Banking Enterprises in the Financing of Public Education, 1796–1866* (Philadelphia, 1945), 10–16, 45–65, 138–42.

16. As quoted, Muscalus, *Use of Banking Enterprises in the Financing of Public Education*, 141–42, and 10–16, 43–65.

17. Hartz, *Economic Policy and Democratic Thought*, 150, 206–7; Hannah, "Financial History of Maryland," 48–56, 67–69, 128–29. For the relationship between volume and large wholesalers, see Porter and Livesay, *Merchants and Manufacturers*, 5–7, 16. For the *Brown* case, see note 11 above.

18. Pierson Muir Tuttle, "A History of Railroad Taxation in New Jersey" (Ph.D. diss., Harvard University, 1920), 1–8; Hannah, "Financial History of Maryland," 48–56, 67–69, 128–29; Hartz, *Economic Policy and Democratic Thought*, 18.

19. See note 15 above.

20. As quoted, Cadman, *Corporation in New Jersey*, 392.

21. Muscalus, *Use of Banking Enterprises in the Financing of Public Education*, 63.

22. Ibid., 16; Hannah, "Financial History of Maryland," 69; *Report of the House of Delegates' Committee on Internal Improvements. . . . Three Important Papers Relating to the Baltimore and Ohio Railroad Company* (Annapolis, 1840), 76; *30th Annual Report of the President and Directors' to the Stockholders of the Baltimore and Ohio Railroad Company* (Baltimore, 1856), 7. This and all subsequently cited pamphlets by or about the railroads are in the Hagley Museum and Library.

23. Wallace, *Rockdale*, 309, 384–85, 389; Hartz, *Economic Policy and Democratic Thought*, 192–204.

24. Muscalus, *Use of Banking Enterprises in the Financing of Public Education*, 12, 63; Hancock, "Industrial Worker along the Brandywine"; Browne, *Baltimore*, 40–46, 101–13, 149–58, 196–215, 224–25, 233–36; Hirsch, *Roots*, 12, 112–15, 120–26, 130–31.

25. Notes 9–13 above.

26. George R. Taylor, *The Transportation Revolution, 1815–1860* (New York, 1968); Peter Temin, *The Jacksonian Economy* (New York, 1969).

27. Taylor, *Transportation Revolution*; David G. Gilchrist, ed., *The Growth of Seaport Cities, 1790–1825* (Charlottesville, Va., 1967); James W. Livingood, *The Philadelphia-Baltimore Trade Rivalry, 1780–1860* (Harrisburg, Pa., 1947); H. Jerome Cranmer, "The New Jersey Canals: State Policy and Private Enterprise, 1820–1832" (Ph.D. diss., Columbia University, 1955); George L. A. Reilly, "The Camden and

Amboy Railroad in New Jersey Politics, 1830–1871" (Ph.D. diss., Columbia University, 1951); Gibb, "The Delaware Railroad to 1837" (Senior thesis, University of Delaware, 1961); Gibb, "The Delaware Railroad" (M.A. thesis, University of Delaware, 1965); Jack C. Potter, "The Philadelphia, Wilmington, and Baltimore Railroad, 1831–1840: A Study in Early Railroad Transportation" (M.A. thesis, University of Delaware, 1960); Ralph D. Gray, *The National Waterway: A History of the Chesapeake and Delaware Canal, 1769–1965* (Urbana, Ill., 1967).

28. Cranmer, "New Jersey Canals," 1–3, 12–13, 31, 33.

29. Ibid., 31, 34, 62.

30. Ibid., 38, 58, 47.

31. Ibid., 100.

32. Ibid., 167–68, 215, 239, 243. The reference to "champagne suppers" is in Reilly, "Camden and Amboy Railroad," 54A.

33. Cranmer, "New Jersey Canals," 245–90.

34. Reilly, "Camden and Amboy Railroad," 45–57.

35. Ibid., 63, 64.

36. See note 27 above.

37. Gibb, "Delaware Railroad," 3; as quoted; Gibb, "Delaware Railroad to 1837," 80–81.

38. Gibb, "Delaware Railroad," 39–43. For the failure of Wilmington's Quaker millers to support the enterprise, see Potter, "PW&B Railroad," 24–30.

39. Gibb, "Delaware Railroad," 15–16; Gray, *National Waterway*, 44–46, 52–61, 67, 82, 92.

40. Gray, *National Waterway*, 92–99.

41. William Wordsworth, *The Complete Poetical Works of William Wordsworth*, 9 vols. (Boston, 1911), 9:233.

42. Hartz, *Economic Policy and Democratic Thought*, 17–19; Cadman, *Corporation in New Jersey*, 389–416; Blandi, "Maryland Business Corporations," 72–88; Hannah, "Financial History of Maryland," 46–125; note 4.

43. Notes 9–24.

44. J. Thomas Scharf, *History of Maryland: From the Earliest Period to the Present Day*, 3 vols. (Hatboro, Md., 1967), 2:143–63, 183–86, 208–16; A Citizen of Maryland, *A Short History of the Public Debt of Maryland and the Causes Which Produced It* (Baltimore, 1845); Hannah, "Financial History of Maryland," 70–131.

45. Ibid.

46. *Report on Internal Improvements Relating to B&O*, (1840), 56–68; Scharf, *History of Maryland*, 2:182–86; Citizen of Maryland, *Short History of the Public Debt*, 32–43; Hannah, *Financial History of Maryland*, 80–87.

47. *Report on Internal Improvements Relating to the B&O*, (1840) 61.

48. Hannah, *Financial History of Maryland*, 90–93; Citizen of Maryland, *Short History of the Public Debt*, 44–46; Scharf, *History of Maryland*, 2:205–11.

49. Hannah, *Financial History of Maryland*, 100, 102–4. The interest jumped

because before 1837 the transportation companies in which the state had invested paid considerable receipts into the state treasury in the form of dividends on stock or interest on bonds. These receipts significantly reduced the interest burden of the state's debt. When the panic hit in 1837 and then deepened into depression afterward, the state's income from dividends and interest fell off considerably, while the shortfall in interest payments, combined with the principal, of the state's whole internal improvement debt continued to grow.

50. Scharf, *History of Maryland* 2:209–10, 212–16; Hannah, *Financial History of Maryland*, 120–31.

51. Hannah, *Financial History of Maryland*, 106–20; Citizen of Maryland, *Short History of the Public Debt*; Scharf, *History of Maryland* 2:212–16. By the 1850s the tax was repealed. But until then it fell hard on the capitalist, as the contemporary polemic by A Citizen of Maryland, *Short History of the Public Debt*, 82, exclaimed, "Thus, in almost every instance, compelling payment upon a much larger amount than the *actual worth of the parties concerned*; for no one, in the slightest degree conversant with mercantile affairs, but knows that the man engaged in trade must at those seasons referred to in the law, have a stock on hand greatly beyond his *actual worth*. When it is remembered that his bills receivable are also taxed and that his whole stake has been subsequently assessed and taxed under another general law, it must be obvious that the license law is unjust, unequal, and oppressive. The farmer, the planter, and all those engaged in agricultural pursuits are exempted from this tax."

52. Hannah, *Financial History of Maryland*, 116–19; Scharf, *History of Maryland* 2:212–14.

53. Hartz, *Economic Policy and Democratic Thought*, is the standard work on Pennsylvania during the antebellum years. Hartz suggested the distinction between the producer and entrepreneurial capitalist but did not treat the distinction analytically, especially as it related to tax policy.

54. Ibid. See also Chris Baer, "Leigh Coal Mine Co. and Region," a superb work of primary research used here with the author's permission; *Compilation of the Laws of Pennsylvania Relative to the Internal Improvements: Together with the Canal and Railway Regulations as Established by the Board of Canal Commissioners* (Harrisburg, Pa., 1840); Homer Tope Rosenberger, *The Philadelphia and Erie Railroad: Its Place in American Economic History* (Potomac, Md., 1975); William B. Wilson, *History of the Pennsylvania Railroad Company* 2 vols. (Philadelphia, 1895).

55. I am indebted to Lee Benson, whose major study of antebellum Philadelphia and statewide political economy is underway, for the point that the legislature was influenced by the wider employment opportunities that canals opened up. Benson's work is corroborated, especially as it relates to local contractors, by my own study of the records included in the *Compilation of the Laws of Pa.*, (1840); and Baer, "Lehigh Coal Co."

56. Wilson, *Pennsylvania Railroad*, "Fourth Annual Report," 44, 49; Baer "Lehigh

Coal Co."; "Fourth Annual Report, 1851, see p. 383, n. 29" *The Pennsylvania Railroad Company Annual Reports*, 2 vols. (Philadelphia, 1847–58) 1:17–18, 36, 47–48; "Ninth Annual Report," ibid., 2:15, 17; "Tenth Annual Report," ibid., 2:11; James A. Ward, *J. Edgar Thomson: Master of the Pennsylvania* (Westport, Conn., 1980), 110–22; Hartz, *Economic Policy and Democratic Thought*, 52, 94, 95, 135–39, 145–49, 152, 158–59, 259, 267–79, 284.

57. Baer, "Lehigh Coal Co."; Yearly, *Enterprise and Anthracite*; Hartz, *Economic Policy and Democratic Thought*, 58–62.

58. Scheiber, *Ohio Canal Era*, 8, 25–26, 28–30, 156–57, 208n, 209n, 278, 296.

59. *Compilation of the Laws of Pa., Relative to Internal Improvements* (1840) is a detailed statutory and fiscal history of the appropriations that created the debt. See Hartz, *Economic Policy and Democratic Thought*, 17–18, 148–60.

60. Ibid.

61. As quoted, Hartz, *Economic Policy and Democratic Thought*, 19; note 41 above.

62. Ibid., 18; Burdine, "Government Regulation," 171–74.

63. Gray, *National Waterway*, 101–21.

64. Ibid., 115–16.

65. Ibid., 116–17.

66. Ibid., 118–21; *Perrine v. Chesapeake and Delaware Canal Co.*, 50 Howard 171–72 (1850).

67. Gibb, "Delaware Railroad," 22–89.

68. Ibid., 90, 45, 96.

69. Reilly, "Camden and Amboy Railroad," 103–95; Cadman, *Corporation in New Jersey*, 111–205.

70. Tuttle, "Railroad Taxation in New Jersey," 34–37; Cadman, *Corporation in New Jersey*, 181, 390–93, 397–99, 401–14, 427–28, 438–39.

71. Tuttle, "Railroad Taxation in New Jersey," 25–31; Reilly "Camden and Amboy Railroad," 110–23.

72. Ibid.; Cadman, *Corporation in New Jersey*, 400; II Zabriskie 623 (1850).

73. Reilly, "Camden and Amboy Railroad," 131.

74. Tuttle, "Railroad Taxation in New Jersey," 42–46.

75. *State v. Mansfield* III Zabriskie 510 (1851); Tuttle, "Railroad Taxation in New Jersey," 46–49.

76. William Bruce Catton, "John W. Garrett of the Baltimore & Ohio: A Study in Seaport and Railroad Competition, 1820–1874" (Ph.D. diss., Northwestern University, 1959), 139–215; *Report of the Select Committee Appointed to Investigate the Affairs of the Baltimore and Susquehanna Railroad Co.* (Annapolis, 1847); *Laws and Ordinances Relating to the Baltimore and Susquehanna Railroad Co.* (Baltimore, 1850); A Marylander, *Objections to Yielding to Northerners the Control of the B&O R.R. on Which Depends the Development of Farms, Mines, Manufactures, and Trade of the State of Maryland* (Baltimore, 1860); Blandi; "Maryland Business Corporations," 56–63, 72–88.

77. Ibid.; *Address and Report of a Select Committee of the Baltimore and Ohio Railroad Co.* (Baltimore, 1848); *18th Annual Report of the President and Directors to the Stockholders of the Baltimore and Ohio Railroad Co.* (Baltimore, 1844); *22nd Annual Report of the President and Directors to the Stockholders of the Baltimore & Ohio Railroad Co.* (Baltimore, 1848); *30th Annual Report of B&O* (1856); *Reports of the Majority and Minority of the Special Committee of the B&O R.R. Co. Appointed to Investigate Its Financial Condition* (Baltimore, 1858); *Report of a Select Committee of the House of Delegates of Maryland Relative to Charges of James E. Tyson against the Baltimore and Ohio Railroad Co.* (Baltimore, 1860); *Report to Investigate the Baltimore and Susquehanna Railroad* (1847), 3–4.

78. *Report to Investigate the Baltimore and Susquehanna Railroad,* (1847), 3–4.

79. *Report Committee on Internal Improvements Relating to B&O,* (1840), 76.

80. *30th Annual Report of B&O* (1856), 7; *18th Annual Report of B&O* (1844), 3; *Report of the Select Committee . . . Whether the Pennsylvania, Delaware and Maryland Steam Navigation Company . . . Have Not Forfeited Their Charters* (Annapolis, 1844), 3.

81. *Report from the Committee on Internal Improvement Transmitting a Communication from the President of the Baltimore and Ohio Railroad Relative to an Increase of Toll for Transportation of Flour* (Annapolis, 1840), 4; *Law and Ordinances Relating to the Baltimore and Ohio Railroad Company* (Baltimore, 1850), 112; *30th Annual Report of B&O* (1856), 11; John A. Munroe, *Louis McLane: Federalist and Jacksonian* (New Brunswick, N.J., 1973), 499.

82. *Report of Charges of James E. Tyson against B&O* (1860), 4; Browne, *Baltimore,* 165; A Marylander, *Objections to Yeilding to Northerners* (1860), 23–24.

83. *Reports of the Majority and Minority of B&O* (1858), 26; *Report of Charges of James E. Tyson against B&O* (1860), 165.

84. *Report of the Baltimore and Ohio Railroad Co. concerning a Tariff of Rates of Transportation on "Main Stem" of Said Road to House of Delegates* (Baltimore, 1844), 5.

85. Catton, "John W. Garrett," 153–67; *Report on Internal Improvements Relating to B&O* (1840), 211.

86. *The Opinion of the Hon. Reverdy Johnson, on the Dividend of the Baltimore and Ohio Railroad* (Baltimore, 1847); *The Opinion of the Attorney General in Reference to the Legality of the Recent Dividend Declared by the Baltimore and Ohio Railroad* (Annapolis, 1847); *A Communication from the Executive to the Senate of Maryland . . . Requesting His Views . . . upon the Subject of the Recent Dividend* (Annapolis, 1847), 5, 7, 8; Catton "John W. Garrett," 147–50.

87. Catton, "John W. Garrett," 71–80, 130–42; *Marshall* v. *Baltimore and Ohio Railroad Co.*, 16 Howard 314 (1854).

88. Catton, "John W. Garrett," 130–215.

89. Hartz, *Economic Policy and Democratic Thought,* 267–85; Wilson, *Pennsylvania Railroad* 1:2–5, 44–52; Ward, *J. Edgar Thomson,* 80–122.

90. Hartz, *Economic Policy and Democratic Thought,* 107–16, 267–85, 295–97, 316–19.

91. Ibid., as quoted, 114.

92. Ibid., 113–21; *Sharpless* v. *Mayor of Philadelphia*, 21 Pa. State Rep. 147 (1853); Cecil, "On Municipal Subscriptions to the Stock of Railroad Companies," *American Law Register*, 2 (1853): 1–20; and Lowrie, J., dissenting, *Sharpless* v. *Mayor of Philadelphia*, ibid., 27–43

93. As quoted, Hartz, *Economic Policy and Democratic Thought*, 119.

94. *Sharpless* v. *Mayor of Philadelphia*, 21 Pa. State Rep. 147, 169–71 (1853).

95. *Sharpless* v. *Mayor of Philadelphia*, *American Law Register* 2 (1853): 41, 42, 43.

96. Hartz, *Economic Policy and Democratic Thought*, 123–25.

97. Ibid., 269–85; Ward, *J. Edgar Thomson*, 110–22; *Mott* v. *Pennsylvania Railroad Co.*, 30 Pa. State Rep. 9 (1858).

98. 30 Pa. State Rep. 9, 26, 27 (1858).

99. Hartz, *Economic Policy and Democratic Thought*, 267–69; Ward, *J. Edgar Thomson*, 110–22.

## 4. Taking Property

1. Taylor, *Transportation Revolution*, 88 and Thomas C. Cochran, *Business in American Life: A History* (New York, 1972), esp. 119–22, 194–96, give probably the most illuminating statement of the dominant view. Of the many works of James Willard Hurst that make this and related arguments, see *Law and Social Order*; "Old and New Dimensions of Research in United States Legal History," *American Journal of Legal History* 23 (1979): 1–20; and Hurst, *Law and the Conditions of Freedom*, 24–26, 63–64. Horwitz, *Transformation*, and numerous publications by Harry N. Scheiber, including "Federalism and the American Economic Order" and "Property Law, Expropriation, and Resource Allocation," accept much of Hurst's view, while going beyond it to stress the importance of social subsidy. See also Hartz, *Economic Policy and Democratic Thought*, 70, 72, 76; John F. Stover, *American Railroads* (Chicago, 1961), 30; Frederick A. Cleveland, *Railroad Finance* (New York, 1912), 54. For a critical reassessment of the general thesis that the principal result of eminent domain was that it subsidized development, see Freyer "Reassessing the Impact of Eminent Domain."

2. *Northern Pennsylvania Railroad Company. Letters of the President and the Chief Engineer* (Philadelphia, c. 1855), 31–36, 37. See also *Report of the Case of Alexander . . . against . . . the Schuylkill Navigation Company . . . Court of Common Pleas of Philadelphia County* (Philadelphia, 1825).

3. *Northern Pennsylvania Railroad Company: Coal Depot Site on the Delaware River* (Philadelphia, 1855); *Philadelphia's Great Northern Route: Northern Pennsylvania Railroad. . . .* (Philadelphia, 1853); *Municipal Subscription Made by the City of Philadelphia . . . to the Capital Stock of the Northern Pennsylvania Railroad Company* (Philadelphia, 1854); *Northern Pennsylvania Railroad Company: Facts Relative to the First Mortgage Loan* (Philadelphia, 1855).

4. *Municipal Subscription by Philadelphia to Northern Pennsylvania Railroad Company* (1854), 5.

5. *Northern Pennsylvania Railroad: Coal Depot Site*, (1855).

6. Ibid.

7. The pamphlets referred to in note 3 above give a comprehensive picture of the financial stresses the Northern Pennsylvania Railroad was experiencing.

8. *Report on Internal Improvements Relating to B&O*, (1840), 69–73.

9. As quoted in Potter, "PW&B Railroad," 52–56; "Twentieth and Twenty-First Annual Report, 1857, 1858," *Organization of the United Companies under the Name of the Philadelphia, Wilmington and Baltimore Railroad* (Philadelphia, 1838–63), 13, 14.

10. Rosenberger, *Philadelphia and Erie Railroad*, 330; Thomas T. Taber III, *The Delaware, Lackawanna & Western Railroad in the Nineteenth Century, 1828–1899* (Williamsport, Pa., 1977), 28 (I am grateful to Christopher Baer who pointed out this example); Wilson, *Pennsylvania Railroad*, 1:20, 28–29.

11. Taber, *Delaware, Lackawanna & Western Railroad*, 51; *Report a Canal to Unite the River Delaware . . . with the Passaic* (Morristown, N.J., 1823), 19; Feldberg, "Crowd in Philadelphia History," 80; *The Proceedings of a Public Meeting of the Citizens of New Brunswick in Reference to the New Jersey Railroad* (New Brunswick, 1849), 8.

12. Frances Grund, *The Americans in Their Moral, Social, and Political Relations* (1837; rept. New York, 1968), 180. For general discussion, see David Grimsted, "Rioting in Its Jacksonian Setting," *American Historical Review* 77 (1972): 361–97, esp. 364.

13. Potter, "PW&B Railroad"; Gibb "Delaware Railroad."

14. The federal provision requiring just compensation is to be found in the Fifth Amendment of Bill of Rights of the U.S. Constitution. Of course, the Bill of Rights did not apply to the states until the Supreme Court decided that it did by applying the Fourteenth Amendment during the twentieth century. As far as I know, all state constitutions recognized in some form the just compensation principle.

15. The statutes of the companies examined are: Pennsylvania Railroad; Northern Pennsylvania Railroad; Pennsylvania & Erie Railroad; Susquehanna Canal Co.; Central Coal Mining and Manufacturing Co.; New Castle & Frenchtown Turnpike & Railroad Co.; Baltimore & Ohio Railroad; Chesapeake & Ohio Canal; Baltimore & Susquehanna Railroad; West Jersey Railroad; New Jersey & Delaware Railroad; New Jersey Railway & Transportation Co.; Morris Canal & Banking Co.; Delaware & Raritan Canal and the Camden & Amboy Railroad; Schuylkill Navigation Co.; Delaware & Schuylkill Navigation Co.; Franklin Canal; Philadelphia, Germantown & Norristown Railroad; Mine Hill & Schuylkill Haven Railroad; West Chester Railroad; Philadelphia, Easton & Water Gap Railroad; Mill Creek & Mine Hill Navigation & Railroad Co.; Ligett's Gap Railroad; Eight Passenger Railroads in Philadelphia; Williamsport & El Mira Railroad; Shamokin & Pottsville Railroad; West Philadelphia Railroad; Ohio & Pennsylvania Railroad; Philadelphia & Reading Railroad; Beaver Meadow Railroad; Philadelphia & Trenton Railroad; Pittsburg

& Connellsville Railroad; Reading & Lehigh Railroad; Sugar Loaf Coal Co.; Tangascootack Coal Co.; Susquehanna & Delaware Railroad; Alleghany Valley Railroad; West Chester & Philadelphia Railroad, Philadelphia Railroad; Lehigh Coal & Navigation Co.; Lackawanna Railroad; Hempfield Railroad; Danville & Pottsville Railroad Co.; Chester Valley Railroad; Catawissa, Williamsport & Erie Railroad; Delaware & Chesapeake Canal; Northampton & Luzerne Coal Co. See also *An Act Regulating Railroad Companies* (Harrisburg, 1849), 68, 56. Contrast the eminent domain provisions of these private companies with that of the Pennsylvania State Works in *Compilation of the Laws of Pennsylvania Relative to the Internal Improvements*, (1840), 8, 17, 27, 29, 38, 66. For lobbying pressures involving eminent domain provisions, see: *Free Legislation for Railroads: A History of the Railroad Conflict in the Eighty-fourth Legislature of New Jersey* (Trenton, 1860), 41–43, 46; Rosenberger, *Philadelphia and Erie Railroad*, 101–2; Wilson, *Pennsylvania Railroad*, 1:10.

16. *Laws and Ordinances Relating to B&O*, (1850), 22–23, is cited as a typical assessment and eminent domain provision.

17. *Barron v. Baltimore*, 7 Peters 243 (1833).

18. *West River Bridge Co. v. Dix*, 6 How. 507 (1848).

19. *Baltimore & Susquehanna Railroad Co. v. Nesbit*, 10 How. 395 (1850).

20. Potter, "PW&B Railroad," 76–77.

21. See statutes and references, note 15.

22. Gibb, "Delaware Railroad," 96–97, 121, 127–28.

23. *Report on Internal Improvements Relating to B&O*, (1840), 6–12.

24. *The Tide Water Canal Company v. Ann Archer*, 9 Gill & J. 479, 322 (Appendix, 1830); *Appeal against a City Railway . . . Philadelphia* (Philadelphia, c. 1856).

25. R. A. Parish to Charles Dillworth, Feb. 13, 1847, Judge John Cadwalader Papers, legal file 52, Historical Society of Pennsylvania.

26. As quoted, James T. Schleifer, *The Making of Tocqueville's Democracy in America* (Chapel Hill, N.C., 1980), 236, 241, 242.

27. Potter, "PW&B Railroad," 51; "Second Annual Report, 1855," *Northern Penn. R.R. Co. Annual Rep. of the Bd. of Dir.* (Philadelphia, 1853–78), 23; Gibb, "Delaware Railroad," 96–97, 121. See also Cochran, *Business in American Life*, 196; Hurst, *Law and the Conditions of Freedom*, 104.

28. *Report on Internal Improvements Relating to B&O*, (1840), 160–64; *Report, Northern Central Railroad, Corporate Mortgage*, 209, 210, L211, Baltimore County, Maryland, Maryland Hall of Records, Annapolis; *Journal of the Pennsylvania Senate* (Harrisburg, 1818–19), 276–79.

29. *Report on Internal Improvements Relating to B&O* (1840), 160–64; Middlesex County, [N.J.] Deedbooks, 34:551–53, 51:372–74, 383–97, 93:215; and Somerset County [N.J.] Deedbooks, 5:395–97, 10:57–65, 81–85, 137–46, L-2:31–33, 414–16 (I am indebted to Christopher Baer for this material); "Fourth Annual Report, 1851," *Pennsylvania Railroad Annual Reports* 1:17. For influence of terrain, see Rosenberger, *Philadelphia and Erie Railroad*, 101–2. It is worth noting that the assessors employed

on the Pennsylvania State Works usually awarded lower judgments than those resulting from voluntary agreement. However, in most cases the property owner was able to appeal these decisions to the legislature which inevitably revised the award upward (Hartz, *Economic Policy and Democratic Thought*, 159–60). Because of this politization of the assessment process, the ultimate result of the condemnation privilege employed on the State Works was similar to that of the private corporations I have discussed in the text.

30. Potter, "PW&B Railroad," 74.

31. "Second Annual Report, 1848," *Pennsylvania Railroad Annual Reports* 1:20–21. See also "Annual Report, 1853, 1854," *Annual Reports . . . of the Pittsburgh & Connellsville R. R. Co.* (Pittsburgh, 1853–63), 14–15, 12–13, 22.

32. Potter, "PW&B Railroad," 51; "Second Annual Report, 1855," *Northern Pennsylvania Railroad Annual Reports*, 23.

33. Wilson, *Pennsylvania Railroad* 1:53–54, 66–69, 38–43; Somerset County [N.J.] Deedbooks, L-1:31–33, L-2:414–16 (I am indebted to Christopher Baer for these references); Rosenberger, *Philadelphia and Erie Railroad*, 217.

34. Whitman H. Ridgway, "A Social Analysis of Maryland Community Elites, 1827–1836: A Study of the Distribution of Power in Baltimore City, Frederick County, and Talbot County" (Ph.D. diss., University of Pennsylvania, 1973); Ridgway, "Maryland Community Leaders and Economic Development, 1793–1836," *Regional Economic History Research Center Working Papers* 2, no. 3 (1978): 1–24; I am indebted to Lee Benson for reference to his work on Philadelphia and Pennsylvania. See his "Philadelphia Elites."

35. Potter, "PW&B Railroad," 17, 25, 27–31, 73; see also Gibb, "Delaware Railroad," 68–92.

36. Potter, "PW&B Railroad," 52, 114–16; Gibb, "Delaware Railroad," 70; *Report of the Committee Relative to the Gettysburg Railroad* (Harrisburg, Pa., 1839) 47; Hartz, *Economic Policy and Democratic Thought*, 148–60; John R. Miele, "The Chesapeake and Ohio Canal: A Physical History" (M.A. thesis, University of Delaware, 1969), 10–11.

37. See notes 35–36 above; Chandler, *Visible Hand*, 45, 52–53, 93–94.

38. Laurie, "Nothing on Compulsion," 94.

39. Potter, "PW&B Railroad," 115–16.

40. Simpson, *Working Man's Manual*, 132–33.

41. *West River Bridge Co. v. Dix*, 6 How. 507 (1848); Friedman, *History of American Law*, 140–41; Will H. Lowdermilk, *History of Cumberland, Maryland* (Washington, D.C., 1878), 374; Rosenberger, *Philadelphia and Erie Railroad*, 173. For suggestive evidence on the general social status of the men who became judges, see Kermit L. Hall, "The Children of the Cabins: The Lower Federal Judiciary, Modernization, and the Political Culture, 1789–1899," *Northwestern University Law Review* 75 (1980): 423–71. See also Edward D. Ingrahm to Jacob Sommer, Sept. 20, 1826, Longwood Manuscript Collection group 8, box 11, Hagley Museum and Library.

42. Isaac F. Redfield, *A Practical Treatise upon the Law of Railways* (Boston, 1858), 133–34, 158.

43. Ibid., 11; J. B. Thayer, *Monthly Law Reporter* 19 (Sept. 1856): 242–30 (1856): 302–25; *New Jersey R. v. Suydam*, 2 Harrison 25, 75 (1839). See also Horwitz, *Transformation*, 63–66.

44. Brackenridge, *Law Miscellanies*, 54. For the English story, see John P. Dawson, *The Oracles of the Law* (Ann Arbor, 1968), 88–95.

45. James Kent, *Commentaries on American Law*, 4 vols., 12th ed. (1873), 1:477; *Queries about the Practicality of Codifying the Laws of Maryland* (Baltimore, 1854), 8. For a more general discussion, see Freyer, *Harmony and Dissonance*, 24–26.

46. Edward D. Ingrahm to Jacob Sommer, Sept. 20, 1826, Longwood Manuscript group 8, box 11, Hagley Museum and Library; *Debates and Proceedings of the Maryland Reform Convention* 1:767–68.

47. Gibb, "Delaware Railroad," 22, 61, 89.

48. Atiyah, *Rise and Fall of Freedom of Contract*, 114–17; G. R. Rubin and David Sugarman, "Introduction," in Rubin and Sugarman, eds., *Law, Economy and Society: Essays in the History of English Law, 1750–1914* (Worcester, Eng., 1984), 85–86; Dawson, *Oracles*, 88–95.

49. See Freyer, *Harmony and Dissonance*, 24–26; notes 41, 44–46 above. For Delaware's developmental lag and similar pressures encouraging underdevelopment elsewhere in the region, see chaps. 2, 3 above.

50. *Queries about the Practicality of Codifying the Laws*, 10.

51. *Gibson & Paschall v. PW&B Railroad*, Judge John Cadwalader Papers, legal file 52, Historical Society of Pennsylvania; *Queries about the Practicality of Codifying the Laws*, 11–16.

52. *Northern Pennsylvania Railroad: Letters of the President and Chief Engineer* (c. 1855), 31–36, 37.

53. Potter, "PW&B Railroad," 108–10.

54. I. Knight and Nathan Roberts, "Commissioners Report to Presidents & Directors of the C&O and B&O," July 2, 1830, Chancery Case File, 6619, Maryland Hall of Records, Annapolis. See also *The B&O R.R. v. C&O*, 144 Chancery Record R.W. (1831), 142–510, esp. 192, 196; ibid.

55. *Report on Internal Improvements Relating to B&O* (1840), 61.

56. *Water Power v. Chambers*, 1 Stock. ch. 471 (1853), involved the owner's change of mind; *Plum v. Morris Canal & Banking Co. and the City of Newark*, 2 Stock. ch. 256 (1854), involved the injunction.

57. *Lauderburn v. Duffy*, 2 Pa. State 398 (1845).

58. *Shrunk v. Schuylkill Navigation Co.*, 14 S. & R. 17 (1826); *Zimmerman v. Union Canal Co.*, 1 Watts & S. 346 (1841).

59. *Henry v. Pittsburg & Alleghany Bridge Co.*, 8 Watts & Serg. 85 (1844); *Monongahela Nav. Co. v. Coon*, 6 Watts & Serg. 101 (1843).

60. *PW&B R. v. Trimble*, 4 Whart. 47 (1838); *Ohio & Penn. R. v. Wallace* 14 Pa. 245

(1850); *Commonwealth v. Erie & N. East R.*, 27 Pa. State 339 (1856); *Foster v. The Cumberland Valley R.*, 23 Pa. 371 (1854); *Barrickman v. The Commissioners of Hartford County*, 11 G. & J. (1839).

61. *Sommerville & E. R. v. Doughty*, 2 Zab. 495 (1850); see also *Tide Water Canal Co. v. Ann Archer*, 9 Gill & J. 479 (Appendix 1839).

62. The controversial case was *Sunbury & Erie R. v. Hummel*, 27 Pa. R. 99 (1856); for more on this case, see: *Lehigh Valley R. v. Lazarus*, 28 Pa. 203 (1857); *Huyett v. Phil. & Reading*, 23 Pa. 373 (1854); Redfield, *Railways*, 155–56. Cases set aside for inclusion of improper factors in assessments are: *New Jersey R. v. Suydam*, 2 Harrison 25 (1830); *Penn. & Reading R. v. Yeiser*, 8 Barr. 366 (1848); *Schuylkill Co. v. Thoburn*, 7 S. & R. 411 (1821).

63. *Harrisburg v. Craigle*, 3 Watts & S. 460 (1842). See also *Gaff v. City of Baltimore*, 10 Md. 544 (1854).

64. *B&O RR v. Israel Thompson*, 10 Md. 76, 87 (1856).

65. *Western Md. R. R. Co. v. Owings*, 15 Md. 199 (1860); *Alleghany v. Ohio & Penn. R.*, 26 Pa. 355 (1855); *Morris & Essex R. v. Newark*, 2 Stock. ch. 352 (1855).

66. *Att. Gen v. Hudson Riv. R.*, 1 Stock; ch. 526 (1853); *Bell v. Gough*, 3 Zab. 624 (1852); *Glover v. Powell*, 2 Stock. ch. 211 (1854), involved rights of owners along navigable streams. The inclusion of consequential damages was decided in *Tinsman v. The Belvidere Delaware R. Co.*, 2 Dutcher 149 (1857).

67. *Phil. & Trenton R. Co.*, 6 Wharton 25 (1840).

68. *The Newville Road Case*, 8 Watts 172 (1839); *Willing v. PW&B R.*, 5 Whart, 460 (1840); *Directors of the Poor v. Railway*, 7 Watts & S. 236 (1844); *Vail v. Morris & Essex R.*, 1 Zab. 189 (1847); *Reading R. R. v. Boyer, ex. of Widow Luther*, 13 Pa. 496 (1850); *Stormfeltz v. Manor Turnpike Co.*, 13 Pa. 554 (1850); *State v. Miller*, 3 Zab. 383 (1852); *Reitenbaugh v. Chester Valley R.*, 21 Pa. 100 (1853); *Coster v. New Jer. RR & Tr. Co.*, 4 Zab. 730 (1853); *Penn. R. v. Keiffer*, 22 Pa. 356 (1853); *Green v. Morris & Essex*, 4 Zab. 486 (1854); *Pittsburgh & Steubenville R. v. Hall*, 25 Pa. 336 (1855).

69. *Rathbone v. Tioga Navigation Co.*, 2 Watts & S. 74 (1841); *Levering v. Railway*, 8 Watts & S. 459 (1844); *Mifflin v. Harrisburg, Portsmouth, M. & L. R. Co.*, 4 Harris 182 (1851); *Commonwealth v. Erie & Northeast R.*, 27 Pa. 339 (1856); *Erie & Northeast R. v. Casey*, 26 Pa. 287 (1856).

70. *Compton v. Susquehannah R.*, 3 Bland 386 (1831); *C&O Canal Co. v. Grove*, 11 G. & J. 269 (1841); *Ross v. Elizabethtown & Sommerville R.*, 1 Spencer R. 230 (1843); *B&S R. Co. v. Compton*, 2 Gill 28 (1844); *Hamilton v. Annapolis & Elk Ridge R. R. Co.*, 1 Zab. 442 (1848); *Coster v. New Jersey R.*, 3 Zab. 227 (1852).

71. *C&O Canal Co. v. B&O R.R.*, 4 Gill & J. 1 (1832); *Patterson Manufacturing Society v. Morris Canal & Banking Co.* (Patterson, 1829), pamphlet, Hagley Museum and Library; *Morris & Essex R. v. Blair*, 1 Stock. ch. 635 (1854). But see *Bellona Co's. Case*, 3 Bland 442 (1831).

72. *Rundle v. Delaware & Raritan Canal Co.*, 14 How. 80 (1852); *Haight v. Morris Aqueduct*, 4 Wash. 601 (1826); *State of Penn. v. Wheeling Bridge Co.*, 13 How. 518

(1851); *Willson* v. *Blackbird Creek Marsh Co.*, 2 Pet. 245 (1829); *Butler* v. *Penn.*, 10 How. 402 (1850), favored corporate or state authority. *Bonaparte* v. *C&A Co.*, 1 Bold. 216 (1830); *Baltimore & Susquehanna R.* v. *Nesbit*, 10 How. 395 (1850); *Barclay* v. *Howell's Lessee*, 6 Pet. 498 (1832; *Perrine* v. *Ches. & Del. Canal Co.*, 9 How. 172 (1849), favored property owners.

73. In states such as Ohio, where eminent domain was enforced by state-appointed appraisers with the authority of the state behind them, such a result may not have been possible (Scheiber, *Ohio Canal Era*, 277–78). But in Pennsylvania, because of the politization of the assessment process, the fact that the legislature routinely overruled the state-appointed appraisers raises a question as to whether Ohio's and Pennsylvania's experience was comparable (see notes 15 and 27 above).

74. Chandler, *Visible Hand*, 88, 138, dated the development of the great railroad systems (which permitted extensive unity of action among railroad executives in many cases) as occurring primarily after the Civil War. In the mid-Atlantic states, as chap. 3 above explained, only the Pennsylvania Railroad and the Baltimore and Ohio Railroad achieved considerable independence, but this was not until after 1860.

## 5. Railroad Accidents and Capitalist Accountability

1. Robert J. Kaczorowski, "The Common-Law Background of Nineteenth-Century Tort Law," *Ohio State Law Journal* 51, no. 5 (1990): 1127–99; and compare: Hurst, *Law and the Conditions of Freedom*, 20–22; Hurst, *Law and Social Order*, 61–62, 80–81; Friedman, *History of American Law* 261–64, 409–27; Friedman and Jack Ladinsky, "Social Change and the Law of Industrial Accidents," in Lawrence M. Friedman and Harry N. Scheiber, eds., *American Law and the Constitutional Order: Historical Perspectives* (Cambridge, Mass., 1978), 268–82; William E. Nelson, *Americanization of the Common Law: The Social Impact of Legal Change on Massachusetts Society, 1760–1830* (Cambridge, Mass., 1975), 246–48; Gary T. Schwartz, "Tort Law and the Economy in Nineteenth-Century America: A Reinterpretation," *Yale Law Journal* 90 (1981): 1717–75; Scheiber, *Ohio Canal Era*, xvii, 7, 28, 90, 94, 272, 355; Roberto Manabeira Unger, *Law and Modern Society: Toward a Criticism of Social Theory* (New York, 1976), 52–54, 273–77; Hurst, *Legitimacy of the Business Corporation*, 33–47; Horwitz, *Transformation*, 85–102, 204–10, 300, 301, 306, 308; G. Edward White, *Tort Law in America: An Intellectual History* (New York, 1980), 3–12.

2. The state and federal cases are discussed below in the fourth section of this chapter. The emphasis upon principles of morality and justice is taken from Kaczorowski, "Common-Law Background."

3. Compare Chandler, *Visible Hand*, 76–78, 82–87, 243–44; Walter Licht, *Working for the Railroad: The Organization of Work in the Nineteenth Century* (Princeton, N.J., 1983), 50, 181–212, 242–43, 260, 263; Wallace, *Rockdale*, 149–50, 186–88, 227–37; Ferguson, "History and Historiography," 6–9; Porter and Livesay, *Merchants and*

*Manufacturers*, 22–23, 57, 72–77; Joyce Appleby, "Commercial Farming and the 'Agrarian Myth' in the Early Republic," *Journal of American History* 68 (1982): 833–49; John F. Kasson, *Civilizing the Machine: Technology and Republican Values in America, 1776–1900* (New York, 1977), 1–107.

4. Foner, *Free Soil*, 21–23; Welter, *Mind of America*, 33, 78, 70–80, 88, 89, 133, 136, 141, 168–69; Appleby, "Agrarian Myth," 847–49; Yearly, *Enterprise and Anthracite*, 15, 19ff.

5. Howe, "Victorian Culture in America," 3–28.

6. Freyer, "Reassessing the Impact of Eminent Domain"; Scheiber, *Ohio Canal Era*, 9, 11–13, 66–67, 88–91, 101–8, 253–54, 271–72, 283–85, 295–96; Hartz, *Economic Policy and Democratic Thought*, 10–15, 41–56, 133–38; Cochran, *Business in American Life*, 119–22.

7. Alfred D. Chandler, Jr., "The Adversaries," *Harvard Business Review* 57 (Nov.-Dec. 1979): 88–92; Thomas K. McCraw, "Rethinking the Trust Question," in McCraw, ed., *Regulation in Perspective: Historical Essays* (Cambridge, Mass., 1981), 4–5; Licht, *Working for the Railroad*, 118–22; P. W. Kingsford, *Victorian Railwaymen: The Emergence and Growth of Railway Labour, 1830–1870* (London, 1970), 22–27.

8. Friedman, *History of American Law*, 410, 412–13, 422, 424; Licht, *Working for the Railroad*, 120–22, 181–212, 242–43; John T. Noonan, Jr., *Persons and Masks of the Law: Cardozo, Holmes, Jefferson, and Wythe as Makers of the Masks* (New York, 1976), 116–17, 136–37. These studies, of course, do not focus on the mid-Atlantic region.

9. Catton, "John W. Garrett," vii, ix; Chandler, *Visible Hand*, 104–26, 134–39; Cadman, *Corporation in New Jersey*, 54–60, 399–401, 427; Ward, *J. Edgar Thomson*, 110–22; Tuttle, "Railroad Taxation in New Jersey," 1–60; Reilly, "Camden and Amboy Railroad," 45–177; Wheaton J. Lane, *From Indian Trail to Iron Horse: Travel and Transportation in New Jersey, 1620–1860* (Princeton, N.J., 1939), 298–300; Kirkland, *Men, Cities, and Transportation*, 263–64; *Communication from the Executive to the Senate of Maryland* (1847), 8; *Laws and Ordinances Relating to B&O* (1850), 51, 52, 92, 94, 112, 118, 154–55, 203; *Report on Internal Improvements Relating to B&O* (1840), 76, 211; *30th Annual Report of B&O* (1856), 7, 11; *18th Annual Report of B&O* (1844), 23; *Report Whether the Pennsylvania, Delaware and Maryland Steam Navigation Company Have Not Forfeited Their Charters* (1844), 3; *Report from B&O Relative to an Increase of Toll for Flour* (1840), 4; *Report of Charges of James E. Tyson against B&O* (1860), 4; *A Marylander, Objections to Yeilding to Northerners* (1860), 23–24; *Reports of the Majority and Minority of B&O*, (1858), 26. The companies whose statutes I have examined are listed in note 15 of chap. 4 above.

10. Hurst, *Law and Social Order*, 80–81; discussion below; Nathan Isaacs, "Fault and Liability," *Harvard Law Review* 31 (1918): 954–79; Thomas G. Shearman and Amasa A. Redfield, *A Treatise on the Law of Negligence*, 2 vols., 4th ed. (New York, 1888).

11. Friedman, *History of American Law*, 261–64, 409–27; Horwitz, *Transformation*, 85–102, 204–10, 300, 301, 306, 308; see also Robert L. Rabin, "The Historical

Development of the Fault Principle: A Reinterpretation," *Georgia Law Review* 15 (1981): 925–61. The formulation given in the paragraph above owes much to Rabin.

12. Schwartz, "Tort Law"; see also Shearman and Redfield, 1:iii; Freyer, *Harmony and Dissonance* 63–75.

13. Kaczorowski, "Common-Law Background," 1128–29. See also Isaacs, "Fault and Liability"; Shearman and Redfield, *Law of Negligence* 1:1–24, 61–70; Charles C. Bonney, *Rules of Law for the Carriage and Delivery of Persons and Property by Railway* (Chicago, 1864).

14. Shearman and Redfield, *Law of Negligence* 1:iii; Bonney, *Rules of Law*, 19, 20, 34, 40.

15. Tocqueville, *Democracy in America* (1945 ed.), 1:280–87, esp. "The jury is, above all, a political institution" (282) and "The jury system as it is understood in America appears to me to be as direct and as extreme a consequence of the sovereignty of the people as universal suffrage" (283); Bonney, *Rules of Law*, 18.

16. For the influence of firms in small towns and rural areas, see Freyer, *Harmony and Dissonance*, 109. David J. Bodenhamer, "The Democratic Impulse and Legal Change in the Age of Jackson: The Example of Criminal Juries in Antebellum Indiana," *The Historian* 55 no. 2 (Feb. 1983): 206–219 discusses well the diversity and impact of jury selection on society and confirms the jury's continuing strength, which was sanctioned by the legislature and the Supreme Court in Indiana. My own work in Pennsylvania, Maryland, New Jersey, and Delaware confirms Bodenhamer's findings. See also Brackenridge, *Law Miscellanies*, 458, 558.

17. Friedman and Ladinsky, "Industrial Accidents," 273; Friedman, *History of American Law*, 422–23; William Henry Swift to A. Phelps, Oct. 7, 1853, in Thomas C. Cochran, *Railroad Leaders, 1845–1890: The Business Mind in Action* (Cambridge, Mass., 1953), 470.

18. "In the District Court for the city and county of Philadelphia," "List of Jurors for December Term 1844, First Period Commencing December 30, 1844" ibid. for "September Term, Second Period Commencing October, 1847" legal file 51, and *Grant* v. *Farnum* legal file 52, Judge John Cadwalader Papers, legal file 52, list of jurors in that case, Historical Society of Pennsylvania.

19. Ibid.; "Laws Relative to Debtor and Creditor," *Hunt's* 2 (1840): 491–92.

20. Thomas Sargent Fernon, *Facts in Detail Relative to the Negotiation of the First Mortgage Loan of the North Pennsylvania Railroad Company* (Philadelphia, 1857), 28.

21. Licht, *Working for the Railroad*, 253–57, summarized the studies supporting the thesis of "community uprisings." For similarities among community responses to railroad accidents, lawyer services, and other issues of conflict, see chap. 1–3 above.

22. See notes 18–20 above.

23. See chap. 3 above.

24. Howe, "Victorian Culture in America," 3.

25. Emile With, *Railroad Accidents: Their Causes and the Means of Preventing Them*

(Boston, 1856), vi; *Report of the Directors of the New Jersey Railroad and Transportation Co. to the Stockholders* (Newark, 1853), 9.

26. "Report of the Committee on Railroads, Relative to Accidents on Railroads," *American Railroad Journal* 25 (April 1852): 262–63; ibid., 16 (1843): 289–90.

27. "Accidents on Railroads," ibid., 25 (1852): 262–63.

28. Bonney, *Rules of Law*, 34.

29. "Railway Morals and Railway Policy," *American Railroad Journal* 27 (1854): 761–62; "Accidents on Railroads," ibid., 25 (1852): 262–63. For definitive discussion of Poor, see Alfred D. Chandler, Jr., *Henry Varnum Poor: Business Editor, Analyst, and Reformer* (Cambridge, Mass., 1956).

30. *Report of the Directors of the New-Jersey Railroad and Transportation Co. to the Stockholders* (New York, 1854), 11.

31. *American Railroad Journal* 16 (1843): 289; "Accidents on Railroads," ibid., 25 (1842): 262–63; 234.

32. Ibid., 10 (1840): 13; "Railway Morals," ibid., 27 (1854): 777.

33. William Henry Swift to A. Phelps, Oct. 7, 1853, in Cochran, *Railroad Leaders*, 158, 470; Friedman and Ladinsky, "Industrial Accidents," 473; Friedman, *History of American Law*, 422–23; Licht, *Working for the Railroad*, 111–18.

34. "Eighteenth Annual Report, 1844," *Organization of the United Companies under the Name of the PW&B*, 11–12; *Report of the Directors of the New-Jersey Railroad* (1853), 9.

35. Licht, *Working for the Railroad*, 201–12, 242–43, 260, 263; Munroe, *Louis McLane*, 505–6; *American Railroad Journal* 31 (June 1858): 389; Cochran, *Railroad Leaders*, 173–74.

36. *Annual Report of the New Jersey Railroad and Transportation Company to the Legislature of New Jersey for 1857* (Trenton, 1858), 13–14, 54.

37. Licht, *Working for the Railroad*, 64–65, 125–47, 134–42, 178–79, 273–74; With, *Railroad Accidents*, ix; *American Railroad Journal* 26 (1853): 502.

38. *American Railroad Journal* 16 (1843): 380.

39. Licht, *Working for the Railroad*, 185–88; Robert G. Shaw, *Down Brakes: A History of Railroad Accidents, Safety Precautions, and Operating Practices in the United States of America* (London, 1961), 39, 41–42, 54, 56–57. I have read through the following railroad company reports made to the New Jersey state legislature for the years 1852–58: New Jersey Railroad and Transportation Co., Camden and Amboy (Joint Companies), Central Railroad, Morris and Essex Railroad Co., Belvidere Delaware Railroad Co., Camden and Atlantic Railroad Co., Paterson and Ramapo Railroad Co., Sussex Railroad Co., Millstone and New Brunswick Railroad Co., Newark and Bloomfield Railroad Co., and Warren Railroad.

40. "Railway Morals," *American Railroad Journal* 26 (1854): 778.

41. Reilly, "Camden and Amboy Railroad," 45–177.

42. *Annual Reports of the Railroad and Canal Companies of the State of New Jersey*

(Trenton, 1857), 40, 42; *Annual Report of the New Jersey Railroad . . . to the Legislature of New Jersey* (Trenton, 1853), 2; ibid. (Trenton, 1857), 28; ibid. (1858), 16.

43. *Annual Reports of the Railroad and Canal Cos. to the Legislature of the State of New Jersey* (Trenton, 1855), 251.

44. *Annual Report of the New Jersey Railroad* (1853), 2; ibid. (1857), 28; ibid. (1858), 16; *Annual Report of the Railroad and Canal Cos.* (1855), 251; *Annual Report of the Belvidere Railroad Co. to the Legislature of the State of New Jersey* (1857), 59.

45. Charles Francis Adams, Jr., *Notes on Railroad Accidents* (New York, 1879), 267; notes 17, 20, 47 above.

46. *Hear Both Sides: Documents and Papers Relating to the Late Camden and Amboy Railroad Accident, at Burlington, N.J.* (Philadelphia, 1855), 10.

47. *Report of the Directors of the New Jersey Railroad and Transportation Co. to the Stockholders* (New York, 1855), 4; ibid. (1853), 9; William Henry Swift to A. Phelps, Oct. 7, 1853, in Cochran, *Railroad Leaders*, 158, 470.

48. *Report of the Directors of the New Jersey Railroad and Transportation Co. to the Stockholders* (Newark, 1857), 3; ibid. (Newark, 1859), 4.

49. "Railroad Accidents," *American Railroad Journal* 26 (Feb. 1853): 117.

50. Licht, *Working for the Railroad*, 198–212.

51. See notes 35 and 36 above.

52. Licht, *Working for the Railroad*, 118–21; Chandler, *Henry Varnum Poor*, 155.

53. *Laws of Maryland*, ch. 309 (Annapolis, 1837); ibid., ch. 346 (Annapolis, 1846); "Accidents upon Railroad," *American Railroad Journal* 16 (1843): 376–78.

54. Bonney, *Rules of Law*, 16, 19.

55. "Railroad Accidents," *American Railroad Journal* 26 (Feb. 1853): 117; "Accidents on Railroads," ibid., 25 (1852): 234.

56. *Paper Book of Plaintiff in Error . . . The Pennsylvania R.R. Co. v. Catharine G. Ogier* (1860), 2; *Pennsylvania R.R. Co. v. Ogier*, 35 Pa. (11 Casey) 60 (1860).

57. See discussion of appellate litigation below. See also Wex S. Malone, "Contributory Negligence," *Illinois Law Review* 41 (July-August 1946): 179; Friedman and Ladinsky, "Industrial Accidents," 279.

58. Shaw, *Down Brakes*, 15; *Hear Both Sides*, 4–5.

59. *Annual Reports of the Union Railroad of the State of New Jersey* (Trenton, 1856), 59.

60. *Annual Reports of the Railroad and Canal Companies of the State of New Jersey* (Trenton, 1856), 10–11.

61. *Annual Reports of the New Jersey Railroad and Transportation Co. of the State of New Jersey* (Trenton, 1854), 250, 254; ibid. (Trenton, 1855), 20; *Annual Reports of the Morris and Essex Railroad Co.* (Trenton, 1854), 259; ibid. (Trenton, 1856), 31.

62. *Annual Reports of the New Jersey Railroad* (1856), 19.

63. *Annual Reports of the Railroad and Canal Cos.* (1857), 6.

64. *Annual Reports of the Union Railroad* (1856), 59.

65. *Annual Reports of the Philadelphia, Wilmington, and Baltimore Railroad to the Stockholders* (Philadelphia, 1858), 15. See also With, *Railroad Accidents*, x-xi.

66. *Kent Commentaries on American Law* 1:473, 477–78; Freyer, *Harmony and Dissonance*, 24–25.

67. William Sampson, "On the Common Law," *North American Review* 19 (1824): 427.

68. *Lehigh Valley R.R. Co. v. Trone*, 28 Pa. (4 Casey), 206 (1857); *Pennsylvania R.R. Co. v. Kelley*, 31 Pa. (7 Casey), 272 (1858); *Goldey v. Pennsylvania R.R. Co.* 30 Pa. (6 Casey), 242 (1858); *Searle v. The Lackawanna and Bloomsberg R.R. Co.*, 33 Pa. (9 Casey), 57 (1859); *Powell v. Pennsylvania R.R. Co.*, 32 Pa. (8 Casey), 414 (1859); *Watson v. Pittsburg & Connellsville R.R. Co.*, 37 Pa. (Wright), 469 (1860); *Barclay R.R. Coal Co. v. Ingram*, 36 Pa. (12 Casey), 194 (1860); *Lehigh Valley R.R. Co. v. Lazarus*, 28 Pa. (4 Casey), 203 (1857); *Mifflin v. R.R. Co.*, 16 Pa. (4 Harris), 182 (1851); *Huyett v. Philadelphia & Reading R.R. Co.* 23 Pa. (11 Harris), 373 (1854); *R.R. Co. v. Yeiser*, 8 Pa. State Rep. (8 Barr.), 267 (1848); *Sunbury & Erie R.R. Co. v. Hummell*, 27 Pa. (3 Casey), 99 (1856); *Northern Central Co. v. Mary Ann Scholl, Adm'r of Elias Scholl*, 16 Mary. Rep. 331 (1860); *Scaggs v. Baltimore & Washington R.R. Co.*, 10 Mary. Rep. 268 (1856); *Baltimore & Susquehanna R.R. Co. v. Woodruff*, 4 Mary. Rep. 242 (1853); *Tinsman v. Belvidere Delaware R.R. Co.* 26 N.J. Rep. (2 Dutcher), 148 (1857).

69. *Pennsylvania R.R. Co. v. Kilgore*, 32 Pa. (8 Casey) 292 (1858); *Sullivan v. Philadelphia & Reading R.R. Co.*, 30 Pa. (6 Casey), 234 (1858); *New Jersey R.R. Co. v. Kenard*, 21 Pa. (9 Harris), 203 (1853); *Pennsylvania R.R. Co. v. Aspell*, 23 Pa. (11 Harris), 147 (1854); *Pennsylvania R.R. Co. v. McCloskey's Admin.*, 23 Pa. (11 Harris), 526 (1854); *Peters v. Rylands*, 20 Pa. (8 Harris), 497 (1853); *Pennsylvania R.R. Co. v. Zebe & Wife*, 37 Pa. (1 Wright), 420, (1860); *Ibid.*, 33 Pa. (9 Casey), 318 (1859); *Flinn v. Philadelphia, Wilmington and Baltimore R.R. Co.*, 6 Del. Rep., (1 Houston), 469 (1857).

70. *Rauch v. Lloyd & Hill*, 31 Pa. (7 Casey), 358 (1858); *Reeves v. Delaware, Lackawana & Western R.R. Co.*, 30 Pa. (6 Casey), 454 (1858); *Pennsylvania R.R. Co. v. Ogier*, 35 Pa. (11 Casey), 60 (1860); *Runyon v. Central R.R. Co. of New Jersey*, 25 N.J. Rep. (1 Dutcher), 556 (1856); *Central R.R. Co. of New Jersey v. Moore*, 24 N.J. Rep. (4 Zabriski), 824 (1854); *Burton v. Philadelphia, Wilmington, and Baltimore R.R. Co.*, 4 Del. Rep. (4 Harrington) 252 (1845).

71. *New York & Erie R.R. Co. v. Harris*, 19 Pa. (7 Harris), 298 (1852); *Keech v. The Baltimore & Washington R.R. Co.*, 17 Mary. Rep. 32 (1860); *Baltimore & Ohio R.R. Co. v. Lamborn*, 12 Mary. Rep. 257 (1857); *Vandegrift v. Rediker*, 22 N.J. Rep. (2 Zabriski), 185 (1849); *Vandegrift v. Delaware R.R. Co.*, 7 Delaware Rep. (2 Houston), 287 (1860).

72. *R.R. v. Norton*, 24 Pa. (12 Harris), 465 (1855); *Ryan v. The Cumberland Valley R.R. Co.*, 23 Pa. (11 Harris), 384 (1854).

73. *Patten v. The North Central R.R. Co.*, 33 Pa. (9 Casey), 426 (1859); *State v. Morris & Essex R.R. Co.*, 25 N.J. Rep. (1 Dutcher), 437 (1856).

74. Passengers won in: *Flinn v. Philadelphia, Wilmington and Baltimore R.R. Co.*, 6 Delaware (1 Houston) 469 (1857); *Peters v. Rylands*, 20 Pa. (8 Harris), 497 (1853);

*Pennsylvania R.R. Co.* v. *McCloskey's Administrator*, 23 Pa. (11 Harris), 526 (1854); *New Jersey R.R. Co.* v. *Kenard*, 29 Pa. (9 Harris), 203 (1853); *Sullivan* v. *Philadelphia & Reading R.R Co.*, 30 Pa. (6 Casey), 234 (1858); *Pennsylvania R.R. Co.* v. *Kilgore*, 32 Pa. (8 Casey), 292 (1858). Passengers lost in: *Pennsylvania R.R. Co.* v. *Aspell*, 23 Pa. (11 Harris), 147 (1854); *Pennsylvania R.R. Co.* v. *Zebe & Wife*, 37 Pa. (1 Wright), 420 (1860); *Pennsylvania R.R. Co.* v. *Zebe et ux*, 33 Pa. (9 Casey), 318 (1859).

75. Property rights upheld in: *Tinsman* v. *Belvidere Delaware R.R. Co.*, 26 N.J. Rep. (2 Dutcher), 148 (1857); *Northern Central Co.* v. *Scholl, Adm'r of Elias Scholl*, 16 Mary. Rep. 331 (1860); *Huyett* v. *Philadelphia & Reading R.R. Co.*, 23 Pa. (11 Harris), 182 (1851); *Watson* v. *Pittsburgh & Connellsville R.R. Co.*, 37 Pa. (1 Wright), 469 (1860); *Powell* v. *Pennsylvania R.R. Co.*, 32 Pa. (8 Casey), 414 (1859); *Goldey* v. *Pennsylvania R.R. Co.*, 30 Pa. (6 Casey), 242 (1858); *Pennsylvania R.R. Co.* v. *Kelley*, 31 Pa. (7 Casey), 372 (1858); *Lehigh Valley R.R. Co.* v. *Trone*, 28 Pa. (4 Casey), 206 (1857). Property rights lose: *Baltimore & Susquehanna R.R. Co.* v. *Woodruff*, 4 Mary. Rep. 242 (1853); *Scaggs* v. *Baltimore & Washington R.R. Co.*, 10 Mary. Rep. 268 (1856); *Sunbury & Erie R.R. Co.* v. *Hummell*, 27 Pa. (3 Casey), 99 (1856); *R.R. Co.* v. *Yeiser*, 8 Pa. State Rep. (8 Barr.), 267 (1848); *Barclay R.R. & Coal Co.* v. *Ingram*, 36 Pa. (12 Casey), 194 (1860); *Lehigh Valley R.R. Co.* v. *Lazarus*, 28 Pa. (4 Casey), 203 (1857); *Searle* v. *Lackawanna & Bloomsburg R.R. Co.*, 33 Pa. (9 Casey), 57 (1859).

76. *N.Y. & Erie R.R. Co.* v. *Harris*, 19 Pa. (7 Harris), 298 (1852) *Keech* v. *Baltimore & Washington R.R. Co.*, 17 Mary. Rep. 32 (1860); *Baltimore & Ohio R.R. Co.*, 17 Mary. Rep. 257 (1858); *Vandegrift* v. *Rediker*, 22 N.J. Rep. (2 Zabriski), 185 (1849); *Vandegrift* v. *Delaware R.R. Co.*, 7 Delaware Rep. (2 Houston), 287 (1860).

77. Railroads lost in: *Burton* v. *Philadelphia, Wilmington and Baltimore R.R. Co.*, 4 Delaware Rep. (4 Harrington), 252 (1845); *Pennsylvania R.R. Co.* v. *Ogier*, 35 Pa. (11 Casey), 60 (1860); *Rauch* v. *Lloyd & Hill*, 31 PA. (7 Casey), 358 (1858). Railroads won: *Central R.R. Co. of N.J.* v. *Moore*, 24 N.J. Rep. (4 Zabriskie), 824 (1854); *Runyon* v. *Central R.R. Co. of N.J.*, 24 N.J. Rep. (1 Dutcher), 556 (1856); *Reeves* v. *Delaware, Lackawana & Western R.R. Co.*, 30 Pa. (6 Casey), 454 (1858).

78. *Patten* v. *North Central R.R. Co.*, 33 Pa. (9 Casey), 426 (1859); *State* v. *Morris & Essex R.R. Co.*, 25 N.J. Rep. (1 Dutcher), 437 (1856).

79. *Ryan* v. *Cumberland Valley R.R. Co.*, 23 Pa. (11 Harris), 384 (1854); *R.R.* v. *Norton*, 24 PA. (12 Harris), 465 (1855).

80. *Powell* v. *Pennsylvania R.R. Co.*, 32 Pa. (8 Casey), 414 (1859).

81. Compare *Sullivan* v. *Philadelphia & Reading R.R. Co.*, 30 Pa. (6 Casey), 234 (1858), with the cases involving livestock wandering on tracks.

82. Licht, *Working for the Railroad*, 197–201, suggested that the fellow-servant rule discouraged employees from bringing suits. Yet Licht also noted that juries generally favored workers, and he ignored altogether the availability of attorneys motivated by the contingency fee, which also could have served as an inducement. Ultimately, probably the most important reason why employees did not sue their employers more often during the antebellum era was that they were more likely to

receive favorable treatment from the railroad as an injured employee seeking mercy from the boss than as a litigant.

83. Railroads lost in: *Lehigh Valley R.R. Co.* v. *Trone*, 28 Pa. (4 Casey), 206 (1857); *Mifflin* v. *R.R. Co.*, 16 Pa. (4 Harris), 182 (1851); *Watson* v. *Pittsburg & Connellsville R.R. Co.*, 37 PA. (1 Wright), 469 (1860). Railroads won in: *Searle* v. *Lackawanna & Bloomsburg R.R. Co.*, 33 Pa. (9 Casey), 57 (1859); *Sunbury & Erie R.R. Co.* v. *Hummell*, 27 Pa. (3 Casey) 99 (1856).

84. *Powell* v. *Pennsylvania R.R. Co.*, 32 Pa. (8 Casey), 414 (1859); *Goldey* v. *Pennsylvania R.R. Co.*, 30 Pa. (6 Casey), 242 (1858).

85. Railroad won in *Barclay R.R. & Coal Co.* v. *Ingram*, 36 Pa. (12 Casey), 194 (1860) but lost in *Tinsman* v. *Belvidere Delaware R.R. Co.*, 26 N.J. Rep. (2 Dutcher), 148 (1857).

86. Railroad won in *Scaggs* v. *Baltimore & Washington R.R. Co.*, 10 Mary. Rep. 268 (1856) but lost in *Northern Central R.R. Co.* v. *Mary Ann Scholl, Adm'r of Elias Scholl*, 16 Mary. Rep. 331 (1860).

87. Railroad lost only in *Huyett* v. *Philadelphia & Reading R.R. Co.*, 23 Pa. (11 Harris), 373 (1854) and won in *R.R. Co.* v. *Yeiser*, 8 Pa. (8 arr.), 366 (1848), *Baltimore & Susquehanna R.R. Co.* v. *Woodruff*, 4 Mary. Rep. 242 (1853); *Lehigh Valley R.R. Co.* v. *Lazarus*, 28 Pa. (4 Casey), 203 (1857).

88. *Pennsylvania R.R. Co.* v. *Kelly*, 31 Pa. (7 Casey), 372 (1858).

89. *McKinney* v. *Neil*, 16 F. Cas. 219 (C.C.D. Ohio 1840) (No. 8,865); *Maury* v. *Talmadge*, 16 F. Cas. 1182 (C.C.D. Ohio 1840) (No. 9,315).

90. *Stokes* v. *Saltonstall*, 38 U.S. (13 Pet.) 181, 190 (1839).

91. 16 F. Cas. 219, 224.

92. *Stokes*, 38 U.S. at 190.

93. *Philadelphia & Reading R.R.* v. *Derby*, 55 U.S. (14 How.) 468, 486 (1852).

94. Ibid., 487.

## Epilogue

1. As quoted, John P. Frank, *Justice Daniel Dissenting: A Biography of Peter V. Daniel, 1784–1860* (Cambridge, Mass., 1964), viii, 289.

2. Genovese, *Political Economy of Slavery*; Genovese, *Roll, Jordan, Roll: The World the Slaves Made* (New York, 1974).

3. Frank, *Justice Daniel*, 244, 246.